Praise for *Reopening Muslim Minds*

"Mustafa Akyol passionately engages in controversial and timely issues, builds upon a wide range of contemporary scholarship on Islam and expands his well-thought arguments by supportive examples and interesting stories. This is a brilliant book."

—Mariam Al-Attar, lecturer of Arabic heritage and Islamic philosophy at the American University of Sharjah, United Arab Emirates, author of *Islamic Ethics: Divine Command Theory in Arabo-Islamic Thought*

"This is a hugely important book. Akyol has dared to destroy one taboo after the other. It should be required reading for all Muslims as well as non-Muslims concerned about the deplorable state of the Islamic world today. I recommend it without any hesitation."

—Murat Çizakça, professor of comparative economic history and Islamic finance at Marmara University, Istanbul, author of *Islamic Capitalism and Finance*

"The tug-of-war in the three monotheistic traditions between reason and revelation is both ancient and fiercely contested, but perhaps never more so among Muslims. We are in Akyol's debt here for penning such an eye-opening history of minority scholars and movements in Islam who from the beginning called for the greater use of reason in theology and law and promoted pluralism and tolerance. Especially in a day when crowds all over the world spill into the streets crying out for freedom and dignity, this is a must-read for Muslims and non-Muslims alike."

—David L. Johnston, affiliate assistant professor of Islamic Studies, Fuller Theological Seminary, author of *Muslims and Christians Debate Justice and Love*

"In this lucid and captivating book, Akyol gives us a most compelling and penetrating plea for reform in Islamic thought. A fervent believer in the universality of reason and freedom, he masterfully links the most debated issues in contemporary Muslim societies to their roots in the past. But for Akyol, history is not an exercise in itself, it is here to teach a lesson. And the lesson is that there will be no lasting political reform in the Muslim world without a much-awaited theological renewal."

—Martino Diez, associate professor of Arabic,
Catholic University of Milan

REOPENING MUSLIM MINDS

ALSO BY MUSTAFA AKYOL

Islam Without Extremes:
A Muslim Case for Liberty (2011)

The Islamic Jesus: How the King of the Jews
Became a Prophet of Muslims (2017)

REOPENING MUSLIM MINDS

———— ••• ————

A Return to Reason,
Freedom, and Tolerance

MUSTAFA AKYOL

ST. MARTIN'S
ESSENTIALS

NEW YORK

First published in the United States by St. Martin's Essentials, an imprint of St. Martin's Publishing Group

REOPENING MUSLIM MINDS. Copyright © 2021 by Mustafa Akyol. All rights reserved. Printed in the United States of America. For information, address St. Martin's Publishing Group, 120 Broadway, New York, NY 10271.

www.stmartins.com

Library of Congress Cataloging-in-Publication Data

Names: Akyol, Mustafa, 1972- author.
Title: Reopening Muslim minds : a return to reason, freedom, and tolerance / Mustafa Akyol.
Description: First. | New York : St. Martin's Essentials, 2021. | Includes bibliographical references and index.
Identifiers: LCCN 2020045304 | ISBN 9781250256065 (hardcover) | ISBN 9781250256072 (ebook)
Subjects: LCSH: Islam—History. | Islamic civilization.
Classification: LCC BP52 .A3635 2021 | DDC 297.09—dc23
LC record available at https://lccn.loc.gov/2020045304

Our books may be purchased in bulk for promotional, educational, or business use. Please contact your local bookseller or the Macmillan Corporate and Premium Sales Department at 1-800-221-7945, extension 5442, or by email at MacmillanSpecialMarkets@macmillan.com.

First Edition: 2021

10 9 8 7 6 5 4 3 2 1

To my beloved sons, Levent Taha & Efe Rauf,
so that they may grow up with both
Islamic faith & universal ethics

Political Islam is only an aspect of the overall problem of Islam in the modern world.

—Ali A. Allawi, *The Crisis of Islamic Civilization*, 2010

The task before the modern Muslim is, therefore, immense. He has to rethink the whole system of Islam without completely breaking with the past.

—Muhammad Iqbal,
The Reconstruction of Religious Thought in Islam, 1930

CONTENTS

A NIGHT WITH THE RELIGION POLICE

Anyone who can liberate the Malay Muslim mind is a dangerous threat. That is why the authorities had to censure Mustafa Akyol. They detained him, interrogated him and made his immediate future uncertain.

—Mariam Mokhtar, Malaysian journalist, Oct 2017[1]

On September 21, 2017, I took the very long journey from the small town of Wellesley, Massachusetts, to Kuala Lumpur, the capital of Malaysia, with no clue about what awaited me in this far end of the world.

At that time, I was a visiting fellow at the Freedom Project at Wellesley College—an initiative aimed at cherishing classical liberal values, such as freedom of speech within American academia. What took me to Malaysia was also a liberal initiative, albeit one that operated within a very different milieu. Named Islamic Renaissance Front, or IRF, this was a small but vocal organization founded by faithful Malay Muslims who challenged the oppressive and intolerant interpretations of Islam in their country—with arguments from Islam itself.

My acquaintance with the IRF had a history. The organization had hosted me in Malaysia three times before, organizing seminars at universities, institutes, and other public venues. In 2016, it also published the Malay version of my 2011 book, *Islam Without Extremes: A Muslim Case for Liberty*. The founding leader of IRF, Dr. Ahmad Farouk Musa, was energized with the attention Malay Muslims were giving to foreign voices like mine. He just had a concern with the "Inquisition," the seriousness of which I had not yet grasped.

On this trip, the first event on my schedule was a panel on how rational theology and philosophy flourished in early Islam and how their later decline marked an "intellectual suicide" that still haunts us—as we shall also see in this book. To an attentive audience, I argued that we Muslims need to revisit some of the ideas that have been banned to us as "heresy" for about a thousand years.

The next day, at another public venue in Kuala Lumpur, I spoke at the second panel on my schedule, which probed a sensitive topic: apostasy from Islam.[2] It is a sensitive topic, because while you may think that anybody has the right to change his or her religion, quite a few Muslims believe that if the abandoned religion is Islam, the apostate deserves a death penalty. This punishment is applicable in about a dozen "Islamic" states, such as Saudi Arabia or Iran, where Malaysians are proudly more "moderate." So, instead of executing the apostates, they send them to rehabilitation centers, where people can be held for six months, so that they can be "educated" and "corrected."[3]

In my speech, I argued that apostates should be neither executed nor "rehabilitated," but just left alone with their conscience. I referred to Islamic scholars who have reformist views on this matter, and also I reminded my audience of a Qur'anic phrase: *La ikraha fi al-din,* or "There is no compulsion in religion."[4] Yes, apostasy was condemned as a capital crime in classical Islamic law, I explained, but this only reflected the medieval norms according to which leaving the religious community also implied political treason. Times have changed, I noted, and our laws and attitudes must change as well.

In the same speech, I also added that if a Muslim loses faith in the religion, dictates would achieve nothing. For faith is a sincere conviction in the heart and mind that cannot be imposed from the outside. "Faith," I emphatically said, "is not something you can *police*."

Well, speak of the devil, as the saying goes, and he shall appear.

As the panel ended and I was getting ready to leave, a group of serious-looking men approached me. "Are you Mustafa Akyol?" asked one of them. I said, "yes," wondering who he was. "*As-salamu alaykum*," the man said. "We are *the religion police*." Then he showed me his card, which defined his job really as "religion enforcement officer."

The officers just wanted to "ask a few questions." Supposedly, they had heard "complaints" about my speech, and now they were to investigate what I had said. "We got the recorded video of your talk," the senior officer said. "We will watch it and then inform you about the next step." He also asked me if I really quoted the Qur'anic phrase "There is no compulsion in religion"? I affirmed, "yes," wondering why that could be a problem.

The officers also noted that they didn't like my lecture planned for the next day—a conversation on my more recent book, *The Islamic Jesus: How the King of the Jews Became a Prophet of the Muslims*. Apparently the problem was the event's subtitle, which read, "Commonalities Between Judaism, Christianity, and Islam." "We don't like that kind of stuff," the senior officer plainly told me, making me recall the obsession in the country of drawing sharp boundaries between Abrahamic religions—to the absurd extent of banning Christians from using the word "Allah," which Arab Christians have used for centuries without any question.[5]

Then, after this short interrogation, the religion police let me go, and I thought that was it.

The next morning, however, I woke up in my hotel room to read in the Malay media that I had been summoned to their headquarters—to the government ministry called Federal Territories Islamic Affairs Department, or, shortly, JAWI. My hosts suggested that we should cancel my last lecture and I should leave the country as soon as possible, to deal with JAWI's questions through a lawyer and from afar. Following this advice, I packed my bags, bought souvenirs for my wife, and headed to the Kuala Lumpur International Airport. Around 8 P.M., I checked in and got my boarding pass. When I arrived at the passport control area, however, I realized that my adventure in Malaysia wasn't yet over.

A VISIT TO THE "INQUISITION"

The female officer who looked at my passport turned a bit nervous when she put my name in her computer. "You need to wait, sir," she said. She then called some police officers, who called other police officers, who soon escorted me to the police unit at the airport. There I learned that JAWI had issued a nationwide arrest order for me, to make sure I didn't leave the country.

That was the beginning of a very long night. I was taken from the airport to a nearby police station, then to another official building, going through sluggish processes and also long distances around the unfamiliar Malay capital. Finally, toward 5 A.M., I was taken to the JAWI headquarters, where I was locked up in a detention room. No one was rude or harsh toward me, but the many unknowns were nevertheless distressing. I kept thinking about my children and my wife, who had given birth to our second son just weeks before my arrival in Malaysia.

In the morning, around 8 A.M., my door was unlocked and I was told that we were heading to the "Sharia court." Finally, after another long drive and some waiting, I entered the court, which must have been the "Inquisition" that Dr. Musa had been talking about. I found two young veiled female officers sitting next to an older religious scholar with a long beard—a *Hakim Syarie,* or "Sharia Judge." For two hours, they questioned why I came to Malaysia, who "abetted" me, and why I did not seek "permission" from the authorities in order to "teach Islam." They were respectful, but also stern. And, astonishingly, they asked again with what authority I quoted the Qur'anic phrase "There is no compulsion in religion."

Finally, there came the happy ending to this dark episode. I rejoiced to hear the sentence "We will release you." "This is a lesson," added one of the female officers, "so don't come back to Malaysia again and teach Islam without permission."

Soon, after eighteen hours under detention, I was let go. The first thing I did was call my wife, Riada. From her, I learned that what saved me was not mere luck. After Dr. Musa notified her of my arrest via phone, she immediately called Istanbul to alarm my father, Taha Akyol, who is a prominent Turkish public intellectual. He sought help from a few of his influential friends, the most prominent of which was Abdullah Gül, Turkey's former president and a rare Muslim liberal democrat. Mr. Gül's Istanbul office immediately got in touch with the office of His Royal Highness Sultan Nazrin Shah, a key ruler in Malaysia's complex federal monarchic system. The Sultan's advisor, Dr. Afifi al-Akiti, a scholar at Oxford University, soon contacted the court's officials. Whatever was said apparently worked. Hours later, Dr. al-Akiti even kindly escorted me to my plane, on which this time I boarded without any trouble.

Yet still, days after my departure, the Malaysian government banned my book *Islam Without Extremes* along with its Malay edition, *Islam Tanpa Keekstreman*. The decision was announced by then deputy prime minister Ahmad Zahid Hamidi, who said the book was "not suitable to the societal norms here."[6] That initiated a long legal process, as the Islamic Renaissance Front went all the way up to the nation's High Court to get the books unbanned. But in April 2019, the High Court upheld the government's prohibition. In return, the Cato Institute in Washington, D.C., which I joined in September 2018 as a senior fellow focusing on Islam and modernity, offered the Malay edition of the book for free, soon to be downloaded by thousands of Malay readers.[7] The Malaysian authorities were not giving up, so we would not give up, either.

"NO COMPULSION"—AND ITS LIMITS

What was it that alarmed the Malay authorities so much about my message? That question was in my mind right from the moment I was let go by the religion police. While seeking an answer, I recalled the bizarre detail in the interrogation: that they were annoyed at me for quoting the Qur'anic phrase "There is no compulsion in religion." It is in a longer verse of the Qur'an, which, in its entirety, reads as follows:

> There is no compulsion in religion: true guidance has become distinct from error, so whoever rejects false gods and believes in God has grasped the firmest hand-hold, one that will never break. God is all hearing and all knowing.[8]

While this verse has always been present in the Qur'an, the short clause at its very beginning took a life of its own in the modern era, providing a universal motto for liberal-minded Muslims. For in just a few simple words, it seemed to rule out any coercion in religious matters. True, the rest of the verse moved on to renounce "false gods" and to proclaim monotheism as "true guidance." That is what religions do: they make a truth claim. But this truth claim remarkably came with a proclamation of "no compulsion," or, in other words, freedom.

However, not all Muslims liked this Qur'anic freedom. I had seen some Saudi translations curtail it by inserting a few extra words, in parentheses, into the "no compulsion" phrase.[9] When I checked the website of JAKIM, the Malaysian Department of Islamic Development, I found out the same thing. The "no compulsion" phrase was written like this:

There shall be no compulsion in religion (in becoming a Muslim).[10]

This little insertion in parentheses had huge consequences, for it reduced the "no compulsion" clause merely to allowing non-Muslims to stay outside of the faith. Those who are already Muslim, however, had no right to leave. They were also subject to coercion in the practice of the faith. This little stroke of a pen, in other words, gave the religion police its very authority to dictate Islam—the very authority I had challenged.

Yet, to be fair, this little stroke of a pen was also not unwarranted, because the "no compulsion" clause in fact had a limited meaning in the eyes of the premodern exegetes of the Qur'an, who built the mainstream Islamic tradition. Some argued that the verse was simply about a specific historic incident without any broader implications. Others suggested that the verse was only about not forcing Christians and Jews to accept Islam, but nothing more. Some even held that the "no compulsion" clause was "abrogated" by other verses of the Qur'an, which commanded war against "those who do not believe in God or in the Last Day."[11] Forcing people to accept Islam "with the sword" does not even count as compulsion, some also argued, because it is only for their own good.[12]

Moreover, a hadith, a saying attributed to the Prophet Muhammad, peace be upon him, further marginalized the spirit of the verse. "Whoever changes his religion," it bluntly read, "kill him."[13] Whether the Prophet of Islam really said this is a good question we will probe in later chapters. But classical scholars took it at face value, reaching a "consensus," or *ijma,* that the apostate must be executed—only after being given a few days to recant.

That is why the Malaysian authorities weren't totally making things up by "editing" the translation of the "no compulsion" clause in order to limit its scope to only those who aren't Muslim yet.

They had the whole weight of the Islamic tradition behind them. In return, liberal Muslims like myself were pushing for something new.

A MATTER OF ENLIGHTENMENT

This story is not meant to discredit Malaysia. It is a beautiful country for which I still have a heart, a country that I would encourage anyone to visit. I also feel lucky that I had this experience there— and not in countries with much harsher laws, such as Saudi Arabia or Iran. Malaysia is indeed more "moderate" when compared to such religious dictatorships, where liberal critics can go through much darker experiences.

The problem isn't about Malaysia, though. It is not about any other specific country, either. It is about an interpretation of Islam that is, by modern standards, authoritarian and intolerant. It manifests itself in laws and institutions that force women to cover their heads, or consider them lesser than men. It jails, flogs, or kills people for criticizing Islam and for even offering alternative interpretations of it. It demonizes Christians, Jews, and others, or even fellow Muslims who happen to be from a different sect.

Mind you: this is a separate problem from terrorism in the name of Islam, as practiced by armed groups such as ISIS, Al-Qaeda, or Boko Haram. Those terrorists are really "extremists," in the sense that their wanton violence, which targets many fellow Muslims, as well, finds a very marginal support in the Muslim world. The problem of religious illiberalism, however, is not marginal. Suffice it to say that more than 60 percent of all Egyptians or Pakistanis believe that apostates must be executed or adulterers must be stoned.[14]

In the West, especially in the past few decades, this problem has attracted a great deal of attention, but its nuances often get lost in the tug-of-war between two opposite camps.

On one side, there are the apologists, who argue that there is simply no problem within Islam today. There are only a handful of extremists, they say, whose zealotry has "nothing to do with Islam." They often have the good intention of defending Muslims from bigotry, but they do this by deflecting attention from real problems.

On the other side, there are Islamophobes, who cherry-pick all the problems within Islam today in order to depict the entire religion in darkest terms. They not only draw an unfair picture of the reality but also promote bigotry against Muslims, which helps only deepen the problem at hand.

So a more fair take on Islam is necessary, which can be helped greatly by a historical and comparative perspective.[15] Islam is the last of the three great Abrahamic religions, and most problems we see in it today have also been present in the other two—Judaism and Christianity. The history of the latter, in particular, includes many episodes of coercion and violence in the name of God. It was only a few centuries ago that "heretics" or "witches" were burnt alive in Europe, and Catholics and Protestants shed each other's blood. In those premodern times, Islam in fact proved to be a more lenient religion. That is why Sephardic Jews migrated to Muslim lands in 1492 to flee the persecution of Catholic Spain. That is why French philosopher Jean Bodin (d. 1596), who pleaded for religious tolerance, praised "the great emperour of the Turks," who "permitteth every man to live according to his conscience."[16]

Things began to change dramatically, however, with the Age of Enlightenment and its brightest creation: liberalism. New values, such as freedom of speech, freedom of religion, or equality before law, emerged, establishing a sense of human rights unmatched in any premodern civilization. Compared to them, the norms of the Islamic civilization looked growingly archaic.

To be sure, since the nineteenth century, some Muslims have taken significant steps to catch up. Recently, British historian Christopher de Bellaigue has summarized these efforts as the "Islamic Enlightenment."[17] Yet this very drive—including its authoritarian strains—provoked "Islam's counter-Enlightenment."[18]

This is a reaction spearheaded by those whom scholar Khaled Abou El Fadl calls "puritans"—a wide range of Salafis, Islamists, and rigid conservatives—who act as the defenders of the Islamic orthodoxy against modern liberal values. For worse, they are often more assertive than the orthodoxy itself, due to both their reactionary nature and the newfound powers of the modern bureaucratic state.

This book is meant to be an intervention into this big crisis of Islam. It aims to help advance the Islamic Enlightenment, by presenting a comprehensive argument for it—and, perhaps more importantly, by dismantling the theological roadblock that obstructs it.

Yet I have an important point to stress: By "Islamic Enlightenment," I really mean *Islamic* Enlightenment. In other words, I am not speaking about a wholesale adoption of Western Enlightenment, which had some dark spots of its own, such as Eurocentrism, racism, "white man's burden," or the illiberal secularism that grew especially in France. I am rather speaking about finding Enlightenment values—reason, freedom, and tolerance—within the Islamic tradition itself.

Luckily, those values really do exist within the Islamic tradition—yet often only as uncultivated seeds, forgotten paths, or even muted voices. And, as a great irony of history, those muted voices have been more impactful on another civilization: the Western world.

And right from that irony, now, we will begin *Reopening Muslim Minds*. We will go back to early modern Europe and look into a philosophical novel that fascinated British, French, German, and Dutch thinkers — a philosophical novel that was written centuries before by an Arab philosopher from Muslim Spain.

The Improvement of
HUMAN REASON,
Exhibited in the LIFE of
Hai Ebn Yokdhan:
Written in *Arabick* above 500 Years
ago, by *Abu Jaafar Ebn Tophail.*

In which is demonstrated,

By what Methods one may, by the meer
Light of Nature, attain the Knowledg
of things Natural and Supernatural;
more particularly the Knowledg of GOD,
and the Affairs of another Life.

Illustrated with proper FIGURES.

Newly Translated from the Original *Arabick*,
by *SIMON OCKLEY*, A. M. Vicar of
Swavesey in *Cambridgshire.*

With an APPENDIX,
In which the Possibility of Man's attain-
ing the True Knowledg of GOD, and
Things necessary to Salvation, without
Instruction, is briefly consider'd.

LONDON: Printed and Sold by *Edm. Powell* in
Black-friars, and *J. Morphew* near *Stationers-hall.*1708.

The cover of the 1708 edition of Simon Ockley's
English translation of *Hayy ibn Yaqzan.*

A SELF-MADE MAN: HAYY IBN YAQZAN

Enlightenment is man's emergence from his self-imposed immaturity. Immaturity is the inability to use one's understanding without guidance from another.

—Immanuel Kant, "What is Enlightenment?" (1784)

In 1671, Edward Pococke, the son and namesake of a famous Arabist at Oxford University, published a book titled *Philosophus Autodidactus*, or *The Self-Taught Philosopher*. This was the Latin translation of an Arabic-language manuscript that his father had encountered some forty years ago in Aleppo, where he worked as a chaplain to the Levant Company. At first sight, the book read like an adventure novel, but it was also a philosophical treatise demonstrating the power of human reason.

What Pococke expected from his translation, that we don't know. But we do know that the book turned out to be a hit. Scholars visiting Oxford soon began begging for copies on behalf of colleagues abroad who had heard of it. The secretary to the British embassy in Paris, who introduced the book to scholars at the Sorbonne who "all read and approved it," regretted that he ran out of copies to distribute. A Swiss colleague of Pococke's asked for a copy for a French bishop who "impatiently expected it."[1]

No wonder several reprints and other translations followed. In

1672, a year after Pococke's Latin translation, the book came out in Dutch. Two years later, an English translation by a Scottish theologian was published, only to be followed by another English translation by a Catholic vicar in 1686, and finally a third translation from the Arabic original in 1708 by Simon Ockley, a professor of Arabic at Cambridge University. In 1726, the book also was published in German.

Philosophus Autodidactus did so well because it fascinated its readers. These included, even much before Pococke's translation, Giovanni Pico della Mirandola, the key philosopher of the Renaissance who wrote the famous *Oration on the Dignity of Man*.[2] Later fans of the book included "natural philosophers," or scientists, as they were called at the time, such as Robert Boyle, who is largely regarded today as the first modern chemist, along with Enlightenment thinkers such as Baruch Spinoza and Gottfried Wilhelm Leibniz. Some scholars think that the book may have inspired John Locke, the father of political liberalism, for his notion of *tabula rasa*, which envisions a free and self-authored human mind.[3] Some also suspect an influence on the author Daniel Defoe, who, in 1719, published what is commonly known as the first English novel: *Robinson Crusoe*.[4]

In fact, some connection between *Robinson Crusoe* and *Philosophus Autodidactus* seems evident, because both books are about lone men living on uninhabited islands. The latter was just more philosophical, was written some six centuries earlier, and its author had a name less familiar to Western ears: Abu Bakr Muhammad ibn Abd al-Malik ibn Muhammad ibn Tufayl.

AN INDIVIDUAL PATH TO WISDOM

Ibn Tufayl (d. 1185/86), as he is shortly called, was an Arab Muslim polymath from Al-Andalus, the medieval Muslim kingdom in southern Spain. He penned treatises on medicine, only one of which survived, and also astronomy, in which he raised serious objections against the Ptolemaic system, which was the dominant model of his time. None of his works, however, have been as influential as the novel that would later make its way into Europe as *Philosophus Autodidactus*. The book's original name, which was also the name of its hero, was *Hayy ibn Yaqzan*, or, literally, "*Alive, The Son of the Awake*."

Hayy's story, which we will now briefly see, begins on a wondrous Indian island, which "enjoys the most equable and perfect temperature of all places on the Earth."[5] It is full of beautiful plants and animals, but the first human who ever appeared on it, as a little baby boy, is Hayy ibn Yaqzan. Regarding his origin, which the author left unclear, we are introduced to two alternative theories. One is that men could come into life on this island "spontaneously without the help of father and mother." The other theory is that a princess on a nearby island feared for the life of her baby and set him aloft—just like baby Moses—to reach a safe shore.

No matter how he appears on the island, the baby Hayy begins his life there all alone, only lucky to be suckled and adopted by a gazelle that we meet as "Mother the Roe." As Hayy grows up, he begins to examine the natural world around him and to draw conclusions. He initially envies the animals for all the defensive weapons that they have but that he himself lacks—horns, teeth, hoofs, spurs, and nails. But then he realizes he has other gifts. His hands are capable of using tools, or making shoes and dresses from the skins of dead animals. He also realizes that he has the power to think, aim, and strategize.

When he is at the age of seven, his mother, Roe, the gazelle, gets fragile and finally dies. Devastated by grief, Hayy wants to do something to bring her to life, and, to that end, he wants to understand why she died. Finding no visible defect on her body, he decides to do that which had been a big taboo throughout the Middle Ages: an autopsy. He uses a sharp stone to dissect the body, and goes all the way to the heart and examines its cavities. Although he can't bring Roe back to life, he figures out how the heart and the blood system work. By analogy, he begins to map out his own anatomy as well. When the body of Roe begins to decay, Hayy also learns from the ravens how to bury it—evoking the Qur'anic story of Abel and Cain.[6]

As he grows up, Hayy gets wiser and wiser, going through seven-year-long phases of maturation. He discovers more and more about the natural world through his evolving capacity for reasoned inquiry. He studies the limbs of animals and classifies them into kinds and species. He also begins to utilize the natural world by controlling fire, spinning wool, building himself a house and a pantry, domesticating birds to help him for hunting, or taming wild horses and asses. Thanks to all his observations and experiments, he acquires "the highest degree of knowledge in this kind which the most learned naturalists ever attained to." In the words of an early twentieth-century French Orientalist, "This part of the novel forms a very interesting and ingeniously arranged encyclopaedia."[7]

Then, at the age of twenty-eight, Hayy begins to focus on physics. He observes how water becomes vapor, discovering the transition from one form to another, recognizing that every transformation and motion must have a cause. Then he gets to the physics of the heavenly bodies. "He considered the motion of the moon and the planets from West to East," we read, "till at last he understood a great part of astronomy."

After all this, Hayy, who is now well in his middle ages, begins to ponder philosophy. What is the origin of all this amazing natural world? he asks himself, and entertains the two grand theories that were bitterly opposed at the time: that the universe was either created ex nihilo, or that it existed since eternity. "Concerning this matter he had very many and great doubts," we read, "so that neither of these two opinions did prevail over the other."

Not being a dogmatic person who would jump to conclusions without evidence, Hayy doesn't end up with a verdict. "He continued for several years, arguing *pro* and *con* about this matter,"

Ibn Tufayl tells us, as "a great many arguments offered themselves on both sides, so that neither of these two opinions in his judgment over-balanced the other." So, on the question of the origin of the universe, Hayy remains skeptical, keeping a position of well-thought uncertainty that you would not see very often in the middle ages—and, well, not today, either.

Hayy does not end up skeptical on the question of God, though. He reasons that both of the cosmologies he considers point to the existence of a deity. If the universe was created ex nihilo, it certainly must have had a Creator. And even if it always existed, it still had to have a Prime Mover—a concept advanced by none other than Aristotle. So, eventually, Hayy gets convinced that there is a "necessarily self-existent, highest and all-powerful Being," which he discovers not through any revelation, prophet, or tradition, but merely his own reason. He becomes a "knower," in other words, more than a "believer."[8]

Finally, Hayy develops a sense of ethics, too. Since there are no humans on the island, this comes out as care for the environment. He strives to attain the Creator's compassion to living beings, by adopting an ascetic vegetarian diet and even caring for the well-being of plants. When he eats fruits, he always preserves their seeds. He also chooses "that sort of which there was the greatest plenty, so as not totally to destroy any species." Such were the ethical rules, we read, "which he prescribed to himself."[9]

A DISAPPOINTMENT WITH THE RELIGIOUS

When Hayy reaches the age of forty-nine, we come to an unexpected twist in the story: a surprise guest from another island.

This other island is not too far from Hayy's secret paradise. But unlike the latter, it is full of human beings who have a religion of their own—a "Sect," as Ibn Tufayl calls it. We are introduced to two men from this island—Salaman, who is the very prince of the place, and Asal, his good friend. The two men are fond of each other, but they are different. Asal is inclined to philosophy, "to make a deeper search into the inside of things," as he also thinks that the scripture of his people's Sect has hidden meanings that require interpretation. Salaman, in contrast, is a more simple man. He follows the scripture faithfully, keeping "close to the literal sense," never troubling himself with different interpretations, and "refraining from such free examination and speculation of things."

As his preference for solitary contemplation over the chatter of society grows, Asal finally decides to change his world. He hires a ship to take him to the uninhabited island of whose beauty he has heard before—the very island of Hayy. Soon after Asal lands ashore, the two men run into each other and both get very surprised. Hayy is all the more surprised, because he has never seen a human before.

The two men become friends. Asal teaches Hayy human language. When he learns his friend's whole story, including the contemplations through which he discovered God, Asal is amazed, for he sees that "the teaching of reason and tradition did exactly agree together."

Asal then tells Hayy his own story and the story of the people on his island. He tells about "the Sect," or religion, his people believe in, whose teachings and practices all make sense to Hayy, who gets eager to see all those curious human beings. While Asal worries that this may not be the best idea, he can't turn down his friend. Luckily, right at that moment, a wayward ship hits the island, giving the two men a chance to go to Asal's homeland.

When they arrive at the city, Asal introduces Hayy to the people, telling his amazing story and praising his deep wisdom. Hayy sees that these common people are quite observant, that they keep "the performance of the external rites" of religion, but this does not stop them from "indulgence in eating" or other things he would consider immoral or unwise. So he begins to share his philosophical insights with the people of the island, only to find them too crude to understand. "He continued reasoning with them mildly night and day, and teaching them the truth, both in private and publick," we read, "which increased their hatred towards him, and made them avoid his company." The islanders were not bad people, Ibn Tufayl explains, but still,

> Through the defect of their nature, they did not pursue it by the right path, nor ask for it at the right door, nor take it in the right manner; but sought the knowledge of it after the common way, like the rest of the world.

Hayy finally realizes that these people are hopeless, as "disputing with them" only "made them the more obstinate." He also decides that the right guide for them is not their reason but their Sect. The ruler, Salaman, should continue keeping them "within the bounds of the law, and the performance of the external rites," as it is better for them to "follow the examples of their pious ancestors and forsake novelties."

At the end of this disappointing exposure to a religious society, both Hayy and Asal decide to leave it in this state of mediocrity, and go back to Hayy's world. "Thus they continued serving God on this island," Ibn Tufayl writes in closing, "till they died."

THE "INWARD LIGHT" IN THE WEST

Hayy ibn Yaqzan, as a tale, was a good read, but that is not why it was important. Like some other powerful works of literature, such as *Utopia* by Thomas More or *Animal Farm* by George Orwell, it was a philosophical novel. It is, in fact, widely recognized as the very first philosophical novel ever written. Its purpose was to elucidate an idea—that man, through reason and inquiry, can both explore and utilize nature, while also figuring out the big questions about existence and ethics. The book was also a tribute to the individual—the rational individual—showing that he or she can find truth, in the words of a modern-day translator of the book, "unaided—but also unimpeded—by society, language, or tradition."[10]

To some modern readers, these may not sound like spectacular ideas, and that is precisely because they are modern readers. We are living within modernity and are often taking its philosophical presuppositions as given. When Ibn Tufayl wrote his story, however, these precepts were quite unusual, if not revolutionary.

Their impact would be revolutionary, too. To get a sense of this, let's take a closer look at Hayy's path to the Anglo-Saxon world. The first English translation of the book, three years after Pocock's Latin text, was penned by a Scottish Christian named George Keith. In his foreword to what he entitled as *An Account of the Oriental Philosophy,* Keith praised Ibn Tufayl, who, despite being an infidel, "hath been a good man, and far beyond many who have the name of Christians."[11] A few years later, in 1678, Keith's friend and student Robert Barclay, in his book *An Apology for the True Christian Divinity,* also praised the story of "Hai Ebn Yokdan . . . a book translated out of the Arabick."[12]

Neither Keith's nor Barclay's admiration for the book was accidental. They were missionaries of a new Protestant sect called the Religious Society of Friends—or, as they became more commonly known, the Quakers.[13] A key element in the Quaker creed was, as it still is, the emphasis on the "inward light," which "teaches us the difference between right and wrong, truth and falseness, good and evil."[14] Every human being had this inner light, Quakers believed, regardless of sect, religion, or race. Every human being, therefore, was equally valuable—an idea whose roots went back to the "Christian humanists" of the Renaissance.

For some other Christians at the time, who believed that light shines only within their church, this universalism was not appealing. When they saw the reference to *Hayy ibn Yaqzan* in Barclay's *Apology,* they happily spotted the origin of the heresy. "Certain adversaries of Quakerism," notes a contemporary Quaker source, "declared that Barclay drew his doctrine of the Universal and Saving Light from this work, a charge which one would think carried its refutation with it."[15] That is why Barclay's reference to "*Hai Ebn Yokdan*" was removed from the later editions of the *Apology*. The "inward light" theology would continue without references to alien sources.

The theology did continue, though, quite successfully, making the Quakers the champions of what we today call human rights. William Penn, a Quaker leader, founded in 1681 the Province of Pennsylvania, which proclaimed religious freedom to all its residents, laying a prototype for the American Bill of Rights. In the next century, Quakers spearheaded the first antislavery organizations on both sides of the Atlantic. Under the leadership of one of their prominent friends, Benjamin Franklin, they became the first to petition the United States Congress for the abolition of slavery. Quakers also played a key role in establishing women's rights, with their rigorous defense of education of girls and women's right to vote. More recently, they have also been instrumental in setting up human rights organizations such as Amnesty International.

In contrast, we Muslims abolished slavery only thanks to the encouragement, even pressure, from Western governments--as we shall see in a later chapter. We still have a hard time accepting religious freedom--as the Malaysian religion police kindly reminded me. Some of us still frown upon the idea of equal rights for women. While our conservative scholars condemn "human rights-ism," our authoritarian leaders who persecute their dissidents despise organizations like Amnesty International for interfering with our supposedly wonderful "domestic affairs."

One wonders why. Why did the ideas articulated in *Hayy ibn Yaqzan* help trigger an intellectual revolution in Europe, whereas they remained feeble in the Muslim world?

To find an answer, we have to look deeper into the world of Ibn Tufayl, the world of medieval Islam. We have to see what this Muslim philosopher was trying to do with his novel and what the odds he was struggling with were. We have to see, more precisely, the stormy sea of theology on which he was trying to steer a battered ship of philosophy.

WHY THEOLOGY MATTERS

[In Islam] legal theory departs from the point where
theology leaves off.

—Wael Hallaq, scholar of Islamic law[1]

If you ask a random Muslim today what brand of Islam he or she
follows, the answer will probably come as either "Sunni," or "Shiite."
The former answer is just nine times more likely, because nearly 90
percent of the world's 1.6 billion contemporary Muslims are Sunni.

And how do the Sunni and Shiite visions of Islam differ? To outsiders, the answer may be surprising. For the big difference is not
about the Qur'an or the Prophet Muhammad, which are held sa-
cred equally by all Muslims. It is rather about who really was the
rightful heir to the Prophet Muhammad as his first caliph, or "successor." Sunnis approve what actually happened in history, honoring the first four caliphs—Abu Bakr, Umar, Uthman, and Ali.
Shiites, in contrast, accept the legitimacy of only Ali and his later
descendants. The big difference between them, in other words, is
different versions of *political history*.

If you want to dig deeper, Sunnis, on which we will mostly focus
in this book, can also tell you their specific *madhhab*, or "school":
Hanafi, Shafi'i, Maliki, or Hanbali, all named after their founders, who all lived more than a thousand years ago. How do they

differ? To outsiders, the answer may be again surprising. For these schools differ on things like whether shellfish is eatable or where hands should be placed during prayer—the *practice* of Islam, in other words, in all its minute details. Because they are schools of *fiqh*, or "jurisprudence," which is the human effort to interpret the Sharia, or the divine law.

To be sure, there is more to Islam than political history and jurisprudence. There are also beliefs, or *aqaid*, about God, His attributes, His relationship with the world and human beings, and the latter's place in the divine scheme. There is also a discipline that studies these beliefs called *kalam*. It literally means "speech," but it roughly corresponds to the Christian concept of theology.

Yet *kalam* has little presence in Muslims minds today. If they are asked about it, most Muslims would be taken by surprise. They may vaguely know themselves as "Ash'ari," or "Maturidi," but with little sense of what these terms entail. Worse, if they try to learn more about *kalam*, religious leaders may advise them to avoid it. "Leave those debates to the *ulama*," or "scholars," one such scholar says. "Just hold on to the *kalima*," which is the simplest declaration of the faith: "There is not god but God, and Muhammad is His messenger."[2]

This faintness of theology, as we will call *kalam* from now on, among Sunnis is not an accident. Because, after the initial centuries of Islam, which were intellectually diverse and vibrant, there happened a "significant decline and marginalization of kalam among Sunnis."[3] Instead, jurisprudence became the primary discipline. As a result, Islamic culture became a "legal culture," focusing on "proper behavior rather than proper belief."[4]

Today, most Muslims are living within this legal culture, which entails a plenitude of dos and don'ts regarding prayer, fasting, almsgiving, ritual hygiene, dress code, dietary laws, family laws, and, most controversially, criminal laws. Non-Muslims also focus on this legal culture, because some of its rules conflict with the modern standards of human rights.

That gap between Islamic jurisprudence and human rights has led, for more than a century now, to various efforts at "reinterpreting" or even "reforming" Islam. Yet, while some steps have been taken, these efforts ultimately hit a rock-solid wall: the divine will, as decreed by the Qur'an and exemplified by the Prophet. Any discussion on whether Muslims should give up corporal punishments, respect free speech, or accept gender equality, for example, faces a strong "no." No, because God and His Prophet said so and so.

But can we try to understand *why* God and His Prophet said certain things in a certain context? Can we figure out their *intentions* and then try to realize them in some other way, if we are in a different context? Moreover, besides religious texts, do we humans have a rational capacity to figure out what is right and wrong? And if we say "no" to this latter question, then how can we know the truth of religion in the very first place?

Such questions will take us from the realm of jurisprudence to what really lies beneath it, which is theology. The very realm, in other words, to which Muslims stopped paying attention centuries ago—although it still silently holds the barriers in their minds.

HOW IT ALL BEGAN

Islam, as the historical religion we know today, was born in the Arabian city of Mecca in the year AD 610. One night, Muhammad ibn Abdullah, a prominent merchant from the wealthy tribe of Quraysh, heard a strange voice in a cave that told him, "Recite." First he was terrified, but thanks to his wife, Khadija, he got convinced that the voice was that of an angel. New revelations confirmed that he was chosen by God to share a dangerous message with his people: that their idols were all false gods. The only true God was "the Lord of the heavens and earth and everything between," and who had sent other messengers before—men such as Noah, Abraham, Moses, or Jesus.[5]

This monotheist campaign soon put Muhammad and his

small group of believers into trouble with the polytheist leaders of Quraysh. Hence, the thirteen years in Mecca, the first phase of Muhammad's mission, passed under fear and persecution. The next phase began when the Prophet fled to Medina, another Arab city that welcomed him, in the year AD 622. The battles between the Muslims of Medina and the revengeful polytheists of Mecca, besides conflicts with shifting allies, went on almost until the very end of the Prophet's life.

Hence, neither Prophet Muhammad nor his fellow believers had the time or the means to produce any literature. The only text that they left behind, besides a few short political treaties, was the Qur'an. After the Prophet, though, Muslim armies poured outside of the barren Arabian Peninsula to take over the more sophisticated centers of the ancient world, such as Palestine, Syria, Iraq, or Egypt, which had rich cultural and intellectual traditions. Eastern Christians in particular had a lot to offer. Their church fathers had wrestled with theological questions that would soon intrigue Muslims as well.

One of these questions soon turned out to be the first big theological controversy in early Islam: Did God create humans with free will? Or did He predestine their fate?

The Qur'an's answer wasn't very clear, but due to the enduring influence of pre-Islamic Arab beliefs, there was "a large element of fatalism or belief in predestination."[6] It was doctrinally defended by scholars who were ultimately called Jabriyyah, or "Compulsionists." For them, all human acts occurred under the "compulsion" of divine predestination. God had simply created some for heaven, others for hell, and each were like "a feather hung in the wind."[7]

But a minority of scholars disagreed, insisting that God gave humans free will—or *qadar*, meaning "power." Their premise was God's justice, which is reiterated throughout the Qur'an. To deprive humans from the freedom to choose and then to reward or punish them for their deeds, they argued, would be injustice, which God would not do. They were called Qadariyah, because they defended human "power" to act independently of God. (Yet later, the term *qadar* was associated with the power of God and became synonymous with predestination, so beware of confusion here.[8])

The tension between these theologies was reflected in an interesting correspondence between Hasan al-Basri (d. 728), a highly respected scholar, and Caliph Abd al-Malik, a member of the Umayyad dynasty, which dominated Islam after the first four caliphs. The Umayyads were staunch supporters of Compulsionism. Hasan al-Basri, in contrast, was a defender of free will. "News has reached the Commander of the Faithful," the caliph thus wrote, referring to himself, "that you would have made statements about the divine decree which are unheard of amongst those who have gone before us." So he ordered, "Write to the Commander of the Faithful, explaining your position and whence you derive it."[9]

A letter like that from an absolute monarch would give chills to most people. But Hasan al-Basri didn't falter. He greeted the caliph with respect, then made his case. "God rewards His servants only on the basis of their works," he wrote, explaining why this requires free will. Then he referred to the Qur'anic verses used by the predestinarians, adding:

> However, Commander of the Faithful, things are not as these ignoramuses, in their error, maintain. Our Lord is too merciful and just and generous to behave like that with His servants. How could He act in this way, if we can read that, "God charges no soul save to its capacity; standing to its account what it has earned, and against its account what it has merited."[10]

This correspondence between Hasan al-Basri and Caliph Abd al-Malik is the earliest document in Islam that deals with the controversy over free will.[11] Some scholars doubt its authenticity and suggest that it may be apocryphal.[12] Even if that is the case, it is an important text showing the early theological battle lines—and that the caliphate had a stake in them.

ARE TYRANTS PREDESTINED BY GOD?

We do not know how Caliph Abd al-Malik reacted to Hasan al-Basri's response to his letter, if he had really received it at all. But we do know that the Umayyad caliphs, with a few exceptions, continued to promote the doctrine of predestination as a part of a "state sponsored orthodoxy."[13]

Some scholars who defied this orthodoxy paid a heavy price. One of them was Mabad al-Juhani, who was executed by crucifixion around the year 700 for promoting free will, along with his role in an insurrection. Another one was Ghaylan al-Dimashqi, who had begun his theological work in the Umayyad court, only to become the "arch heretic" in early Islam. For the sole crime of championing free will, he was brutally executed in the year 743. First his hands and feet were amputated, according to one account, then he was hanged.[14]

One wonders why the Umayyad rulers were so obsessed with a deeply theological question. The answer is what you may guess: this theological question had political implications. Unlike the first four caliphs, who had come to power with some consultation in the community, the Umayyads had come to power by sheer force. Their founder, Muawiyah I, had fought with Ali, the fourth caliph, in the first *fitna*, or "civil war." Muawiyah's son, Yazid, brutally killed Ali's son, Hussein, along with all his family members, in the horrendous massacre at Karbala. With all this violence, along with their corruption, nepotism, hubris, and Arab supremacism, Umayyads made many enemies.

In return, they needed all the support they could enlist—and there was no better supporter than God. First, they began to call themselves "Caliph of God," instead of the more modest title, "Caliph of the Prophet." Second, they used Compulsionism to insinuate that their rule was predestined by God. "These [Umayyad] kings," as their victim al-Juhani said with contempt, "shed the believers' blood, take their money, and then say, 'our actions are ordained by God.'"[15] One of these "kings" executed an innocent man, only to claim that he did "as was written in the book of fate."[16] Compulsionism was a perfect cover for all their misdeeds. Therefore, in the words of contemporary scholar Suleiman Ali Mourad:

> In order to disseminate this ideology, the Umayyads enlisted in their service a number of religious scholars and poets whose task was to provide a religious defense of the predestination doctrine. It was these scholars who furnished a number of hadiths that depict the prophet Muhammad and his companions defending predestination and condemning freewill.[17]

In contrast to predestination, belief in free will led to the questioning of political authority: "If individuals were accountable for their actions, then were so governments."[18] That is why, throughout the Umayyad rule, the doctrine of free will was often connected with "agitating for a new political order."[19]

The Umayyads ruled for about ninety years. After their fall, Compulsionist doctrine lost some of its impetus. Mainstream Sunni Islam, as we shall see, tried to develop a difficult middle position between predestination and free will—that there is predestination, but humans still "acquire" it with their free choice. "Human beings *perform*," in other words, "the actions which God *creates*."[20] Yet this painstaking theological mishmash was necessitated by the invention of Compulsionist texts, especially hadiths by the Umayyads and their allies.[21]

Compulsionism would be used again and again, in different phases of Muslim history, including the modern times, to promote a fatalistic worldview that often helped those in power.[22] These include Arab dictators such as Jamal Abd al-Nasser or Saddam Hussein, who, while owning their successes, repeatedly referred to fate "to rationalize defeat."[23] In face of the traumatic Arab defeat by Israel in the Six-Day War of 1967, Nasser had publicly evoked an Arab proverb, *La yughni hadharun an qadar,* or "Precaution or alertness does not change the course of fate."[24] As Arab scholar As'ad Abu Khalil observes, such "invocation of the notion of the inescapability of destiny" only helped "the absolution of Arab regimes and armies from any responsibility for the defeat at a time of mounting public criticism."[25]

Meanwhile, in contrast to Sunnis, the Shiites, who also had predestinarian views in the beginning, growingly found them dissuasive. The reason, again, had something to do with politics: "The fact that they were not in power" implied to them "that there is no such thing as complete predestination."[26]

There is a lesson that must be taken from this very first doctrinal war in Islam: Islamic theology, and all the clashes and schisms within it, did not develop in a vacuum. It developed under the tutelage of despotism, which dominated Islam since its very first century and influenced it for its earthly goals and ambitions—a crucial fact to which we shall return.

A THEOLOGY OF JUSTICE, FREEDOM, AND REASON

One of the pupils of Hasan al-Basri was a man named Wasil ibn Ata (d. 748). He embraced his master's defense of free will and its basis in God's justice, but he disagreed with him on other matters. Ultimately, he decided to "withdraw" and establish his own school, which soon became known as "those who withdraw," or Mu'tazila.[27] It was a school that would soon spark the greatest theological controversy in early Islam, one whose repercussions are still felt today.

Mu'tazila scholars, some of whose important works came to light only in the late twentieth century, were not always uniform in their views, but they all held certain tenets that offered a systematic theology upholding human *freedom* and *reason*.

The first principle in this theology was God's *justice*. This was, according to the Mu'tazila, the most definitive attribute of God— even more so than His omnipotence. Yes, God was all-powerful, but His power was not arbitrary; it was rather constrained with the principles of justice. As Mankdim Shashdiw (d. 1034), a Mu'tazila scholar from the Zaydi tradition, put it:

> His acts are all good, He does not do evil, He does not fail to perform what is obligatory on Him, He does not lie in His message nor is He unjust in His rule. He does not torment the children of pagans for the sins of their fathers. He does not grant miracles to liars, and He does not impose on people obligations that they can neither bear nor have knowledge of. . . .
> If obligation is imposed on a person and he fulfills it as he is bidden to, then He will necessarily reward him.[28]

The controversial suggestion here was that there were "obligatory" and "necessary" things for God, such as doing what justice, as we humans understand it, would entail. This implied that God was "bound by the same code of value as human beings," which was the Mu'tazila's very point—but also, in the eyes of their opponents, their very heresy.[29]

From God's justice came the principle of man's freedom. Since God promised humans reward or punishment in the afterlife, He must have given them free will. So humans are autonomous in their choices, the Mu'tazilites insisted, to the extent that they are the "creators of their own acts." Abu'l-Qasim al-Balkhi (d. 931) put it this way:

> [God] does not create the acts of human beings, but it is the latter who do the acts they have been commanded to do and prohibited from doing, by virtue of the capacity for action [*qudra*], which God has created for them and instated within them, that they may obey through it and desist from disobedience. . . .

And He willed—great and exalted is He—that they might come
to believe out of their own accord and not by compulsion, that
they may thus be tried and tested.[30]

From the principle of man's freedom, there came the Muʿtazila
emphasis on *reason*. Human reason, they argued, was a gift of God
to find truth—even when there is no revelation. Yes, God had told
us via revelation that murder is wrong and that saving an innocent
soul is right. But revelation was not *constituting* such truths, it was
only *indicating* them.[31]

From the principle of reason, there came the need for allegorical interpretation of revelation. There could be tensions between
reason and the text of the Qur'an, the Muʿtazila realized, and in
this case the latter had to be interpreted. The Qur'an itself, no wonder, had made a distinction between its "definite" and "ambiguous"
verses.[32] For the Muʿtazila, the main concern here was some of the
anthropomorphic descriptions of God in the Qur'an—such as His
"hands," "face," or "throne," which they insisted to take as allegorical rather than literal. But they were opening a door of figurative
interpretation that could get wider over time.

Finally, the Muʿtazila had a strong position on a peculiar question on the nature of revelation: Is the Qur'an "created" or "uncreated"? The defenders of the latter view held that the Qur'an,
as God's speech, was coeternal with God Himself—only to come
down to seventh-century Arabia to become a physical book. (Like
the divine Logos in Christianity, which was "with God at the beginning," only to come down to first-century Judea to become
flesh.[33]) Worrying that this would compromise Islam's staunch
monotheism and would also require predestination, the Muʿtazila
insisted that the Qur'an was "created." It was God's speech, for sure,
but God had spoken "in time."

With such views on God, man, and scripture, which we will explore more deeply in the chapters ahead, the Muʿtazila was offering
not just a rational theology but also a dignified anthropology. God

had created human beings, but only to give them freedom and reason. Hence their doctrine of free will was also called *tafwid,* or "delegation," meaning that "God has delegated to men power and authority to act independently of himself."[34] This was a theology that empowered human beings, in stark contrast to the Compulsionist doctrine that intentionally disempowered them.

Lenn E. Goodman, one of America's foremost historians of philosophy, makes good sense of what this all means. "Although the Mu'tazilites were hardly liberals," he reminds us, "their *kalam* is, in many ways, a form of humanism"—because it preserves human free will and "deems human reason competent to judge justice and injustice, even on God's part."[35]

This is not because Mu'tazilites were secular "freethinkers," as some early Orientalists had wrongly thought, and some Muslims still wrongly assume. They were rather sincere believers in Islam, and, in fact, even often "persons of uncommon piety."[36] No wonder their ultimate aim was to defend Islam rationally in the face of the puzzling questions from other traditions. They were "missionaries on the frontiers of Islam," in other words, who realized that a powerful faith should first make rational sense.[37]

THE BIRTH OF MUSLIM PHILOSOPHY

In the year AD 750, the Umayyad dynasty was overthrown with a violent revolution led by a rival Arab family, the Abbasids. The latter had gathered the support of many disenfranchised groups, ranging from Shiites to non-Arabs and even non-Muslims. They seized the caliphate, moved its center from Syria to Iraq, and, like most revolutionary movements do in the beginning, initiated a brighter era. But again, like in the history of most revolutionary movements, the brightness would not last for too long.

The Mu'tazila, whose forerunners were persecuted under the Umayyads, found first freedom under the Abbasids, then even endorsement. The latter crystalized under the rule of Caliph al-Ma'mun (r. 813–833), who is one of the most interesting political figures in Islamic history—a kind of enlightened despot, who was eager to pursue knowledge, from the meaning of Egyptian hieroglyphs to the exact size of the earth.[38] He embraced the Mu'tazila doctrine of the created Qur'an, and while that in itself would have been fine, he also imposed it. He initiated *mihna*—which means "trial" but is also dubbed as "inquisition"—to force all scholars to accept that the Qur'an is created. This authoritarian policy would prove disastrous and would only help delegitimize the Mu'tazila, although they probably weren't directly responsible.[39]

Meanwhile, the same al-Ma'mun supported another institution, a better one: *Bayt al-Hikma*, or "House of Wisdom," which was originally founded by his father, Caliph Harun al-Rashid. Established in Baghdad—the new, slick, and splendid Abbasid capital whose circular design was a tribute to geometric teachings of Euclid—this was an institute devoted to studying *ulum al-awa'il*, or "sciences of the ancients." Thanks to a diverse team of experts, including many Christians, Greek classics that were lost in Europe but preserved in Eastern churches were translated into Arabic. These included the works of mathematicians like Pythagoras and Euclid, physicians like Hippocrates and Galen, thinkers like Plato and Plotinus, and most important, Aristotle, who is widely considered the father of Western philosophy.

One of the scholars hosted at the House of Wisdom was al-Kindi (d. 873), the first Arab philosopher who penned an impressive literature on astronomy, medicine, chemistry, mathematics, metaphysics, and music. "We ought not to be ashamed of appreciating the truth and of acquiring it wherever it comes from," he wrote, "even if it comes from races distant and nations different from us."[40] He was followed by al-Farabi (d. 950) and Ibn Sina (d. 1037), both from Central Asia, who advanced what is now called the "Peripatetic Arabic School," in reference to the Peripatetic School in Ancient Greece.

For these medieval Muslim thinkers, as well as their counterparts in the West, "philosophy" had a much broader meaning than it has today. It covered all the diverse areas of human knowledge that we would now categorize into diverse disciplines. The term "PhD," which means "Doctor of Philosophy," and which you can get in almost every academic field, is a relic from this all-encompassing meaning of the term.

The Mu'tazila was the very first school in Islam to be influenced by the Greek philosophical heritage—but by its "method or technique, rather than of substance or content."[41] That is why they were *mutakallimun*, or "theologians," and not *falasifa*, or "philosophers." But these two intellectual trends in early Islam had a commonality in championing human reason as a source of wisdom independent from revelation. That is why they would soon be lumped together, and delegitimized forever, as the deviant branches of the true faith.

THE FIDEIST COUNTERATTACK

While Islam's rationalists were enjoying the support of the early Abbasid caliphate, the more conservative forces were regrouping. They were concerned both with rational theology and its influence on jurisprudence. Since they wanted to minimize the scope of reason and fill the void with hadiths, or sayings attributed to the Prophet, they became known as *Ahl al-Hadith,* or the "People of Hadiths."

The standard-bearer of this movement was Imam Ahmad ibn Hanbal (d. 855), who wrote one of the first books of hadith: the *Musnad,* a collection of some twenty-seven thousand reports, which he reportedly chose from a staggering pool of seven hundred thousand. Not surprisingly, most of these hadiths reflected Hanbal's own theological views, which were, on almost every single issue, the exact opposite of those of the Mu'tazila. For Hanbal, God's justice was beyond our comprehension, Qur'anic statements about God's attributes had to be accepted "without asking how," and the Qur'an itself was "uncreated"—a view that Hanbal defended, heroically as one must grant, despite the persecution he went through under al-Ma'mun's *mihna*.

Hanbal's collection also included the narrations that the Compulsionists had put into circulation to vindicate predestination. One of them read:

> God, Almighty, took a handful of mud and said: "These are [the people] in paradise and I do not care." He took another handful and said: "These are [the people] in Hell and I do not care."[42]

This not-so-dignified view of human nature did not grant much authority to reason. Reason, for Hanbal and his followers— the Hanbalites—was only good for comprehending God's commandments, not to speculate on them, let alone to search for truth independently. Hence they renounced the very notion of *kalam*, the discipline of theology, as a heretical "innovation," or *bid'a*. The fact that neither the Prophet nor his companions engaged in theology, for them, was enough of a reason to reject it. With this rigid dogmatism, the Hanbalites were building the far-right—or ultraorthodox—end of the Sunni spectrum, which would be revived in the modern era under the banner of Salafism, and its specifically Saudi version, Wahhabism.

Yet the real challenge to the Mu'tazila soon came from a more refined version of Hanbalism, which would ultimately form the backbone of Sunni Islam. It was founded by a scholar named Abu al-Hasan al-Ash'ari (d. 936), and thus would be called Ash'arism. Interestingly, al-Ash'ari was initially a Mu'tazilite. Around the age of forty, however, he had a Road to Damascus moment. Word has it that in his dreams he saw Prophet Muhammad, who told him repeatedly three times to "support what is related from me," meaning the hadiths. This made al-Ash'ari jump on the Ahl al-Hadith bandwagon, and to vehemently oppose the Mu'tazila doctrines that he knew well.

In literature, it is sometimes said that al-Ash'ari developed "a middle position" between the rational Mu'tazila and the anti-rational Hanbalites, but that is not very accurate. What he really did was to use the Mu'tazila method of rational argumentation to defend the Hanbali doctrines. "We hold firmly, professing what Ibn Hanbal professed," al-Ash'ari himself had affirmed, "because he is the excellent imam and the perfect leader."[43] Ironically, though, the very fact that he engaged in kalam, a deviant "innovation," still made al-Ash'ari a heretic in the eyes of the Hanbalites, who went as far as overturning his tombstone in the graveyard at Baghdad.[44]

In Islam: A Contemporary Philosophical Investigation, modern-day academic Imran Aijaz makes a useful classification of these early theological schools. Accordingly, the Mu'tazila corresponds to "theistic rationalism," which seeks harmony between faith and reason, both of them being independent sources of knowledge. In contrast, Hanbalism and Ash'arism are stricter and milder versions of "fideism."[45] The latter term, which comes from the Latin word fides, or "faith," literally means faith-ism. "Faith does not stand in need of rational justification," it holds; "faith is rather the arbiter of reason and its pretensions."[46]

The late George F. Hourani, the British-born Lebanese scholar and one of the towering experts on classical Islamic thought, also had offered a helpful schematization. In his definition, the Mu'tazila had accepted two sources of knowledge: "Revelation and independent reason." For the Ash'arites, the formula was: "Revelation supplemented by dependent reason." And for the Hanbalites, it was: "Revelation alone."[47]

A SOLDIERLIKE OBEDIENCE

These millennium-old formulations in Islam are still very important—because they are still very definitive. Most Muslims, under their influence, still value reason only, at best, as "dependent reason."

To see what this means, let's take a look at the writings of Sayyid Abu al-A'la Mawdudi (d. 1979), the Pakistani Sunni thinker who had a profound influence on Islamist movements all across the globe. His take on reason was quite interesting. On the one hand, he eagerly appreciated reason and its use for Islam, in articles such as "Islam is a Scientific and Rational Religion," and "Rational Proof of the Muhammadan Prophethood." He repeatedly argued that human reason, when rightly applied, would bring all reasonable humans to the truth of Islam.

Once people arrived at the truth of Islam, however, things would dramatically change. Reason was not a guide anymore, for Mawdudi, but rather a devious voice to restrain. In an article aptly titled "The Deception of Rationalism," he wrote that a person is either a Muslim or a non-Muslim. If he is a Muslim,

> this means that he has surrendered to God and to the Prophet as the prophet of God. It also means that he accepts that if God's Prophet communicated a certain law from God, he will obey it without asking "how and why." He has no right to require a rational proof for each individual law. As a Muslim, he has only to ascertain whether the Messenger of God promulgated a certain law or not. If the law is proven by a traditional proof, he must obey it immediately. He can seek a rational proof in order to attain repose of the heart and further insight. But until then, he must bow his head, obey orders and consider the traditional proof as [sufficient] proof for acquiescence.[48]

Mawdudi also used the example of a soldier in an army. No army could exist, he noted, if each soldier questioned the rationale behind the orders issued by the commanding generals. The soldiers, rather, had to obey the orders, fully and immediately, without asking "how and why."[49]

Mawdudi was not an outlier. His notion of a soldierlike obedience to religious texts reflects the mainstream religious mindset in broad parts of the Muslim world today. Conservative scholars emphatically advocate it, saying, "We hear and we obey, whether we understand or not."[50] For them, this is the true expression of Muslim piety.

Yet, as we saw, there was an alternative piety in Islam. It appreciated reason not only as a vehicle to bring outsiders to the religion but also a guide for the insiders to think critically. Now we will take a closer look at this latter view. We will especially focus on a crucial dilemma that marked the deepest gap between the Mu'tazila and the Ash'arites—a dilemma that still holds the key to the biggest padlock on many Muslim minds.

ISLAM'S "EUTHYPHRO DILEMMA"

Does the divine law define justice or does justice define the divine law? . . .

If the divine law is prior to justice, then the just society is no longer about rights of speech and assembly, or the right to explore the means to justice, but simply about the implementation of the divine law.

—Khaled Abou El Fadl, contemporary Muslim scholar[1]

As I was writing this book, I was blessed with the joy of raising two little lovely sons, the five-year-old Levent and the three-year-old Efe. While I gave them all my love, I also had to educate them sometimes with warnings. When one grabbed his brother's toys, for example, I had to tell him, "No, don't do that." Or when one yelled at the dinner table making everyone annoyed, I again had to tell him, "No, don't do this."

In one such parental guidance moment, my younger son turned to me with some cute frustration and asked the magical question: "Why?"

In return, I had two options. I could either explain why it was wrong to grab his brother's toy or to disrupt a family dinner. I could explain that by doing these, he would upset the people that loved him, and therefore his act would be *wrong in itself*. Or, I could issue a more simple dictum: "Don't do this, *because I say so!*" In this case, what made the act wrong would be not something inherent in it, but rather my authoritative *command* about it.

To put things in a theoretical framework, let's call this second approach—the "because I say so" approach—the *parental command theory*. To children, it implies that elders establish what is right and wrong, and hence good kids should always obey their parents' commandments. In contrast, let's call the first approach—where you explain to your kid why it is wrong to monopolize toys or disrupt a dinner—the *ethical objectivism theory*. To children, it implies that there are objective rights and wrongs out there in the world, about which their more knowledgeable parents are educating them but which the kids can also figure out by themselves.

Probably all parents who are reading these lines are familiar with both approaches, and they may be using both of them depending on the circumstances. For there certainly will be moments where you need the swift "because I say so" approach, for example, to protect your child from imminent danger.

However, a child raised mainly with the parental command theory instead of the ethical objectivism theory may end up being an immature person—as studies already indicate.[2] This is because the parental command theory will not help the child develop an inner conscience based on ethical values such as respect, fairness, or honesty. It can only teach him a set of rules, which will never be enough to account for all the complex situations the child will face in the ever-expanding life experience.

It can even make the child a little literalist hypocrite. He can grab his brother's chocolate cake, for example, and when you chide him for that, he can respond, "Well, you said, 'Don't take his toys.' You did not say anything about chocolate cakes!"

DIVINE COMMAND AND HUMAN REASON

This book, of course, is not about pedagogy. Also, no example is perfect when it comes to comparing God with His creatures. Yet still, the example above can help give a sense of the theological puzzle that we will now probe. You should just replace parents with God, and replace children with humans. And you should also replace *parental command theory* with *divine command theory*.

The puzzle is this: When God tells us "do this," or "don't do this," does He educate us about objective values in the world that we could also understand on our own? Or, does He merely give us bare commandments whose very value comes from nothing but God's own authority?

This is a question that long predates Islam. As far as we know, it was first addressed by Socrates, in his famous dialogue with a man named Euthyphro. Accordingly, the two Athenians, while both waiting for their hearings at the city's court, discussed what "piety" means. "Piety," argued Euthyphro, "is what is pleasing to the gods." In response, Socrates asked him, "Is the pious loved by the gods because it is pious? Or is it pious because it is loved?"[3]

In other words, was piety defined subjectively by the gods' will? Or rather, was gods' will defined objectively by what piety is? The question became known in philosophy as the "Euthyphro Dilemma."

Socrates lived in a polytheistic culture of "gods," but the dilemma proved relevant for monotheists as well. In Christianity, scholastic theologians like William of Ockham (d. 1347)—whose "razor" became famous as a principle of logic—took the side of the divine commandment theory. A like-minded theologian, Pierre d'Ailly (d. 1420) also believed that God "does not command good actions because they are good, or prohibit evil ones because they are evil." Quite the contrary, he argued, "these are good because they are commanded, and evil because prohibited."[4] This view also became known as *voluntarism,* because of its emphasis on God's will, or *voluntas.*

Other Christian scholars disagreed. Perhaps the most important was Saint Thomas Aquinas, who accepted that behind God's commandments there are objective moral values, "to which all men are forced to give their assent."[5] This view, in contrast to voluntarism, became known as *intellectualism,* implying that God's commandments are intelligible.

Intellectualism led to the concept of "natural law," which presumes that there are inherent ethical qualities, and also "rights," in nature that are knowable by human reason. The concept became quite popular during the Enlightenment, influencing thinkers such as the German philosopher Gottfried W. Leibniz. "It is generally agreed that whatever God wills is good and just," he wrote, adding:

> But there remains the question whether it is good and just because God wills it or whether God wills it because it is good and just; in other words, whether justice and goodness are arbitrary or whether they belong to the necessary and eternal truths about the nature of things.[6]

Leibniz himself was on the side of "necessary and eternal truths about the nature of things." So were most other Enlightenment thinkers, including John Locke, the father of classical liberalism, who wrote, "God himself *cannot* choose what is not good."[7] French thinker Montesquieu (d. 1755), who had a big impact on liberal political theory and even the United States Constitution, made the same emphasis in his landmark book *The Spirit of Laws.* Laws arise from "the nature of things," he argued, and it is absurd to think "there is nothing just or unjust but what is commanded or forbidden by positive laws."[8]

THE GAP ON *HUSN* AND *QUBH*

The Euthyphro Dilemma divided early Islam, as well: the Mu'tazila and the philosophers championed intellectualism, while the Hanbalites and the Ash'arites defended voluntarism.

This is evident in the long debates that the Mu'tazila and the Ash'arites had over the matter of *husn* and *qubh,* or "good" and "evil." Mu'tazila scholars insisted that acts such as "thanking a benefactor" (*shukr al-mun'im*) or "pursuing fairness" (*insaf*) were "good in itself," and this was knowable to all humans through reason. Similarly, acts such as lying, theft, or murder were "bad in itself," and this was also knowable through reason. This example of theirs was a case in point:

> One who finds a sick blind man on the verge of death in a desolate desert will know by reason alone that he is obligated to help, even where he expects that his help will only burden him and not benefit him in any way.[9]

Here we can sense that this "reason" of the Mu'tazila included what we would today call "moral intuition." Hence, one of the modern scholars who studied Mu'tazila ethics, George F. Hourani, likens it to "British intuitionism," whose advocates include G. E. Moore, W. D. Ross, and the famous C. S. Lewis.[10] The last, while being a faithful defender of Christianity, believed that morality was intuitive for all humans. Hence he disagreed with some other Christians who believed "the world must return to Christian ethics in order to preserve civilization." That is not needed, C. S. Lewis explained, because the "natural moral code" is universal.[11]

Since there is such a natural moral code, the Mu'tazila similarly argued, values existed "before the existence of revelation" (*min qabla wurud al-shar'*).[12] Even without religion, therefore, there would be morality. Only the rituals of religion, such as fasting, praying, or dietary requirements, the Mu'tazila argued, were knowable solely by revelation.[13]

Religion, in this view, did not claim to redefine the whole world, but rather operated in a world of objective facts and truths. The Sharia, argued one of the most astute Mu'tazila scholars, Abd al-Jabbar (d. 1025), "does not change the facts," as "will or intention . . . has no effect upon the truth of things."[14] The Sharia rather only "indicates" what is objectively right and wrong. In the words of al-Jabbar:

> Prohibition from the Exalted [God] is an indication that something is evil, as *the indicator indicates the thing as it is* . . . not that it becomes what it is by indication.[15]

In strong contrast to this ethical objectivism, there was the divine command theory of the Ash'arites. For them, all the good acts such as "thanking a benefactor" or "pursuing fairness" were not good in themselves. Neither bad acts such as theft or murder were bad in themselves. They were categorized as such only because God says so—and not by "the mind's intuitive judgment."[16] Al-Kiya, an Ash'arite from the twelfth century, put their position very clearly:

> We refuse to say that its being good or being bad is grounded in any essential property [of the act] . . . Good and bad are grounded simply in God's command and prohibition.[17]

Another prominent Ash'arite, al-Baqillani (d. 1013), also put it quite clearly: "All acts are evil only because they are evil by way of revelation. If revelation did not make them evil, they would not be evil."[18]

Therefore, if revelation said something totally different, then all the moral values would be totally different. "Lying is wrong, since He declares it to be wrong," al-Ash'ari, the very founder of the school, argued. "[But] if He were to command it, there would be no argument to the contrary."[19]

The Ash'arites did not disagree with the Mu'tazila that Allah is a just God. But His justice did not mean much for them, because since there were no objective values in the world, whatever God does would be, by definition, just. In contrast, the Mu'tazila believed that God is "necessarily just in the same sense that our reason understands justice."[20]

With its theology of an arbitrary God, Ashʿarism was saving itself from wrestling with what traditionally has been the greatest intellectual challenge to any theistic religion: the problem of evil. Because as good and evil lost their objective meanings, asking why there is evil in the world became a meaningless question.[21]

Yet with this slavish fideism, Ashʿarism was sacrificing other things. One was the very goodness of God, for which there was no criteria left. This was a God that could even "make harmless animals, children and insane persons suffer—and not compensate them."[22] As put by the great philosopher and mystic Frithjof Schuon—also known as Isa Nur al-Din—this "arbitrary and willful God" was not really "lovable."[23]

WHAT DOES THE QUR'AN SAY?

In Islam, on any issue, the primary source is the Qur'an, the Book of God. So the rift between the divine command theory and ethical objectivism must be judged by the Qur'an as well. And, at first, a simple clarification must be made: the very fact that the Qur'an includes divine commandments does not mean that it supports the divine command theory. This is a wrong assumption that both Muslims and non-Muslims can unconsciously make. The late Fazlur Rahman (d. 1988), one of the key pioneers of modernist Islamic thought, had criticized this assumption when he noted:

> There is a fairly common view among modern scholars, according to which this uncompromisingly transcendentalist picture of God, entailing a denial of trust in natural properties . . . and freedom of the human will, is to be based squarely on the Qur'an or is, at least, the most logical development of its teaching. This judgment, examined in the light of the Qur'an itself, seems considerably less than a half-truth.[24]

Finding divine command theory in the Qur'an would be indeed "less than a half-truth," arguably even less, because the Qur'an itself often presents divine commandments with intelligible reasons. It bans "strong drink and games of chance," *because* they would "cast among you enmity and hatred."[25] It bans "the flesh of swine," *because* "that surely is unclean."[26] Or while commanding Muslims not to insult pagan gods, it says, "Revile not those unto whom they pray beside God, *lest* they wrongfully revile God through ignorance."[27]

Moreover, in many verses, the Qur'an commands Muslims to do *adl* (justice) or *khayr* (goodness), or to refrain from *zulm* (transgression) or *sharr* (evil), without further explaining what such ethical concepts entail. In the words of contemporary Islamic scholar Khaled Abou El Fadl, this means "the Qur'an presumes that its reader has a degree of moral sense." The Qur'an also describes itself as a "reminder," reminding people "of the truth and values that should be innately known to them."[28]

Another key concept in the Qur'an which seems to support ethical objectivism is *ma'ruf*. In dozens of verses, Muslims are called upon to "do the *ma'ruf*," which is often translated as "doing good." Yet the exact meaning of the term is not "good" but "known." From this, A. Kevin Reinhart, a contemporary scholar on Islam, in an impressive linguistic and scriptural study of the term, infers an important conclusion: "The Qur'an assumes that some part of the good enjoined by the Qur'an is known without revelational stipulation."[29] There is, in fact, wisdom in the Qur'an's repeated use of "unspecified terms for good," for it is "a goad to ethical reflection and the open-textured search for ethical knowledge."[30]

Unfortunately, Reinhart adds, the Islamic tradition gave very little attention to this open-ended sense of the *ma'ruf*. In commentaries of the Qur'an, it remained "a plain-Jane word that seems to compel little interest."[31] In Islamic jurisprudence, it was reflected only by recognizing the *urf*—a term that comes from the same root of "knowing" but which implies only local customs and traditions of societies. However, "known" could be much more than that, opening a door to all kinds of human knowledge.

One must add to all this the very basic fact that in the Qur'an, the term "reason," or *aql*, is always used with positive connotations. The aspect of human nature that the Qur'an does warn against is not reason, but *hawa*, or "whimsical desire." It is quite telling, though, that the fideist movement in early Islam went as far as seeing reason itself as *hawa*. That is why they labeled the Mut'azila, along with more rational jurists, as *ahl al-ahwa*, or "people of desires."[32]

In short, while the post-Qur'anic Islamic tradition is another story, on the Euthyphro Dilemma, we can see the Qur'an as on the side of ethical objectivism. Scholar of religion Daniel Brown, who sees a problem with "extreme theological voluntarism" in Islam, also agrees with this verdict, granting: "the voluntarist position seems to have only weak support in the Qur'an."[33]

But weak support does not mean no support. The Ash'arites referred to the Qur'anic verses that emphasize God's omnipotence and His unbounded will. They also referred to a prophetic story that is all too familiar to not only Muslims, but also all their Abrahamic relatives, Jews and Christians, as well.

MAKING SENSE OF ABRAHAM'S KNIFE

It is one of the most dramatic stories of the Bible. Abraham, God's chosen, is blessed in his late age with a child named Isaac, who becomes a much beloved son. Yet Abraham receives one day a chilling commandment from God to offer Isaac as a sacrifice. He obeys the Lord, takes the poor child to Mount Moriah, and bounds him on an altar, with a knife in his hand. Yet at the last moment before Isaac is slaughtered, an angel stops Abraham, telling him, "Now I know that you fear God."[34] Then a miraculous ram appears, which Abraham sacrifices instead of his son.

What is the moral lesson of this story? It is a tough question discussed for centuries in the Jewish and Christian traditions. For ethical objectivists, who believe that God commands only what is objectively good, the story has "often been an embarrassment." In contrast, fideists have celebrated the story as an illustration of "unquestioning obedience to the divine command."[35] One of the most sophisticated voices in this camp was the Danish Christian philosopher Søren Kierkegaard (d. 1855), who, in his famed book *Fear and Trembling*, saw in the sacrifice story a justified "suspension of the ethical" based on trust in God.[36]

On the other hand, for the Enlightenment thinker Immanuel Kant (d. 1804), Abraham's blind obedience to a divine command for murdering his own child was not an example to follow but an error to avoid. This was, alas, the mindset behind religious fanaticism. It was the very mindset, Kant warned, of the "Grand Inquisitor," which tortured heretics for the sake of God, and of the holy warriors who wielded the sword "to raze all unbelievers from the face of the earth."[37]

A somewhat similar dispute on the sacrifice story took place in Islam as well, because the same story, albeit with some nuances, also exists in the Qur'an. There, too, Abraham has a beloved son—who is unnamed but was later identified in the Muslim tradition as Ishmael. There, too, Abraham comes close to slaughtering his own son, just to obey God, but is stopped at the last moment by an angel and a miraculous ram. The story is also very central to Muslim practice: one of the two major religious holidays in Islam is the Eid al-Adha, or the "Feast of Sacrifice," where all able Muslims are called to sacrifice a lamb, at least, to walk in the footsteps of Abraham.

So what are Muslims supposed to understand from this chilling story? The Ash'ari view was articulated by great Qur'anic exegete Fakhr al-Din al-Razi (d. 1210). According to him, God had first commanded Abraham to sacrifice his own son, but then later "abrogated" this command with a second one that saved the child. But did the initial commandment, to slaughter an innocent child, amount to something evil? Razi declined to concede that, because for him, "to judge the Divine command on the basis of what seems good or evil to human reason [was] invalid."[38]

The Mu'tazila, as one could expect, could not accept this explanation. We know this from Razi himself, who writes in his exegesis that the Mu'tazila struggled to find an alternative explanation to the story. They suggested, "Abraham was actually never commanded to carry out such a sacrifice." He was only commanded with making preparations, to "be ready to follow the command to sacrifice *if* it were given."[39] Razi seems to think that this was too much hairsplitting, which it really was.

Yet one of the most articulate Mu'tazila scholars, Abd al-Jabbar, came up with a better solution, based on a careful reading of the Qur'anic sacrifice story, which has a significant difference from the Bible. In the latter, Abraham receives an explicit commandment from God to sacrifice Isaac. In the Qur'an, though, Abraham only has a dream in which he sees himself sacrificing his son. He then consults his son, and they together decide that this is a commandment from God. But this was a wrong interpretation of the dream, Abd al-Jabbar argued, as dreams are not necessarily revelations. "How can it be a command from Allah," he asked. "He could see anything in his dreams."[40]

Two centuries after al-Jabbar, a towering name from the Sufi tradition, the scholar and mystic Ibn al-Arabi (d. 1240), would offer the same interpretation. Accordingly, Abraham's dream was not a divine commandment to sacrifice his son. Abraham had just misinterpreted the dream's lesson, and God had "rescued his son from Abraham's misapprehension."[41]

Today, more than a billion Muslims around the world recall Abraham's ordeal every year in the Eid al-Adha. Only very few of them are, however, aware of this alternative interpretation of the story. For just like various other gems within the Islamic tradition, it got lost under a thick layer of orthodoxy.

THE ASH'ARITE VICTORY AND ITS AFTERMATH

Today, if you read a standard mainstream Sunni text about different sects and schools in early Islam, you are likely to see the Mu'tazila listed as one of the "deviant sects" that luckily died out. You may also see that Ash'arism is praised as the main pillar of the true faith. The obvious reason for that is that the big war of ideas between these two schools of theology gradually ended with the victory of the Ash'arites. The winners, naturally, established themselves as the guardians of truth and depicted their rivals as the misguided. They even burnt the latter's books.[42]

That is why our knowledge about the Mu'tazila is in fact quite limited. It was even more limited until 1951, when the lost writings of Abd al-Jabbar and two of his students were found in an ancient library in Yemen, where vestiges of Mu'tazilism had survived within the Zaydi tradition. Besides such rare original texts, what we know about the Mu'tazila comes from mainstream Sunni sources who summarized their views only to refute them.

A particularly important figure in this Ash'arite victory was Abu Hamid al-Ghazali (d. 1111), who, by most measures, goes as the most influential Sunni theologian of all times. He left behind a complex literature that showed nuances over time, but he clearly opposed the rationalism of both the Mu'tazilites and the philosophers while adopting some of their tools. Hence, he was more open to reason than stricter Ash'arites—some of which blamed him for "swallowing" too much philosophy—yet he still allowed it only as *dependent* reason.[43] "The intellect only demonstrates the truthfulness of the prophet," he wrote in his last and greatest work on law, *Al-Mustasfa*, "and then absolves itself."[44]

Al-Ghazali was among what scholars call "late Ash'arites," who were more refined than earlier ones.[45] They admitted that acts, by looking at their effects, could be defined as "good" and "bad"—but only in matters not judged by religion. They still refused, in other words, to link objective moral values to Islamic jurisprudence.[46] The most rational of them was probably Fakhr al-Din al-Razi, who turned "increasingly eclectic and independent of traditional Ash'ari thought," going as far as arguing that when revelation and reason contradict, the latter must reign supreme.[47] Meanwhile, even within Hanbalism, there appeared a rationalist strain—a "middle position between Mu'tazilism and Ash'arism"—which seems to be allowed by the very vacuum created by the sect's original rejection of all theology.[48]

More significantly, there emerged another school of Sunni theology offering an even bolder middle position between Ash'arism and Mu'tazila. Named after its eponymous founder, Abu Mansur al-Maturidi (d. 944), a scholar from modern-day Uzbekistan, this school mitigated Ash'ari doctrines: that humans had more power in the "acquisition" of acts created by God, and also that "good and bad" were knowable by reason to some extent. Al-Maturidi also described a more reasonable God. To questions such as "Can God punish one who obeys Him?" or "Can God hold man responsible for what he cannot do?" his answers were "no," in contrast to the Ash'ari "yes."[49] The Maturidi school spread among Turks, Persians, and other Central Asians, in tandem with the Hanafi school of jurisprudence endorsed by the Ottoman Empire.

All these nuances and divergences mean that all Sunni Islam cannot be labeled as fully fideist. Rational approaches never fully died out, and they popped up in unexpected places. There were schools with nuanced positions, and scholars who went against their purported traditions.

Yet still, it is fair to say that the Sunni worldview has been defined primarily by Ash'arism—and certainly not by the Mu'tazila. As Fazlur Rahman, the eminent Muslim modernist, lamented, even Maturidism, which held "more reasonable views than Ash'arite theology . . . was eventually drowned by Ash'arism in medieval Islam."[50] This is true even for the Ottoman tradition, whose Maturidi affiliation was for a long time eclipsed by Ash'arism.[51] Meanwhile, Shiite Muslims, despite their relative openness to Mu'tazila influence, also denied that good and evil are discernible by individual human reason, and instead "postulated an infallible imam as the source of sure knowledge."[52] Sufis often attached a similar infallibility to the master, or shaikh, of their particular order.

An interesting attempt to reopen the discussion was by the great Ottoman Sultan Mehmed II, also known as "The Conqueror" for seizing Constantinople in 1453 from the Byzantines. In line with his liberal spirit of interest in arts and sciences, along with his tolerance to Christians and Jews, Mehmed II also wanted to open some closed doors in Islam. Among these was the old question, "Can reason know the goodness of good and the badness of bad?" He ordered a team of prominent scholars to write separate treatises on the matter, to be discussed at his court. The manuscripts, which were sitting for centuries at the Süleymaniye Library in Istanbul, were studied only in the 2010s by Turkish academic Asım Cüneyd Köksal.[53] From them, we know that one of the most prominent Ottoman sultans found the discussion crucial and wanted to revitalize it. But we do not know whether this effort had any significant influence.

Today, opinion polls held in the Muslim world indicate how powerful divine command theory still is. To the question "Is it necessary to believe in God in order to be moral and have good values?" 99 percent of all Egyptians say "yes." They are followed by 98 percent of Indonesians, 97 percent of Jordanians, 90 percent of Bangladeshis, and 88 percent of Pakistanis. (In comparison, the same question is answered affirmatively only by 10 percent of Swedes, 39 percent of Germans, and 57 percent of Americans.)[54] Overwhelming majorities in Muslim societies, in other words, cannot imagine that morality may have a source other than religion—such as human intuition and reason.

What has been the practical results of this worldview? In the next few chapters, we will investigate this question.

For a heads-up, let's just recall the example related in the beginning of this chapter—the example of raising children mainly with a "parental command theory" and its dos and don'ts. I suggested that it would not help children develop an inner conscience based on ethical values, and could rather make them immature, literalist, and even at times hypocritical. So let's see whether the divine command theory had similar effects on Muslim societies.

4

HOW WE LOST MORALITY

Since they have a religion, they act like they don't need morality anymore.

—Amin Maalouf, Lebanese-French author[1]

Woe to you, teachers of the law. . . . You clean the outside of the cup and dish, but inside they are full of greed and self-indulgence.

—Jesus of Nazareth[2]

I have spent most of my life in Turkey, a predominantly Muslim country. I have also lived through the grand political revolution that Turkey went through in the first two decades of the twenty-first century. It was a revolution that replaced the almost century-long hegemony of the more secular Turks with the hegemony of religious conservatives. From politics to bureaucracy, from business to the media, in almost all walks of life the conservatives replaced their enemies and "took their country back."

In the early stages of this story, it seemed quite promising, giving hope to many, including myself, that a Muslim liberal democracy was in the making, as I argued in an optimistic chapter on Turkey in my 2011 book, *Islam Without Extremes*. The reason was because, at that point, the religious conservatives in power had been implementing the political reforms the European Union required and the tiny band of Turkish liberals always aspired. Soon after that, however, as religious conservatives consolidated power, the mood began to change. It became gradually obvious that the liberal reforms of the earlier years were just to disempower the old secular establishment, especially the overbearing military, notorious for its coups against elected governments. Worse, the new ruling elite soon began to adopt the authoritarian ways of the old ruling elite—often only with more fervor.

In short, the dreams of a free, open, and democratic "New Turkey" fared badly, at least for that moment, against a grim picture of authoritarianism. Meanwhile, the unabashedly Machiavellian tactics of the new ruling elite initiated a new discussion in the country about what kind of people these religious conservatives really are. For they had ended up doing everything that they themselves used to condemn as unjust and cruel—only more aggressively. This included jailing political dissidents with trumped-up charges. It included creating a venomous media, which intimidated and slandered anyone who dared to criticize those in power. The religious conservatives also plundered state resources, with unforeseen levels of corruption, cronyism, and nepotism. A cultish group among them—called "Gülenists"—systematically cheated on exams to advance its members in the bureaucracy, fabricated evidence to put opponents in prison, and even attempted a failed coup, as a part of an intra-conservative power struggle.[3]

A CASE OF IMMORAL PIETY

Most Turks who despised this sea of *ahlaksız dindarlık*, or "immoral piety" were the secularists, who kept telling the liberals, "We had warned you about these people," despite the fact that their own history wasn't much better. Meanwhile, there were also some rare conservatives who had the conscience, and the spine, to speak out. One was Mustafa Öztürk, a popular theologian and opinion writer. "For the next 40 to 50 years, we Muslims will have no right to say anything to any human being about faith, morals, rights and law," he wrote in 2017. "The response, 'We have seen you as well,' will be a slap in our face."[4] Another prominent theologian, the former mufti of Istanbul, Mustafa Çağrıcı, also lamented about "the growing gap between religiosity and morality." In the past, he recalled, conservatives like him would typically argue, "There could be no morality without religion." But now, he wrote, he had to argue, "There *should* be no religion without morality."[5]

What was the exact problem here? For some, the problem was the usual corruption that comes with power. It was also the age-old problem of hypocrisy. The religious conservatives, according to this view, were just failing to live up to their highest ideals—which is a problem one can see in every tradition, every society.

For those who could read between the lines, however, the problem involved something different, something deeper. Because for all the immoral things they did, the conservatives had found religious justifications. Prophet Muhammad had reportedly said, "War is deceit," and since they were at a political war—with secularists, rival groups, "imperialists," or "Zionists"—they could use all kinds of tricks, lies, and libels.[6] A verse in the Qur'an said, "Relatives have prior claim over one another," so packing the bureaucracy with your own relatives was just fine.[7] Or while the Sharia had condemned *riba,* or interest, it had no clear rules about public tendering, which the religious conservatives in power twisted repeatedly—a staggering number of 186 times over a period of sixteen years—for the immediate benefits of their cronies.[8]

In other words, the problem was not that the religious conservatives were not pious enough. The problem was that theirs was a piety that did not make them moral people.

I have seen this problem in my native Turkey, but it is certainly not limited to it. The late Egyptian scholar Nasr Abu Zayd also observed a "religiosity devoid of ethics" in his nation, where "mosques are full, but corruption is rampant."[9] The Iraqi statesman Ali A. Allawi also has experienced an Islam that is "increasingly devoid of any deeply ethical content."[10] Qatar-based academic Omar Edward Moad also witnessed "outward religiosity without moral conscience."[11]

In Turkey, one of the prominent critics of this problem was theologian Ali Bardakoğlu, who served as the country's top cleric at the Directorate of Religious Affairs in the early years of the conservative ascendance, when things still looked promising. In a 2017 article, Bardakoğlu admitted that there is "a serious problem with morality" in his own country, only to add that "the lack of virtues and morals is rampant" in the whole Muslim world. He then nailed the origin of the problem: in a long historical process, Islamic jurisprudence had become "a pile of rules," among which morality had "evaporated."[12] "Of course," Bardakoğlu added, "this is related to the connection between religion and reason, with the issue of *husn* and *qubh* [good and bad]."[13]

TWO MEASURES OF LEGITIMACY

Bardakoğlu's intuition was right on point, because the "immoral piety" we see in the contemporary Muslim world is rooted in Ash'arism and its equation of ethical value with divine commandment. This worldview equates morality with religious law. So, by definition, whatever the law bans becomes immoral, as whatever the law permits becomes moral. The question whether the law's verdicts are moral or not is hardly asked—simply because there is no independent moral criteria left to judge the law.

As a stark example, consider the case of child marriage. To many of us today, a "marriage" between a nine-year-old girl and a sixty-year-old man would seem deeply abusive. But for an ultraconservative Muslim thinking on Hanbalite or Ash'arite precepts, it may be simply *halal,* or "permissible." That is because in the classical age of Islam, there was no clear definition of the marriageable female age, and menstruation was typically seen as the legitimate age for consummation. This was, arguably, normal for premodern times, when most societies equated puberty with adulthood. Today, however, thanks to a plenitude of experiences, reports, and studies, we know that child marriage is absolutely disastrous for little girls. We also have a better alternative for their teen years, which is called "education." But who cares about all that, if your only criteria for judging the "good" and the "bad" are the millennium-old rules of Islamic jurisprudence?

In classical Islam, the first warning sign for this problem was the emergence of *hiyal,* or "legalistic trickery." This referred to the solutions jurists offered to circumvent the prohibitions of the law while still observing the letter of the law. The charging of interest was banned by the Sharia, for example, but you could still charge interest without calling it as such. (A borrower could "sell" some property to a money lender and then buy it back immediately for a higher price.[14]) While such tactics offered some helpful pragmatism in the face of rigid rules, they also opened the way for sheer hypocrisy. A famous case was that of a rich man who "granted" much of his wealth to his little children right before the annual date of the zakat tax, only to get it back after paying his taxes.[15] This wasn't moral but it was legal. And the latter was what really mattered.

The problem became more acute over time, especially with modernity: modern life produced many new areas of human activity and knowledge, whereas Islamic jurisprudence kept offering the same old rules that were now too archaic or too inadequate. The ethical rules humanity developed for these new areas were "un-Islamic," so they were unaccepted. The result was ethics-free zones in which one could surf at will.

Take, for example, the notion of "ethical journalism." It includes principles such as "truth and accuracy," "independence," and "fairness and impartiality." When you present a point of view, accordingly, you should also give voice to alternative views. When you criticize somebody, you should give them a right to respond. But I remember reminding these to an Islamist Turkish journalist, only to get a dismissal of "all this Western blah-blah." For him and his comrades, there was simply nothing *haram* (religiously banned) about what they were doing: war propaganda against the enemy. It was even an act of piety.

Perhaps the same Islamist Turkish journalist would be in favor of ethical journalism if he himself were the target of smear campaigns—as was really the case in Turkey in late 1990s, when secularists had the upper hand. But this would be a mere tactic, as it really turned out to be, revealing not any real ethics but rather the lack thereof.

Ali Bardakoğlu, the wise theologian, pointed out this double standard problem as well in his 2017 book, *Facing Our Muslimhood in the Light of Islam.* Quite a few Muslims in the world today, he observed, are "two-world-ed." This means, he wrote:

> Muslims have two measures of legitimacy in their minds, two separate ways out. When it is convenient, there is the law of the [secular] state, the order of society, there are bylaws, there are regulations. But if these do not work, the legitimacies in your mind come into play—a [religious] permit that you gave to yourself or that you have taken from someone opens your way. Furthermore, if you belong to a *tarikat* [a religious order or cult], you will have even a third measure of legitimacy, a third way out. [Yet] it is impossible for a person with three different measures of legitimacy to appear as a trustable person. . . . For nobody can have a guarantee on which measure of legitimacy that person will use to proceed at any given moment.[16]

The solution to this grand problem lies in harmonizing the "two worlds." That means accepting that besides Islam's own specific principles and rules that bind its own believers, there are also universal principles and rules that bind all people—and the two are not alternatives. But that in itself requires removing the theological roadblock on defining the "good" and the "bad" with human reason.

THE OVERINCLUSIVE WORLD OF FATWAS

While one consequence of Ash'arism has been the rejection of ethical values that come from the outside, another consequence has been the growth of a dry legalism within.

American Muslim scholar Sherman Jackson is among those who captured the nature of the problem here. The Ash'arites, he writes, defined revelation as "the only source of moral value." From this came the inevitable result: "Every question human beings might pose in moral terms could be addressed as such on the basis of scripture."[17] Therefore, "in the aftermath of the Mu'tazila defeat," an "over-inclusive scripturalism" dominated the Islamic world.[18] It was a scripturalism that turned even trivial questions into religious problems. Muslims began to worry about things like, "Should one wear one's wrist-watch on the right wrist or on the left wrist?"[19]

To see what this looks like in practice today, one has to take a look at the world of fatwas. The term, which entered Western parlance with the infamous 1989 "death fatwa" of Ayatollah Khomeini on author Salman Rushdie, of course merely means "legal opinion." It is typically a statement by a trained Muslim mufti, or a "fatwa giver," on a question that often comes from an ordinary Muslim. What is stunning is the scope of the minute details of life that fatwas cover. A quick research on popular "online fatwa" services shows that ordinary Muslims are curious about questions such as these:

"Is it permissible to shower while standing?"
"In cutting fingernails, [do] we need to start in the index finger of the right hand followed by the rest of the fingers?"
"Can you be naked in front of animals like birds?"

"How can a person conceal himself from the *jinn* [genies] when in the toilet?"[20]

Most such questions receive detailed, serious answers from scholars. When it is asked, "Is it permissible to urinate while standing?" the answer is, "It is allowed, but disliked." Then comes a long explanation of how the Prophet Muhammad himself urinated.[21] There are even reported hadiths on this matter: "If anyone tells you that the Messenger of Allah urinated while standing, do not believe him, for I (always) saw him urinating while sitting down."[22] Such things are seen as important, because "imitating" exactly what the Prophet did in all such mundane details of life—from how to eat food, drink water, or leave a beard—is seen as a "morally praiseworthy act independent of the contents of the action."[23]

Then there are matters of sex. A question comes from a Muslim who is "confused about suckling wife's breasts." The fatwa comforts him: "You may suck your wife's breasts. If the milk flows and you drink, this does not affect the marital relations. Only the suckling that takes place during the first two years is considered in the Sharia."[24] Another Muslim wonders if bestiality—sex with an animal—invalidates one's *Hajj*, or pilgrimage, or Ramadan fasts. The answer is that bestiality is impermissible, but according to most scholars, "committing bestiality does not invalidate the *Hajj* or fasts."[25]

The point in fatwa culture is to legislate every minute detail of life and every possible question, so nothing is left for individual Muslims to decide on their own. And while muftis offer all this extreme legalism, conservative lay Muslims ask only more of it. Instead of struggling with "the pangs of personal conscience," in the words of Abou El Fadl, "the average Muslim projects the burden of morality onto the law."[26]

The obvious danger here is that once you have the right fatwa, you can easily justify things that are objectively unethical. Shaikh Hamza Yusuf, a prominent Muslim scholar in the

West, frankly admitted this problem in an intra-Muslim conference in 2018. "Some fatwas are dangerous," he said; others "are ridiculous."[27] But on what basis could Muslims question and oppose such bad fatwas? Could they, for example, rely on their consciences?

THE SHAKY GROUNDS OF CONSCIENCE

"Conscience" is a term that comes from the Latin word *scientia,* or "knowledge." With the prefix *con,* it means "knowing with." It implies that we humans have an internal source of knowing what is right and wrong, even if we aren't guided by outside sources such as religion and culture.

The origin of the concept goes back to Socrates, who spoke of a *daimonion,* or an "inner voice," which turned him away from doing wrong things. It found a strong basis in Christianity, thanks mainly to Saint Paul, who wrote that while the Gentiles didn't know God's written law, "the requirements of the law are written on their hearts, their consciences also bearing witness."[28] Enlightenment thinkers further elevated conscience as the source of "the individual's moral autonomy," while also coining the political term "freedom of conscience."[29] More recently, scientists have presented evidence that there is really something innately moral in human nature, as our brains are "configured to form bonds, to cooperate, and to care."[30]

But what is the place of conscience in Islam?

Contemporary Muslims can think that we have the exact same notion—in Arabic, "conscience" is called *damir,* and in some other languages, such as Turkish, it is called *wijdan.* However, research shows that these two terms acquired the meaning of "conscience" only in the nineteenth century, and with the influence of translations from Western literature, sometimes by Arab Christians.[31] In contrast, in the classical era, *wijdan* was used by Sufis to designate "encounter with God," and *damir* was used to refer to "innermost, secret thoughts," which were not necessarily virtuous.[32] Al-Ghazali, for example, wrote that God sent His prophets to cleanse people's *damir* "from the seductions of the deviant."[33]

That is why some prominent modern Muslim scholars—Fazlur Rahman and Farid Esack—argued that the Islamic term for conscience must rather be the Qur'anic term *taqwa*.[34] This makes sense in the light of the very first mention of the term in the Qur'an: it says that after creating the "soul," God inspired to it "its wickedness and its *righteousness*," the latter being *taqwa*.[35] However, as anyone familiar with the Islamic tradition may know, what *taqwa* came to mean in Islam is "God-fearing piety," often expressed as meticulous observation of the Sharia.[36] *Taqwa*, in this more established sense, is an internal drive for *doing* the right thing, but not a capacity for *figuring out* the right thing.

The truth is that, in mainstream classical Islam, there really was no well-defined concept of conscience as an independent source of moral authority.[37] Such a moral authority was precisely what the "intuitionist" ethics of the Mu'tazila entailed—but Mu'tazila itself was precisely the road not taken. Conscience still remained in the air, naturally, but to act only implicitly. Hence, when jurists followed the "call of conscience," they had to "construct a fortress of juridical reasoning and legal language to create the impression that they are not ruling according to the dictates of philosophy or ethics, but law."[38]

Meanwhile allusions to conscience in the founding texts received only limited attention. One of them is a remarkable hadith in which the Prophet gets asked by his companion, Wabisah ibn Ma'bad, on what it means to be a good person. In return, the Prophet says:

> *Consult your heart.* Righteousness is that which makes the soul feel tranquil and the heart feel tranquil. And sin is that which makes the soul waver and the breast uneasy.[39]

An exceptional voice in classical Islam that embraced this message was the great Sufi master Jalal al-Din Rumi (d. 1273). "You have a spiritual organ within," he wrote, "Let it review the fatwa of the muftis and adopt whatever it agrees with."[40] But muftis themselves, and the orthodoxy they upheld, were not impressed. Some, including al-Ghazali, argued that the advice "consult your heart" was valid only for Wabisah himself. Others said it can't be that narrow, but it must be still valid for only people like Wabisah, whom the Prophet "knew to be a person of faith and understanding."[41] Sunni sources still quote this hadith only by taking great pains to emphasize that the heart can't actually override the law.[42] They say that the hadith is valid only "if the person giving the ruling does not have any strong [textual] evidence to support his conclusion." And even in that case, those who can trust their hearts are only "who are true believers and who are knowledgeable of the Shariah."[43]

All this legalism is justified with an understandable concern: that humans can tilt the law out of *hawa*, or "whimsical desire." But the opposite risk, that law itself can be used to serve immoral ends, is often overlooked. Conscience, which can balance the law, does not count as a moral authority. It can even be suppressed as *waswasa*, or "the whispering of devils," which is precisely what a former extremist regrets to have done during his radicalization.[44]

THE NEED FOR A MORAL REVIVAL

What do Muslims think of this law-versus-conscience dilemma today? There are no polls that I am aware of, so I decided to carry out my own little poll among my fellow Turks in January 2019. To some 450,000 followers on Twitter, I posed the question "If a jurisprudential verdict conflicts with your conscience, which one would you question?"[45] Among the 5,500 people who answered, 37 percent said that it is conscience that must be questioned. One of them, to make his case, even referred to Abraham's sacrifice story, which we examined in the previous chapter: "Abraham listened to God's commandment," he reminded me, "not his conscience."[46] He gave me, in other words, a crash course in Ash'arism, whose grip on the mind of the more conservative Turks was evident.

This strong belief in divine command ethics, which may be stronger in much of the Arab world than in relatively more secular Turkey, is also a constant source of religious authoritarianism. For if morality equals obedience to divine commands, all you can do to uphold morality in a society is to *enforce* those commands. That is why Islamist movements aspiring for a "moral revival" in Muslim societies focus on establishing the Sharia, as they understand it, with dictates such as forcing all women to veil themselves, banning alcohol or nonmarital sex, or enforcing public prayer and other Islamic observances.

In fact, Muslim societies do need a "moral revival"—but of a different kind. What is needed is to revive objective ethical values and "to liberate the captive conscience," as the late Egyptian scholar Gamal al-Banna (d. 2013) put it.[47] This requires a whole new approach to education, and a new genre of art and literature—like the works of the great Egyptian authors of the mid-twentieth century Abbas Mahmud al-Aqqad, Khalid Muhammad Khalid, and M. Kamel Hussein, who elucidated conscience as the "inner voice of God."[48] With such new inputs to society, we need a new culture in which morality doesn't "evaporate" among jurisprudential rules, but rather interprets them—and, if necessary, reforms them.

What is also needed is to open up and reconnect with the rest of humanity, because since ethical values are universal, there may be things to learn from other cultures who may have cultivated the same values in their own traditions. They may have developed, for example, concepts such as ethical journalism, academic integrity, business ethics, legal ethics, even sexual ethics, as contemporary scholar Kecia Ali has argued well.[49] They may also have their own flaws and shortcomings, to which our tradition may help—but only if we can connect it to universality.

This may come as a shocking proposal to the Islamists, who typically believe in the exact opposite, thinking that "immorality" pours in from the outside, especially the West, against which Muslim societies should seal their gates. But that is because by morality they mean nothing other than divine command ethics. It is also because their predecessors were the very ones who shut the gates of Islam to universality in the first place. We will now see how that happened—and what its cost has been.

HOW WE LOST UNIVERSALISM

The tension between divine command ethics and philosophical ethics in Islam . . . overlaps with the one between
revelation-based communitarianism and reason-based
universalism.

—Oddbjørn Leirvik, comparative theologian[1]

Reason without Islam cannot, on its own, tell good from
evil. . . . [Hence] there is no source of justice or truth outside of Islam.

—Necmettin Erbakan (d. 2011), Turkish Islamist politician[2]

"A wise visitor from outer space who dropped in on Earth a millennium ago," an American journalist once suggested, "might have
assumed that the Americas would eventually be colonized not by
primitive Europeans but by the more advanced Arab civilization."[3]
That is because a millennium ago, the civilization of Arabs—or,
more precisely, Muslims—was clearly "the most advanced in the
world."[4] Muslims were the leading figures in astronomy, physics,
mathematics, medicine, and optics, in addition to philosophy, law,
economy, architecture, urban planning, and even music. In comparison, Christendom was lagging behind the Muslim world by all
measures.

Today, it is common among Muslims to long for this "golden age" of Islam. But there is not enough introspection about how it came to be and why it faded away. For many pious believers, there is a simple explanation found in piety itself. Accordingly, early Muslims were so successful because they were zealous for their religion, and hence God rewarded them with wisdom, power, and glory. But then Muslims turned sinful, and this time God punished them by empowering their enemies. So, the same reasoning goes, Islam's majesty will come back only when Muslims turn devout again, only when they become "real Muslims."

Yet this romantic explanation has little basis in facts, which do not show any evidence of Muslim societies becoming less religious over time. In fact, as the late great Turkish intellectual Erol Güngör once pointed out, there are reasons to think that Muslim societies turned often more religious in times of decline—not as the cause of any defeat, but to find moral strength against it.[5]

If we stick to facts, on the other hand, we can find a different explanation to the majesty of the early Islamic civilization: that it was unusually cosmopolitan—"even more cosmopolitan than the Hellenistic and Roman world had ever been," in the words of Italian historian Giorgio Levi della Vida.[6] While we call it "Islamic," Muslims did not constitute its majority until the eleventh century, and they also proved open to the learning from all the diverse cultures they ruled, inherited, or even merely heard of.[7] As Vartan Gregorian, an Iranian-born Armenian American academic, aptly summarized:

> Not merely translators, the Abbasids collected, synthesized and advanced knowledge, building their own civilization from intellectual gifts from many cultures, including the Chinese, Indian, Iranian, Egyptian, North African, Greek, Spanish, Sicilian and Byzantine. This Islamic period was indeed a cauldron of cultures, religions, learning and knowledge—one that created great civilizations and influenced others from Africa

to China. . . . There was just one science—not a separate "Christian science," "Jewish science," "Muslim science," "Zoroastrian science" or "Hindu science"—for the Abbasids, who were apparently influenced by numerous Qur'anic references to learning about the wonders of the universe as a way to honor God. Thus, reason and faith, both being God-given, were combined, mutually inclusive and supportive; Islam was anything but isolationist.[8]

This "exceptional absorptive quality" was really the secret of early Islam.[9] No wonder other civilizations that have shown the same quality, such as ancient Rome or modern-day America, have also flourished remarkably well.

Yet this cosmopolitan spirit did not last for too long, because its theological basis came into question. Those who championed reason—first the Mu'tazila and then "the philosophers"—were blamed for heresy. Fideist theologies that dominated the scene allowed, at best, "dependent reason," radically minimizing the sources of wisdom that Muslims could learn from. If reason by itself could not find any truth, why would Muslims care about what the Greeks or other infidels said about the nature of things?

Therefore, it is not an accident that cosmopolitanism flourished in Islam only before the full consolidation of Sunni orthodoxy. The first wave was the "Abbasid golden age" mentioned above, roughly from the mid-eighth to the mid-ninth centuries. Another "humanist renaissance" took place under the Buyids, a Shiite dynasty that ruled from the mid-tenth to the mid-eleventh centuries. Persian Muslim thinker Ibn Miskawayh (d. 1030), a student of Christian scholar Yahya ibn Adi, developed a virtue ethics inspired by the Greek notion of *eudaemonia*, or human happiness and flourishing.[10] Like the Mu'tazila, Ibn Miskawayh considered reason as "the vicegerent of God in man."[11] From this premise, he developed a notion of *insaniyya,* or "humanity," "a universalist term that was coined precisely in this period."[12] He believed that Muslims should be educated by both the Sharia and also universal norms of ethics. Yet he left little trace in the Muslim world. "Rarely in the later history of Islamic ethics" would such "humanistic views and speculative excursions be seen again."[13]

TWO VIEWS OF HUMAN NATURE

A key matter at hand here was whether Muslims should see an affinity with all humans—or only with other Muslims. Both views existed in early Islam, but the latter proved more definitive.

This can be seen in the different attitudes toward *adamiyyah*—another term for "humanity," deriving from the name of Adam, the first man. It is rooted in the Qur'an, which says, "We have honored the children of Adam," implying an honor given to all humanity. This basis allowed the rise of a "universalistic school" in Sunni Islam—most popular among the Hanafis—which conceptualized universal *huquq al-adamiyyin*, or "human rights."[14] But the bulk of the Sunni tradition was defined by the "communalistic school," whose theological basis was Ash'arism. Accordingly, humans had rights only if they were Muslims, or if they were granted "protection" by Muslims as subdued *dhimmis* or contracted *maahids*. Other non-Muslims counted as *kafir harbi*, or "enemy infidel," who had no inherent rights thanks to their mere humanity.[15]

In fact, for all Muslim schools of thought, the Qur'anic notion of *fitra*, or the primordial "human nature," could have been a strong basis for humanism.[16] But a hadith was used to close that door. "Every child is born on *fitra*," it read, "but his parents convert him to Judaism, Christianity or Zoroastrianism."[17] From this statement, many concluded that *fitra* equals Islam. Therefore, instead of imagining a common human nature they share with other people, Muslims began seeing other people as corrupters of their nature. That is why today some English translations of the hadith above don't even use the term *fitra* and write it simply as "true faith of Islam." For the same reason, converts to Islam are told that they are in fact "reverts"—reverts back to their own nature.

Yet the famous *fitra* hadith had an earlier version that put it in a context—and also a different sense. Accordingly, in a campaign against Arab polytheists, some Muslim soldiers had killed the former's children, thinking, "Are they not the children of polytheists?" But the Prophet admonished them, saying, "Every individual is born with the same pre-disposition (*ala al-fitra*) until his tongue is made Arabic, and his parents make of him a Jew or a Christian."[18] This could well mean that children are born neutral—without any language or religion. And the point was their innocence, not their Muslimness.

No wonder there have been dissenters to the view that *fitra* equals Islam. One was the eleventh-century Iberian scholar Ibn Abd al-Barr, who wrote that babies are born not *ala al-Islam* (on Islam) but rather *ala al-salama* (on peace), the latter meaning, "a state of perfection, devoid of both good and evil, of belief and unbelief, a neutral state, but with the potential to become a Muslim."[19] In the twentieth century, Tunisian scholar Ibn Ashur developed the idea, defining human nature with universal traits such "reasoning" and "moral and sound judgement." He even added "civilization building," as reflected by "the attempts of small children to construct tombs out of sand."[20] But such universalist definitions of human nature have remained marginal, even unheard of.

Contemporary Muslim thinker Abdulaziz Sachedina offers some helpful insights about the problem here. "In line with the Ash'arite theological voluntarism," he explains, most Sunni scholars denied "the innate moral worth of humanity." Consequently, these scholars rejected "a natural system of ethics," seeing it as "alien" and "un-Islamic." This also meant that Islam could not "participate" in a universal moral order; it could only aspire to build its own.[21]

That is why, after the initial centuries of cosmopolitanism and creativity, Muslim thought growingly became insular and self-referential. Hence, Islamic civilization lost the very "exceptional absorptive quality" that made it great in the first place. What emerged, rather, was a pervasive "lack of curiosity" about the rest of the world, which impeded progress in the late Islamic civilization.[22]

LESSONS OF SLAVERY AND ABOLITION

Before modernity, the insularity of Muslim thought did not appear as a burning problem. Islam had its own values and systems that worked for its time. By some measures, it was even ahead of its time. In that Islamic universe, there was a notion of common humanity, and also human rights, but only in a hierarchical sense: At the top of the pyramid, there were free Muslim men. They were followed by Muslim women, Muslim slaves, non-Muslims *dhimmis*, non-Muslim slaves, and finally the *zanadiq* and the *murtaddeen*, or "heretics" and "apostates," who had no rights at all.

With modernity, however, there emerged in the West new ideas about human rights. One of them was the revolutionary creed that all men are created equal, and thus none of them deserved to be slaves. It was championed by the abolitionist movement that was born in late-eighteenth-century England and which soon spread to America and other Western nations. In a long battle that lasted for almost two centuries, slavery was banned in all countries in the world, marking "the most important libertarian accomplishment in history."[23]

So, where did we Muslims stand in this history?

Let's see. Like most civilizations, the Islamic civilization had slavery. It had "moderated the institution and mitigated its legal and moral aspects," and in practice Islamic slavery was often "milder than its Western counterparts."[24] But it was still slavery. During the Ottoman Empire, slave traders were hunting people, often women, with raids among non-Muslim peoples in Africa,

Circassia, and Georgia, to sell them in the slave markets of Istanbul, Basra, or Mecca. The prices for white females were often higher than black ones. Among male slaves, the most pricey were the eunuchs, whose sexual organs were removed with extremely painful and risky operations, so they could take care of their master's women without posing a sexual risk.[25]

The movement to eradicate this social evil began not in Istanbul or Cairo, but in London.[26] In the late 1830s, the British and Foreign Anti-Slavery Society, which had spearheaded emancipation throughout the British Empire with the Abolition Act of 1833, began lobbying Her Majesty's government to push on other governments, including the Ottomans. Soon the British ambassador in Istanbul, Lord Ponsonby, began talking to Ottoman officials about this new strange idea that all slaves must be freed. Not getting a very enthusiastic response, he wrote back to London in December 1840:

> I have mentioned the subject and I have been heard with extreme astonishment accompanied with a smile at a proposition for destroying an institution closely interwoven with the frame of society in this country, and intimately connected with the law and with the habits and even the religion of all classes, from the Sultan himself down to the lowest peasant. . . . I think that all attempts to effect your Lordship's purpose will fail, and I fear they might give offence if urged forward with importunity. The Turks may believe us to be their superiors in the Sciences, in Arts, and in Arms, but they are far from thinking our wisdom or our morality greater than their own.[27]

But honestly, on this particular matter of slavery, the British wisdom and morality had indeed become superior to those of the Turks. To his credit, Abdulmejid I, a reformist Sultan who introduced many great reforms during his definitive reign, 1839–1861, didn't prove obstinate and complied with the British calls. In 1847, he issued an imperial edict banning African slave trade in the Persian Gulf and also abolishing the Istanbul slave market. In the next two decades Ottoman authorities actively suppressed the slave trade in Africa, the Mediterranean, Circassia, and Georgia.[28] Meanwhile, a new genre of Ottoman intellectuals, who were grounded in Islam but also influenced by Western liberalism, produced a new literature that generated a new conscience. One of these was *Sergüzeşt* by Samipaşazade Sezai, a novel on the touching story of a Caucasian female slave, which had an impact on Ottoman readers similar to that of *Uncle Tom's Cabin* on American ones.[29]

At the same time, Tunisia, an exceptionally bright spot in the whole Muslim world, both then and now, officially abolished slavery in 1846. In 1863, the mayor of Tunis, Husayn Pasha, even wrote a letter to the US consul general in town to urge the Americans to join the slavery-free world.[30]

Yet not all Muslims welcomed the movement against slavery, and those who opposed it had a strong case—that it was sanctioned by religion. One of them was the grand sharif of Mecca, Abd al-Muttalib ibn Ghalib, who launched a rebellion against the Ottomans in 1856, partly in defense of slavery, declaring "the Turks have become apostates."[31] Ottomans subdued the revolt, but slavery persisted on the Arabian Peninsula for many decades to come. In Saudi Arabia and Yemen, it would be abolished only in 1962. In 1981, the Islamic Republic of Mauritania would become the last country on earth to accept abolition.

The emancipation process was so stalled, partly because conservative clerics "felt uneasy about jettisoning too much of what their illustrious predecessors had elaborated."[32] There were pioneering scholars, such as the prominent Indian Muslim reformist Sayyid Ahmad Khan (d. 1898), who wrote many articles on *ibtal-i ghulami,* or "abolition of slavery," by relying on the Qur'an's "freedom verses."[33] But more conservative groups in the subcontinent, such as the Deobandis of Pakistan, were still defending slavery, on Islamic grounds, in the mid-twentieth century.[34] In Mauritania, as late as in 1997, a scholar declared that abolition "is contrary to the teachings of the fundamental texts of Islamic law."[35] In Saudi Arabia, as late as in 2003, Shaikh Saleh al-Fawzan, one of the highest-ranking jurists, argued that slavery is lawful in Islam and it should be legalized. He also accused Muslim scholars who condemned slavery as "ignorant" and even as "infidels."[36]

Today, there are hardly any Muslim authorities left that defend slavery—except the horrendous ISIS, the terrorist group which reestablished slavery in the middle of Iraq and Syria in the mid-2010s. But we Muslims should think about why it has been that difficult to come to this point.

The answer is not simply because slavery exists in the Qur'an. It exists in the Bible, too, but this didn't stop some Christians from becoming champions of abolition. Moreover, the Qur'an's treatment of slavery could in fact be understood as an inspiration for abolition, as Cardinal Charles Lavigerie, who led French missions in Muslim Africa, wrote in 1888:

> The Qur'an does not enjoin slavery, but merely permits it. Indeed, the Qur'an goes further, because it places the liberation of captives at the top of the list of merciful deeds, through which believers may be worthy of heaven. Strictly speaking, nothing would prick the consciences of Muslims in the abolition of slavery. However, habits are there, and have acquired a sacred character through their very antiquity.[37]

So, the problem wasn't the Qur'an but a certain mindset that couldn't imagine the Qur'an's praise of manumission, or "freeing a neck," as an inspiration for universal emancipation. It was a mindset that also stuck to tradition and couldn't imagine a new world where all human beings could be free. And when such a new world was presented by the West, the same mindset rejected it on principle. Because non-Muslims, by definition, couldn't have any moral wisdom.

Today, the resistance to abolition is a faded memory among Muslims, but the same mindset resists other liberal values that are promoted again often by the West—values such as freedom of speech, freedom of religion, or gender equality.

Of course, the same West has come to us, Muslims, not always with humane ideals but also inhumane deeds, such as colonialism, occupation, plunder, and domination. That has been a big part of the problem, as it is really hard to appreciate modernity when it comes to you at the barrel of a gun—even as a pretext for that gun. With all that imperialism, which has served their narrow *interests,* modern Western powers have repeatedly betrayed their better *values.* The history of this Western hypocrisy cannot be criticized enough.

Yet there is another part of the problem, which is the focus of this book. It is the Islamist resistance to modern liberal values, which often uses "anti-imperialism" as its own pretext for illiberalism. Scholar Khaled Abou El Fadl observes how this resistance works today, with the help of cultural relativism:

> Islam, it is argued, has its own set of standards for justice and righteousness, and it is of no consequence if those standards happen to be inconsistent with the moral sensitivities of non-Muslims. This argument was repeated often in the context of justifying and defending the Salman Rushdie affair, the destruction of the Buddha statues in Afghanistan, and the treatment of women by the Taliban.[38]

So, how does one argue against that? "I think that any effort to deal with this issue," Abou El Fadl suggests, "must start by acknowledging that Islam itself, like all religions, is founded on certain universals, such as mercy, justice, compassion, and dignity."[39] That is absolutely right. But how can we do that, if we are stuck with a theology that insists that values such as mercy, justice, compassion, and dignity have simply no meaning other than what the Sharia decrees?

HUMAN RIGHTS VS. ISLAMIC RIGHTS?

This background may help explain why some Muslims have been uncomfortable with the Universal Declaration of Human Rights, or UDHR, which was adopted by the United Nations General Assembly in 1948, in the aftermath of the horrors of World War II. The document proclaimed "the inherent dignity and . . . the equal and inalienable rights of all members of the human family," and referred to the "conscience of mankind" as an implicit source for these values.[40]

But not everyone could fully accept these notions. One of them was the Pakistani Islamist Mawdudi, who penned in 1976 an alternative text to the UDHR titled *Human Rights in Islam.* The book proclaimed human equality "irrespective of any distinction of color, race or nationality." It conspicuously excluded gender and religion, which are, of course, the real contentious issues regarding Islamic law.[41]

This work was followed by joint Muslim declarations such as the Universal Islamic Declaration of Human Rights, which was presented by a Muslim NGO in 1981, and the Cairo Declaration of Human Rights in Islam, which was signed by most Muslim-majority governments in 1990.[42] Both of these texts affirmed many of the rights proclaimed by the UDHR, but also offered some serious limitations. While the UDHR affirmed the "freedom to change [one's] religion or belief," for example, the Cairo Declaration not only skipped that freedom but also condemned "exploiting ignorance" to make people choose a religion other than Islam.

What is also significant in both of these "Islamic" documents is that they root the notion of human rights in nothing but the divine law. In the Cairo Declaration, in particular, "all the rights and freedoms" are declared to be "subject to the Islamic Shari'ah." We

read, for example, "every man shall have the right to free movement," but only "within the framework of the Shari'ah." Everyone
also has the "right to express his opinion freely" as well, but again
only "in such manner as would not be contrary to the principles of
the Shari'ah." Islamic law, in other words, is the basis, and the limit,
to all human rights.

At this point, some Muslims can wonder what is wrong with
this. What is wrong for believers to derive human rights from the
divine? There is nothing wrong, but there is something missing:
while there is a strong sense of God-given human rights that we
understand through divine law, there is no sense of God-given human rights that we can understand through human faculties such
as reason and conscience. The Mu'tazila and the philosophers of
Islam had the latter vision. So had the Founding Fathers of the
United States who found it "self-evident," in a historic assembly
in 1776, "that all men are created equal, that they are endowed by
their Creator with certain unalienable Rights."

Yet if reason is not a guide for anything, that it cannot establish any value, then there is simply no need—in fact, no justification—to look beyond the borders of revelation.

Ebrahim Moosa, a leading scholar of contemporary Muslim
thought, explains in a critical essay how this mindset works among
contemporary Muslims. "Muslims can engage in discourses of justice, egalitarianism, freedom, and equality," he observes, "only if
there is some semblance that the scripture or the Prophet or some
of the learned savants (imams) of the past endorsed, hinted, or
fantasized about the possibility of such discourses."[43] This has led
to the development of a particular intra-Muslim rhetoric, he adds,
where justification comes only from classical texts:

> In order to persuade people in public discourse today, the most
> effective psychological trick to play on unsuspecting Muslim
> audiences is to say that some past authority—Tabari, Abu
> Hanifa, or al-Shafi'i—held such an enlightening position on

matter X, so why do you lesser mortals not adopt it? The greater the vintage of the authority, the more persuasive the argument will sound to folks, even if the rationale of the argument and its substance make no sense at all. These may sound like anecdotal stereotypes, but this happens repeatedly in Muslim communities, even among secularly educated lay Muslims.[44]

But what if we can't find any exceptionally "enlightening position" in the past, especially on issues that our forbearers have never encountered? Can we take steps based merely on our reason? Unfortunately, Moosa says, quite a few Muslims are hesitant to do that, as they "discredit the legitimacy of their experience in the present and refuse to allow this experience to be the grounds for innovation, change, and adaptation."[45] As a result, as another Muslim scholar, Muqtedar Khan, points out, "most Muslims understand Islamic scholarship as knowledge of past opinions about Islam rather than new thinking. . . . They live under the tyranny of past opinions."[46]

THREE STRATEGIES: REJECTION, APOLOGY, AND INSTRUMENTALISM

Of course, all cultures do change and evolve, and Muslim cultures have been changing and evolving as well, especially in the past two centuries. Ideas of individual freedom, religious liberty, or gender equality have been making inroads all across the Muslim world, bringing in new attitudes and new laws. The almost-universal acceptance of the abolition of slavery, which we saw, shows that progress does take place. The same can be said for novelties such as constitutional government, popular elections, or modern education, which have gained at least widespread acceptance in many parts of the Muslim world.

But there is also a powerful obstacle in the same world that slows, halts, and even sometimes reverses progress: the "puritans," meaning Salafis, Islamists, and other rigid conservatives.[47] They are determinedly loyal to the "no-value-in-the-absence-of-revelation" tradition.[48] So, they are determinedly trying to prevent or undo all the "un-Islamic" inputs the Muslim world has amassed in the past two centuries. The evils they condemn typically include "rationalism," "liberalism," and "feminism." Some even include "human rights-ism."[49]

Yet even these "puritans" are not monolithic, and the positions they take regarding universal values fall into a spectrum. Based on my own observations over the decades, I believe there are three main strategies on this spectrum.

The first one is outright *rejection* of the universal, which is the strategy of hard-liners. For them, all the values Muslims need come from the Sharia, whereas all "man-made" ideas are by definition "falsehood." A key ideologue of this trend was the Egyptian scholar Sayyid Qutb (d. 1966), who had labeled everything outside of Islam, even mere secular knowledge, as aspects of *jahiliyya,* or the pre-Islamic "ignorance" that Prophet Muhammad had come to eradicate. His targets included "philosophy, the interpretation of human history, psychology, ethics, theology, comparative religion, sociology."[50]

Such ideas, we must note, have real consequences. "Today, many Muslim puritans come to the West," observes Abou El Fadl, "to learn the Western physical sciences while hoping to insulate themselves from the influence of Western culture by refusing to study the humanities or social sciences."[51]

In contrast to such hard-liners, there is the opposite end of the spectrum, the strategy of the moderates, which is *apology.* According to them, the modern world has really produced some good values and systems, but we shouldn't forget that all these were already and fully established by Islam. Is democracy a good thing? Yes—and Islam already introduced the best democracy with the "consultation" principle of the Qur'an, and the "election" of the first four caliphs. Are human rights good values? Yes—and Islam already enacted the best human rights standards fourteen centuries ago. What about slavery? Well, Islamic slavery was quite gracious, and modern humans are "slaves" to money anyway. While the defenders of this approach may have their hearts in the right place, their superficial arguments often avert an honest reckoning with reality.

Then somewhere between rejection and apology, there lies the third and most popular strategy, which is *instrumentalism*. Its adherents, just like the hard-liners, do not believe in universal norms, but they also see no problem in making use of them as long as they are helpful. Their unprincipled pragmatism can bear some helpful moderations, but it also can add to the problem of immorality, which we addressed in the previous chapter. It is the very problem Turkish theologian Ali Bardakoğlu describes regarding the Muslims who have "two measures of legitimacy," and who can freely "surf" between them.[52]

What we really need is to build harmony between the tenets of Islam, which need some fresh interpretations, and the universal values of humanity. (To use an academic genre, what we need is not "Islamization of knowledge," but "integration of knowledge."[53]) Those universal values of humanity are a work of cumulative conscience that has evolved over time with big trials and errors, big efforts and sacrifices. Islam, too, played an important role in this global history. The Qur'an proclaimed the sanctity of human life, for example, by condemning female infanticide—a horrific custom in pre-Islamic Arabia. Or it was Islam that introduced an egalitarian culture to India, whose caste system had degraded large swaths of people to subhumans. But the British also served the same purposes by banning *sati* or "wife burning," another horrific custom among Hindus, or, earlier, by building the foundations of democracy with the Magna Carta. Christianity eradicated horrendous traditions of human sacrifice among pagan peoples, and the American civil rights movement won a victory against the venomous racism among the whites. Moral progress, which we can detect with our inherent conscience, took place in various episodes in human history, sometimes thanks to religious texts, sometimes thanks to reason, and sometimes with a combination of both.

So instead of seeing anything outside of Islam as darkness, we Muslims should accept that there are objective values of "good" and "bad," and the human struggle to discover, articulate, and advance them is a universal cause in which we have a place—but not the only place. Only then can we break our self-containment and reconnect with the rest of humanity.

HOW THE SHARIA STAGNATED

The received formulation of Islam, which came to its full
fruition in the fourth century of the Islamic era and which
has ever since been regarded as being most uniquely and
decisively Islamic, has proved to be a most formidable
barrier to any change. . . . I do not know of any parallel in
the history of any other religion.

—Fazlur Rahman (d. 1988), Islamic scholar[1]

Today few issues about Islam are as controversial as the Sharia, a
word often translated as "Islamic law." The reason is obvious: Sharia, as interpreted by traditional jurisprudence (*fiqh*), has serious
conflicts with modern standards of human rights. These include
harsh verdicts for "apostasy" or "blasphemy," as we will see more
closely in later chapters. They include legal discrimination against
women or non-Muslims. They also include corporal punishments
such as flogging, stoning, amputation of hands, and beheading.

Muslims who are eager to implement these commandments are
often called Salafis or Islamists. Besides them, there is a broader
range of conservatives who may not implement the controversial
commandments, but also don't dare to question them. Their solution is to argue that the Sharia can be established only when the
right social conditions are built. To begin amputating hands for

theft, for example, you must first eradicate poverty so that no one will be too desperate to steal. But you still can't give up on the ideal.

That is why when Islamic scholar Tariq Ramadan called, in 2005, for a worldwide Muslim "moratorium" on corporal punishments, stoning, and the death penalty, the response he got was "either deafening silence or defensive posturing."[2] The reason was clear: How dare we give up the commandments decreed by none other than God?

Yet there is a different way to approach this burning matter: it is to look deeper into God's commandments by bringing more *reason* into the process of understanding and interpreting them. To do, in other words, what Ash'arite theology has not allowed Muslims to do throughout the past thousand years.

To see this theological hurdle, we can take an expert view from Wael Hallaq, a professor of Islamic law at Columbia University and one of the leading scholars in the field. In *A History of Islamic Legal Theories,* he notes:

A salient characteristic of pre-modern legal theory is the great attention it accords to the literal interpretation of the Qur'an and the Sunna. The language of these two sources was construed to have a direct and literal effect on law cases that required solutions. No amount of interpretation in this theory could have changed, for instance, the legal effect of the Qur'anic verse that allots the male heir twice the share of the female. Furthermore, the theological postulate that sustained most legal theories, of Ash'arite inspiration, states that man's intellectual capabilities are thought to be insufficient to determine the rationale behind God's revelation. God's wisdom, deeply embedded in His Sharia, is simply incomprehensible for humans.[3]

An example of this theological postulate was given, quite emphatically, by al-Qushayri, an eleventh-century Ash'arite scholar from Khorasan. In his exegesis of the Qur'an, he quoted the long verse that bans men from marrying certain women—such as their mothers, daughters, sisters, and various relatives—only adding the following note:

> The attempt to find the meanings behind the[se] prohibitions is an impossible matter, because *the law does not need to be justified.* . . . Rather [God] prohibits what He wills for whom He wills, and likewise gives permission. There is no underlying cause (*'illa*) for the laws at all. If the prohibited women were to be the permissible ones, or the permissible women were to be the prohibited ones, then that would be allowed.[4]

So incest was wrong only because God said so. If He said it was right, then it would be right. Human intuitions, value judgments, and rational considerations did not matter. Only God's bare commandments did matter, because they not only indicated but also constituted moral truths. And since there were no moral truths outside of the Sharia, there was also no ground from which one could look back at the Sharia—and dare to reinterpret it.

INHERITANCE, WOMEN, AND JUSTICE

To see the problem here in action, let's take a closer look at the example that Hallaq gave above: "the Quranic verse that allots the male heir twice the share of the female." Plainly, it reads, "Concerning your children, God commands you that a son should have the equivalent share of two daughters."[5]

This verse has been the basis of an unequal inheritance law in Muslim societies, which has been kept in practice up to date all across the Arab world. In fact, when I was working on this book, the only Arab country that came close to ending this system, Tunisia, was debating an "equal inheritance law," which was championed by the country's progressives but strongly opposed by various

Islamic groups. Those who opposed the law, which was made up of some 63 percent of all Tunisians, including 52 percent of women, had a powerful reason: unequal inheritance was God's verdict.[6] That should have been the end of discussion.

Yet according to al-Tahir al-Haddad (d. 1935), an exceptional Islamic scholar from, again, Tunisia, a discussion was possible—and necessary. In his controversial 1930 book, *Our Women in the Shari'a and Society,* he argued that the Qur'an's regulations about women, which were all progressive for their time, had to be understood in the context of seventh-century Arab society. In that society, "women did not participate in warfare, and were under men's protection." Men, therefore, had more economic burden, and giving them a bigger share of inheritance was only fair. But in the modern world, the socioeconomic conditions had become very different, the economic burden on the genders was now often equal, so inheritance had to be shared equally as well.[7] In general, Muslims had to focus on the "Qur'anic strategy," such as empowering women, rather than literal commandments.[8]

For these ideas, al-Haddad was harshly criticized and even condemned as an "apostate." Ez-Zitouna University, where he was educated, revoked his degree, and his friends and colleagues deserted him. At the young age of thirty-five, "in poverty and isolation," he died of tuberculosis.[9]

All that rigidity was only to be expected—for reasons of jurisprudence, and, deep down, theology. For to be able to share al-Haddad's reasoning, one first had to have a mindset of evaluating what "justice" objectively means, and then expect from God a law of inheritance that is objectively just. When God's literal command does not appear to be just, the same mindset would look for an alternative interpretation, such as looking into the specific context of the command and then reinterpreting it according to the new social conditions.

The Mu'tazila approach to the Qur'an would allow such a rational reinterpretation. In fact, it would even require it. Mu'tazila scholars such as Abd al-Jabbar and his student Mankdim had argued that *tafseer*, or exegesis of the Qur'an, "should not be done by one who does not have the prior knowledge of the justice of God through reason."[10]

Yet this was precisely what the Ash'arites would not concede. For them, there was no justice that stood outside of the Sharia and that humans could know through reason. For them, the Sharia came first, and justice followed—not the other way around.

THE DECLINE OF *RA'Y*

To see the impact of Ash'ari theology on Islamic law more structurally, we can look at the rise and the decline of *ra'y*. It is an Arabic term that is translated often as "considered opinion," or "common sense." It comes from the same root as "seeing," so it is also translated as "seeing with reason."[11] We know that it was used by the Prophet Muhammad, when he reportedly said, "I decide between you on the basis of my *ra'y* in cases about which no revelation has been sent down to me."[12]

This precedent allowed some jurists in the second century of Islam, especially those in cosmopolitan cities of Iraq such as Kufa and Basra, to rely on *ra'y*, alongside of the Qur'an, as a source of Islamic jurisprudence, in order to address new questions. Hence, they became known as *Ahl al-Ra'y*, or "People of Reason." Among them were the prominent Abu Hanifa, whose later followers would form the Hanafi school of law, which, despite losing much of its early rationalism over time, remained as the most flexible of the four Sunni schools.

But the "People of Reason" were rebuked by other scholars, often from the more parochial areas, who saw *ra'y* as whimsical. Instead, they wanted to secure all jurisprudence on a textual basis. Since the Qur'an offered only a very limited number of commandments, they filled the vacuum with hadiths, or "sayings," which were oral traditions about the words and deeds of the Prophet.

So they began collecting and canonizing the hadiths, which ultimately made up a much larger textual resource than the Qur'an. Hence, they were known as *Ahl al-Hadith,* or "People of Hadith." Among them was the famous Ahmad ibn Hanbal, the archrival of the Mu'tazila, whose followers developed the most puritanical of the four Sunni schools.

It is this latter camp, the "People of Hadith," that ultimately gave Sunni Islam its main color. Those who advocated *r'ay* either died out or had to restrain themselves.[13] In the end, "Even the term *ra'y,* having been so deeply associated with arbitrary forms of reasoning, was completely abandoned."[14] Hence, today while every Muslim knows what hadiths are, few of them would know what *ra'y* is.

Vestiges of *ra'y* still survived in Sunni Islam, but in limited ways. Imam al-Shafi'i, who founded the principles of the whole Sunni legal system, established that there are four sources of law. The first two, which were most definitive, were the Qur'an and the Sunna, or Prophetic example, as extracted from the hadiths. In addition to these "transmitted" (*naqli*) sources, there were two "rational" (*aqli*) ones: "consensus" (*ijma*) of scholars on a certain matter, and "analogy" (*qiyas*), which helped infer new laws from the ones established by the Qur'an and the hadiths.

Yet even here, boundaries were drawn. As al-Ghazali explained, "consensus" was based on not any trust in human judgment per se, but on the famous hadith stating, "My community will not agree on error."[15] (It would also lead to none other than the tyranny of the majority—even a long-gone majority.) As for "analogy," it gave reason only "a role subsidiary to that of the revealed sources."[16]

The most significant vestige of *ra'y* in Sunni jurisprudence was the concept of *maslaha,* or "human interest," which was accepted as a fifth source of law by the more flexible schools: the Malikis and the Hanafis, the latter just using a different word for it, which was *istihsan,* or "to consider something good." But al-Shafi'i, the big authority, spurned these notions "as based merely on free human reasoning guided by personal interests and whims."[17] That is why even Malikis and Hanafis growingly limited the scope of *maslaha,* restricting it only to cases on which the Qur'an or hadiths were silent.[18] In tandem with this process, later Malikis denied what seemed to them as an excessive rationalism of their founder.[19]

Notably, all this gradual decline of *ra'y* in jurisprudence was a consequence of what was happening in theology. As Wael Hallaq observes:

> The fact that the legal theorists thought it worthwhile to devote some of their energy to the rebuttal of certain theological doctrines indicates the relevance of these doctrines to the issues raised in legal theory. And it seems that most of this energy was expended in defense of the Ash'arite conception against Mu'tazilite theology . . . [and] the Mu'tazilite tenet that human acts are either good or bad, and that the mind, independent of revelation, is capable of determining which act is good and which bad. . . . The relevance of this tenet to the concerns of legal theory is readily obvious, for it runs in diametrical opposition to the most fundamental principle of Sunni jurisprudence, namely, that God decides on all matters and that the human mind is utterly incompetent to function as a judge of any human act.[20]

In short, as a result of the Ash'ari victory in theology, reason lost its initially high standing in Islamic jurisprudence. *Ijtihad,* or reinterpretation of the law, became possible only when there is no clear Qur'anic or prophetic injunction about a certain matter. This did not necessarily close the proverbial "gates of *ijtihad.*" But it kept those gates quite narrow.

Yet the world was constantly introducing new realities, and the narrowness of the gates was making it hard to catch up. For example, modern banking introduced a new concept of a mutually agreed upon reasonable interest rate, which was different from what the

Qur'an condemned as *riba*—a practice of mafia-style usury where the creditor unilaterally added an excessive "increase" to a debt when the debtor failed to pay in time.[21] But most Muslim jurists have proven hesitant, to date, to reinterpret the existing laws in the light of such new realities. The reason, as Rumee Ahmed, a contemporary scholar of Islamic law, observes, is rooted in their theological convictions:

> For a variety of reasons, jurists are hesitant to derive any new laws, especially when they challenge existing ones. What jurists tend to do instead is assume the authority of historical Islamic laws, even when those laws do not make sense, since sensemaking is a function of the human intellect, which is itself subject to corruption.[22]

Not too surprisingly, this legal stagnation had big costs for the world of Islam. Economic historian Timur Kuran has demonstrated some of them in his seminal book *The Long Divergence: How Islamic Law Held Back the Middle East.* Accordingly, Islamic law had in fact initially helped Muslim economies by stimulating commerce, honoring contracts, and securing private property. "Starting around the tenth century," however, "it began to act as a drag on development," by precluding "private capital accumulation, corporations, large-scale production, and impersonal exchange."[23] That is why credit practices in eighteenth-century Damascus hardly differed from those of the tenth century.[24] In the meantime, however, a whole new world was created in the West.

THE THEORY OF *MAQASID* AND ITS LIMITS

Despite all these impediments to rational reinterpretation, the Sunni jurisprudential heritage bears a promise for the future: the theory of *maqasid,* meaning "objectives" or "intentions," of the Sharia. The theory held that God decreed all His laws to

protect human *maslaha,* or "interest," which were often defined as
the protection of five key values: life, religion, property, lineage,
and intellect.

It may seem paradoxical that this rational approach to law was
developed by late (and more nuanced) Ashʿarite scholars such as
al-Juwayni, al-Ghazali, and al-Razi. But the paradox is resolvable.
Precisely for their distrust in human reason, the Ashʿarites believed
that the Sharia must cover all aspects of life, leaving minimum
room for what we would today call "secular law." But they also
knew that explicit commandments in the Qurʾan and hadiths
are finite. To extend these commandments to new situations, they
needed the aforementioned method of *qiyas,* or "analogy." And for
that, they needed to designate the *illa,* or "efficient cause," behind
certain commandments. For example, to extend the Qurʾanic ban
on wine to all other intoxicants, they had to designate the *illa* as
averting intoxication, which in itself served the higher objective of
"protecting the intellect." That is why, despite their theological un-
easiness with reason, they carved a practical space for it in the field
of legal theory.[25]

However, this space remained limited precisely due to theological constraints. Many Ashʿari jurists kept insisting that the
illa of a divine commandment could be "only discovered in the
divine text."[26] Only if God explicitly expressed His intention, in
other words, we would be able to speak about it. Al-Razi was
mocking these more literalist scholars when he said, "Were they
to hear the word 'purpose' [with regard to God], they would
accuse the one uttering it of unbelief."[27] In the words of Rumee
Ahmed:

> Jurists were worried that if they were to clearly identify the le-
> gal objectives, then they would effectively be saying that they
> had thereby captured the underlying, divine intention behind
> God's laws. That was to be avoided at all costs; most jurists in-
> sisted that God's logic is beyond all human comprehension,

and so no one can ever definitively know the true intent behind God's laws. . . . For that theological reason, jurists were adamant that the *maqasid* should never be thought of as objectives that explained the *intention* behind God's laws, but rather as explanations for the *existence* of certain laws.[28]

Moreover, even for al-Ghazali and al-Razi, the *maqasid* "were not conceived as purely theoretical objectives that underpin the law, but they were themselves derived from existing laws."[29] In other words, laws came first and *maqasid* were derived from them, not the other way around.

An exceptional scholar who took the *maqasid* theory to a higher level was Abu Ishaq al-Shatibi (d. 1388), a Maliki jurist from Granada, Spain. His context had helped him recognize "the grave need of his time to adopt Islamic legal theory to new social conditions."[30] Growing economic activities in trade were demanding "freedom of contract," whereas jurists were stuck with mere analogies to "the early Medinese practice of agrarian partnership."[31] This was the very problem of law becoming "a drag on development," in Timur Kuran's words.

To find a solution, al-Shatibi elevated *maslaha*, or "human interest," to "an integral principle that unifies Sharia."[32] To take this step in jurisprudence, he made the theological argument that God acts "according to the best interests of His subjects," and that those subjects can understand their interests.[33] By doing so, al-Shatibi was silently giving up on strict Ash'arism and "treading in the footsteps of the Mu'tazila."[34]

Precisely for this reason, al-Shatibi has been rediscovered in the modern age by reform-minded Muslims who are looking for a way forward. But in his day and age, he was less popular. His views remained "either opposed or ignored for centuries," only to be rediscovered and popularized by late-nineteenth-century Islamic modernists, such as Muhammad Abduh.[35] Najm al-Din al-Tufi (d. 1316), another unusual scholar who argued that *maslaha* could override even the Qur'an and Sunna, "quickly fell into oblivion."[36] His view was "a type of utilitarianism, like that of Jeremy Bentham and John Stuart Mill," and it was discredited for giving too much authority to "fallible human reason."[37]

The obstacle these pioneering scholars all faced was the theological postulate that did not allow too much reasoning about the "intentions" of the divine. The same theological postulate never allowed the *maqasid* theory to form the basis of an Islamic version of natural law—something that only the Mu'tazila could fully develop.[38] The *maqasid* theory itself was "marginalized," as most classical books of Islamic jurisprudence did not even assign a section or chapter to it.[39]

CAN WOMEN TRAVEL NOW?

To see a contemporary example of how conservative Muslims are still uneasy about any reformism based on the *maqasid* approach, let's look at a 2013 fatwa by a scholar at *Darul Iftaa*, or "Home of Fatwas," based in Leicester, United Kingdom. The scholar gets asked whether a Muslim woman can travel alone without a "male guardian," despite the hadiths that rule against that. In his response, he first acknowledges that this limitation on the woman was "to take care of her reputation, dignity and safety." He then says:

> Some contemporary people argue that travelling in modern times have changed from how it was in the time of the Messenger of Allah . . . It is not like how travelling was in the past. It is not filled with the dangers of the waterless deserts, encounters with thieves, highway robbers, etc. Now travelling is by various modes of transportation that usually gather large amounts of people at a time, such as planes, cars, buses, ships, etc . . . Thus, this provides plenty of confidence and reliability, removing feelings of fear for the woman.[40]

So, since we today live in a much safer world, can women freely travel now, as their safety was the underlying concern?

You may think that this would make sense. But our scholar emphatically says no. He accepts that protecting women from obvious dangers could well be the *hikma* (wisdom) behind barring them from free travel. (*Hikma*, roughly, is another term for *maqasid*.[41]) Yet, he insists, we must still implement any ruling of the Sharia regardless of whether we see its wisdom being fulfilled or not. Yes, the world may change, he adds, but "rulings that are based upon clear texts of the Qur'an and Sunnah can never change." Therefore, he decrees, "It will not be permissible for a woman to travel over 48 miles [the distance of three days, measured in seventh-century terms] in order to visit her family and friends, acquire knowledge or any other social reason."[42]

A NON-ASHARITE SHARIA

For all these reasons, Mariam al-Attar, a contemporary scholar of Islamic ethics and law who put much research and thought into this matter, is right to argue that the *maqasid* theory was a promising vision in classical Islam that failed to achieve much. It was only used to justify the existing laws, she notes, but never "to infer laws or to check the appropriateness of some existing rules."[43] Today, it can be a basis for renewing Islamic law, she adds, but first, we need to "establish it on non-Ash'arite basis."[44]

What would that exactly mean?

It would mean focusing on the *maqasid* of the Sharia instead of its rules, and making the former a legitimate basis for reinterpreting those rules. It would ultimately mean, in the words of contemporary scholar Ebrahim Moosa, seeing the Sharia "as a set of ethical and moral norms, rather than a set of rigid rules or laws."[45]

We also don't have to limit these norms to the five values mapped out by classical jurists. Ibn Ashur (d. 1973), the longtime chief justice and top cleric of Tunisia, had expanded them by reminding us of a much-forgotten legal maxim. *Al-Shari mu-tashawwif li al-hurriyyah,* or "The Lawgiver aspires for freedom."[40] So, the Sharia's intentions included "freedom" as well. And this implied both freedom from slavery, as classical jurists thought, and also, in Ibn Ashur's words, "one's ability to act freely and handle one's affairs as one likes, without opposition from anyone."[47]

Ibn Ashur also corrected a problem with the classical *maqasid* terminology: by "protection of religion," traditional scholars meant only the protection of Islam. (That is actually how they justified the execution of apostates.[48]) So he reworded the notion as "freedom of beliefs," extending the protection to all beliefs.[49] He even substantiated "freedom of expression," including "the freedom to pursue knowledge . . . produce intellectual works, and to publish one's views."[50]

If we Muslims begin to see the Sharia through such an objective-oriented lens, our sense of what is "Islamic" may radically change. An example is the "Islamicity Indices," published every year by a team of US-based Muslim academics. What they do is rank the world's countries based on values that they take as the intentions of the Sharia—values such as safety and security, socioeconomic justice, health care, or business environment. The countries that get typically the highest scores are New Zealand, Sweden, Netherlands, and Ireland—not Saudi Arabia, Iran, or Afghanistan. In fact, no Muslim-majority country ever enters the top forty in the measure of "Islamicity."[51]

If all this ethical approach to the Sharia sounds too "modernist"—a term that is often used disparagingly in the Muslim world—then let the last word go to Ibn Qayyim al-Jawziyya (d. 1347), the unorthodox Hanbali scholar who had come close to the Mu'tazila in accepting "the capacity of the human mind to discern the *illa* behind most of the rulings of the Sharia," while also granting that values like "justice" or "welfare" have "an objective existence . . . apprehensible by human reason."[52] On what the Sharia really means, he said the following:

Sharia is all about wisdom and achieving people's welfare in this life and the afterlife. It is all about justice, mercy, wisdom, and good. Thus, any ruling that replaces justice with injustice, mercy with its opposite, common good with mischief, or wisdom with nonsense, is a ruling that does not belong to the Sharia, even if it is claimed to be so according to some interpretation.[53]

HOW WE LOST THE SCIENCES

Before about 1050, science [in the Muslim world] was understood to be common to all humanity . . . After about 1050, the process is set into motion which culminates in the creation of . . . an alternative science which belongs not to all humanity but to Muslims alone: "Islamic" philosophy, "Prophetic" medicine, "Islamic" astronomy.

—Dimitri Gutas, eminent professor of Arabic and Islamic Studies

In January 2020, the world began to hear about a strange new virus that appeared in Wuhan, China. In a matter of weeks, the world also realized that this was only the beginning of a once-in-a-century pandemic.

Soon, health experts began calling for a precaution against the invisible enemy: "social distancing." This required people to stay at home, as much as possible, and also avoid public gatherings, including communal religious services in churches, synagogues, and, of course, mosques.

The Muslim world, by and large, heeded this call. In a few weeks, despite some objections or hesitations, communal prayers were suspended in most Muslim-majority countries, including Saudi Arabia, which also did the unforeseen and the unthinkable:

close down the Holy Kaaba in Mecca and the Prophet's Mosque in Medina.

For Muslims, like for others, none of these lockdowns were easy. Luckily, there was a hadith in the authoritative *Sahih al-Bukhari* that seemed to support social distancing: "If you hear of an outbreak of plague in a land, do not enter it; but if the plague breaks out in a place while you are in it, do not leave that place."[2] The hadith quickly became popular among Muslims, helping many connect the requirements of modern science with the wisdom of their faith.

Yet there were also Muslim dissenters—especially in Pakistan, where some stubborn imams refused to vacate their mosques. Moreover, they had a counter-hadith to support their case: *La adwa*, as they kept reiterating, which means "No contagion."[3] This short phrase was a part of a longer hadith, which is again in *Sahih al-Bukhari*, in its "Book of Medicine," and it reads as follows:

> Allah's Messenger said: "There is no *udwa* [contagious disease], nor *safar* [a serpent in bellies], nor *hama* [omens from birds]." A Bedouin stood up and said, "Then what about my camels? They are like deer on the sand, but when a mangy camel comes and mixes with them, they all get infected with mange." The Prophet said, "Then who conveyed the (mange) disease to the first one?"[4]

Yes, who had made the camels sick? And what was the lesson in questioning the Bedouin's simple but sensible observation of contagion?

IS THERE REALLY "NO CONTAGION"?

Two of the three notions denied in the hadith above—*safar* and *hama*—were superstitions among pre-Islamic Arabs that are forgotten today.[5] However, *adwa*, or "contagious disease," is a scientific fact. But the hadith above seems to both deny its existence, and also challenge the Bedouin's observation that confirms its existence.

If you read contemporary translations or interpretations of this hadith, you will probably see disclaimers against such a conclusion. It often comes as an explanation in parentheses: "*La Adwa*, or no contagion (conveyed without Allah's permission)." In other words, we are noted that the Prophet was not denying the transmissibility of certain diseases, but only emphasizing that it was happening under divine authority, like everything else.

However, in the pre-modern Islamic world, this hadith was often taken more literally: that there is really no such thing as a contagious disease, and that sickness is always created by God, directly and metaphysically, in each and every person.[6] Scholars such as Abu Ubayd al-Qasim ibn Sallam (d. 838) made this case strongly, adding that to believe otherwise is a weakness in faith.[7] Others realized that contagion really takes place, "yet they found themselves in the very difficult position of having to reconcile a saying of the Prophet . . . with the reality."[8]

The issue became most burning in the mid-fourteenth century, when the Black Death—the most fatal pandemic known in human history—ravaged not just Christian Europe but also large parts of the Muslim world. Scholars such as Ibn al-Wardi (d. 1349), Ibn Lubb (d. 1381), or Ibn Hajar al-Asqalani (1448) kept insisting that the plague was not a contagion, but a divine decree for each individual. Some even suggested that God was punishing chosen victims by sending them *jinn*, or demons, "to pierce them internally."[9] Therefore, those who were struck by the plague were not "in themselves dangerous," and Muslims had no reason to "avoid each other."[10] They rather had to stick together and take care of the sick, which was certainly a moral call, but also an unwise one that ruled out quarantine and isolation.[11]

The scholars who made these arguments also spanned the contrarian hadiths that did not fit into their view. One was a narration where the Prophet says: "Do not place the healthy camels with the sick ones."[12] Did this mean that, despite the other narration about mangy camels, the Prophet actually believed in contagion? No, our scholars said. The Prophet took this precaution only because "credulous and uneducated Muslims might be fooled by the apparent existence of contagion to believe that diseases have the ability to transmit themselves."[13] For if Muslims belived in that, then they would be "positing the existence of a causative agent other than God," which would mean slipping into "polytheism."[14]

There were also several critics of this view, and none was bolder than Ibn al-Khatib, the grand vizier of Granada, and an ideological heir to Ibn Tufayl, the author of *Hayy ibn Yaqzan*.[15] In 1349, he wrote a treatise titled *The Satisfaction of the Questioner Regarding the Appalling Illness*. The "appalling illness" was the Black Death, and according to Ibn al-Khatib, its contagious nature was clear from observable facts:

> The existence of contagion is established by experience, study, and the evidence of the senses, by trustworthy reports on transmission by garments, vessels, ear-rings, by the spread of it by persons from one house, by infection of a healthy sea-port by an arrival from an infected land . . . by the immunity of isolated individuals.[16]

But what about the "no contagion" hadith? Ibn al-Khatib gave the sober answer of a rational believer: "If the senses and observation (*al-mushahada*) oppose traditional evidence (*al-dalil al-sam'i*), the latter needs to be interpreted."[17] Otherwise, he warned, Muslims would be "engaging in suicidal behavior," or they would be doing "malice" to other Muslims by putting them in grave danger.[18] He also rebuked the scholars "who ignored contagion, forbade flight, and forced people to remain congregated"—all the unwise clerics, in other words, who rejected social distancing.[19]

Sadly, though, by being a voice of reason, Ibn al-Khatib was putting his own life in danger. He attracted the wrath of the chief judge, Al-Nubahi, who condemned him for "innovation" and "philosophy," and got his books publicly burnt in the market square of Granada. In 1374, Ibn al-Khatib also got arrested with the charges of *zandaqa*, or heresy, got tortured, and finally got strangled to death.[20] He was buried the next day, but an angry mob turned his grave and put his dead body into flames. Hence people would later call him "the man of two deaths."[21]

After al-Khatib, there were other reasonable voices that valued "senses and observation," yet still the "no contagion" view remained influential in Islam, until modern developments in the early nineteenth century. These included the European-inspired Ottoman Quarantine Reform of 1838—a "turning point," after which contagion was taken seriously.[22] As scientific facts and methods became more established, the interpretations of the *la adwa* hadith also turned less literal. But the old view has survived in ultraconservative pockets, including, apparently, Pakistan's rigid clerics.

Today, most Muslims do belive in the existence of contagion—including the latest one, COVID-19, which had locked me in while writing these lines. But why were so many Muslim minds so persistent for so long in denying it?

The reason was not just the "no contagion" hadith, as there were contrary hadiths as well. The real reason was a theological creed called "occasionalism." It is a key component of Ash'arism that we have not discussed so far. But now we will.

A WORLD WITH NO "CAUSES"

"Occasionalism" is the Western term for an originally Ash'arite doctrine: that natural events are mere "occasions" for God to create things—rather than nature having a causal order of its own. Matter has no inherent qualities in itself, accordingly, and there are no "laws of nature" either. God just creates and re-creates everything, at every instant, simply as He wills. Luckily, God does this recurrent creation in a very orderly way, and that is why we have the illusion of causality that helps us live in an orderly fashion. Yet what really keeps things in order is not nature's own workings, but God's "habits." He may, of course, alter these habits whenever He wills, which is how miracles happen.

Al-Ghazali had explained all this in *The Incoherence of the Philosophers* with his famous example of how cotton gets combusted when it touches fire. Those philosophers explain the combustion with natural "causes," such as the chemical properties of cotton and fire, he wrote, only to add:

> And this is one of the things we deny. On the contrary, we say: The one who enacts the burning by creating blackness in the cotton, [causing] separation in its parts, and making it cinder or ashes is God, either through the mediation of His angels or without mediation.[23]

To grasp the worldview of occasionalism better, we can also think of a computer game. When you play such a game, you will have the illusion that objects interact in a system of causality. When you hit a fence with a racing car, for example, the fence may get broken. Yet what really breaks the fence is not the car, which has no causal power, but the computer's processor that is "re-creating" every instance on-screen, all separately, all one by one.

The result of this worldview was to think that according to the will of God, anything could happen at any moment. Ibn Hazm (d. 1064), whose literalist Zahiri school agreed with the Ash'arites on various themes but not occasionalism, put it this way:

> Ash'arites reject all natures. There is no heat in fire, or coldness in snow, or natures in beings. . . . There is no intoxicating quality in wine, or a nature in sperm. They said God creates whatever He wants. He could create a camel from human sperm or a human from a donkey's sperm.[24]

For the Ash'arites, occasionalism was closely linked to voluntarism—in fact, it was the very basis of it. "Good" and "bad" could not be judged by human reason, as voluntarism holds, because the very causality of actions, which would make them produce good or bad outcomes, was ruled out by occasionalism. For example, me slapping you in the face cannot be defined as "bad" unless there is a God-given rule against it, because there is no causal relation between the move of my hand and the pain you will feel on your face. Ash'arite scholar al-Kiya gave a similar example when he referred to a man who said, "I ate and was sated." This was a wrong thing to say, he wrote, because:

> what the individual ate did not strictly speaking cause him to be sated; rather God simply caused things to happen in their usual sequence by making satiety occur after the act of eating. So, also God makes things happen in their usual sequence by making what is advantageous occur after a certain act . . . [or] what is disadvantageous occur after a certain act.[25]

While occasionalism served voluntarism, the two doctrines served the same purpose: the "vindication of the absolute omnipotence and sovereignty of God and the utter powerlessness of the creature without Him."[26] God was simply doing whatever He wills: as He was unconstrained by values of ethics, He was also unconstrained by laws of nature.

In contrast to the Ash'arites, the Mu'tazila and the "philosophers" believed that entities had "necessitating natures." They also held that there is "a certain intelligibility of causal relations." So God would not create a camel from human sperm or human from a donkey's sperm, because that would mean violating the very nature of things that He himself created. That emphasis on the realness of nature made some Ash'arites, such as al-Baqillani, rebuke the Mu'tazilites as *Ahl Al-Tib'a*, or "People of Nature."[27]

Hence it is probably not an accident that the most significant natural scientist of the early Islamic civilization was a Mu'tazila scholar: the prolific al-Jahiz (d. 868), whose encyclopedic *Kitab al-Hayawan,* or "Book of Animals," not only describes more than 350 species with beautiful illustrations, but also argues that animals "engage in a struggle for existence," and "develop new characteristics . . . transforming into new species." He has been rightly called a precursor of the modern theory of evolution.[28] Al-Jahiz's naturalism had also allowed him to refute the racist views that were common at his time, as he argued that black skin color is not the sign of a "curse" from God, but merely the impact of being more exposed to the sun.[29]

MEANWHILE, IN CHRISTENDOM . . .

While occasionalism seems to be a doctrine first developed by Ash'arites, it soon influenced Christendom, persuading initially some medieval theologians, and later, in the seventeenth century, a few Cartesian thinkers.[30] The most famed among the latter was the French priest and philosopher Nicolas Malebranche (d. 1715). "There is only one true cause, because there is only one true God," he argued; "the nature or the force of everything is merely the will of God."[31]

Malebranche was criticized by Enlightenment philosopher Leibniz, who saw occasionalism as a doctrine of "perpetual miracles," which left behind "nothing in the nature of objects."[32] Another critique came from John Locke, who wrote a seventy-page-long essay titled *An Examination of P. Malebranche's Opinion of Seeing All Things in God.* The problem with occasionalism, Locke argued, is that it turns the universe into "a clock which can strike only if the maker interferes with its workings."[33] This made men "merely an occasional cause for God's producing certain motions in him," and it reduced their will to "an irresistible fatal necessity."[34] But Locke didn't publish the essay during his lifetime, hoping that occasionalism "would not spread, but was like to die of itself, or at least to do no great harm."[35]

The Christian alternative to occasionalism was the view that while God created the whole universe as the "First Cause," He had also allowed "secondary causes" to operate within His creation. Saint Thomas Aquinas articulated this view in his *Summa Theologica*. God gave "the dignity of causality" to His creatures, he explained, "not on account of any defect in His power, but by reason of the abundance of His goodness."[36] The view has been called "concurrentism," as it implies a concurrence between the acts of God and the acts of creatures. There is also a third view called "conservationism," which implies that God created the universe and "conserves" it, but "creatures are causally active in bringing about their natural effects" and "God's contribution is remote or indirect."[37] In these views, "the supernatural" does not "replace . . . the natural," but rather "guides and completes" it.[38] And this acknowledgment of nature calls for its study, whereas occasionalism "plunges us into radical skepticism about the external world."[39]

In Christendom, it was first concurrentism, then conservationism, that won the day. That allowed Sir Isaac Newton's view of a clocklike universe, which was created by God but also had "laws" to run on its own—laws that men could discover and also utilize. This allowed the modern scientific revolution, which was based on "an unprecedented faith in reason and the rational ordering of the natural world."[40]

In Islam, however, due to the dominance of Ash'arism, occasionalism became, and has remained, the dominant theological view.[41] And just like voluntarism, it had some influence on Muslim minds, as we have already seen in the longtime denial of contagious disease. It also had a broader impact on the fate of Muslim science, to which we now turn.

THE RISE AND FALL OF MUSLIM SCIENCE

Two chapters ago, I noted how advanced the medieval Islamic civilization was, especially when compared to Europe. A big part of this success was due to the accomplishments in science. Muslim astronomers had greatly advanced human knowledge about the motion of heavenly bodies and even laid the foundation of the Copernican Revolution. Muslim physicians figured out how blood circulation works and how the structure of the eye operates. Muslim mathematicians were so advanced that their contributions to the West are still traceable in terms that originated from Arabic: "algebra" comes from *al-jabir,* which literally means "the union of broken parts"; and "algorithm" comes from the very name of al-Khwarizmi, the Persian Muslim mathematician who worked at the famous House of Wisdom.

That is all why Adam Smith, to many the greatest economist of all times, had praised "the empire of the Caliphs" under which "the ancient philosophy and astronomy of the Greeks were restored and established," and revived "the curiosity of mankind."[42]

It would be wrong to think, though, that Islam's scientific achievement was limited to reviving ancient sources. Muslims not only inherited but also advanced and even corrected their precedents. Among their own contributions was the very notion of "experiment," which was first systemized by Ibn al-Haytham, widely known today as the father of optics. His *Book of Optics,* penned in AD 1021, refuted the established ancient Greek view that eyes emit the rays of light to see, demonstrating, quite to the contrary, that objects remit rays into the eyes. To prove his theory, al-Haytham used a variety of experimental apparatuses, such as specially arranged dark chambers, mirrors, and viewing tubes. His method, which he called *i'tabara,* was rightly translated by his medieval Latin translator as *experimentare.*[43]

However, recalling this golden age of Muslim science, which we Muslims often do with nostalgia, only raises a big question: What happened to that age? Why is it that, at some point, the Europeans began to take off, while Muslims did not?

An early answer was offered by Ernest Renan (d. 1892), the famous French Orientalist who had an unmistakable bigotry against all "Semitic" religions, including Islam. It was al-Ghazali and his occasionalism that killed sciences in Islam, Renan argued, setting the stage for a popular narrative. In return, for more than a century, first Muslim intellectuals and then Western anti-Orientalists spent much ink to debunk this theory, which indeed was devoid of nuances, including the complexities of al-Ghazali.[44] However, now there is a third view suggesting that the Ash'ari worldview indeed "obfuscated" the more scientific worldview of the philosophers, by ending "the open-ended rational investigation of all reality," and reducing philosophy to the defense of "one pre-determined thesis." A sign of the narrowing scope of rational inquiry was the flourishing of "esotericism" and "various occult sciences"—such as *ilm al-huruf,* or "letterism," which supposedly maps the future by counting numerical values or Arabic letters.[45]

Here is the more simple problem with occasionalism: it allows practical science but it discourages theoretical science. You can observe the falling of an apple from a tree regardless of whether you call its cause "gravity" or "God's habit." But while you can empirically study gravity, you can't empirically study God's habit.

In his book *Islam, Science, and the Challenge of History,* professor of history Ahmad Dallal shows how this problem indeed hindered sciences in classical Islam. The great Qur'anic commentator al-Razi, for example, had written about astronomy, but only to emphasize that the motions of heavenly bodies come not from any inherent nature of themselves, but rather God's will. Night and day, for example, were "due not to the motion of the sun," but rather an angel was assigned "to move each heavenly body or planet when [the sun] rises and sets."[46] Or the growth of a leaf on a tree was something that the "human mind is incapable of comprehending." So humans had to "concede that their creator is beyond full comprehension and admit his utmost wisdom."[47]

Dallal points to an important nuance here: the Qur'an repeatedly calls on humans to reflect on the created world and to realize the majesty of God. This invitation can be an encouragement for science—but only if you also accept that the inner workings of nature are comprehensible. Yet this is not what many classical scholars seem to have thought. "The ultimate purpose of reflection," they rather thought, "is to establish the limitations of human knowledge and our inability to comprehend creation, not to establish a scientific fact."[48]

An interesting example of this approach was presented by Adud al-Din al-Iji (d. ca. 1355), a strict Ash'ari scholar, who in his famous book *Kitab al-Mawaqif* offered a critique of astronomy. His problem was with the idea that celestial bodies moved with "the principle of uniform and circular motion." This mechanistic model, he emphasized, went against the theological principle that every object is dependent on the will and act of God. As Abdelhamid I. Sabra (d. 2013), one of the great experts on medieval Muslim science, observes:

> The specifically Ash'arite doctrine of pervasive contingency comes to the fore in al-Iji's argument against any inherent inclination to circular motion: to assume the existence of such an inclination is to attribute the motion to something that necessarily and by itself . . . brings about the motion—which al-Iji, of course, cannot accept.[49]

The geocentric Ptolemaic model that al-Iji criticized was in fact wrong, and hence it would be soon replaced by the heliocentric models of Copernicus and Keppler. But al-Iji's problem was with "causal explanation per se, rather than with any specific astronomical system."[50] So he argued "against any human attempt to explain the heavens," and decreased "astronomy's intellectual prestige."[51] His book would be widely used in the Sunni Muslim world, including Egypt's prominent Al-Azhar University, well into the mid-twentieth century.[52]

WHAT IS GEOMETRY GOOD FOR?

Abdelhamid I. Sabra, who has brought al-Iji's occasionalist critique of astronomy to academic attention, was an Egyptian historian of science who studied with the great philosopher Karl Popper in London and taught at Harvard University for decades. He helped highlight the great scientific achievements of the medical Islamic civilization. It was Sabra who published Ibn al-Haytham's majestic seven-volume *Book of Optics*, with translation and commentary, along with several other significant works.

Sabra also pondered why sciences declined in Islam. While admitting that it is difficult to pin down a definitive answer, he pointed to the gap between the mindset of "the philosophers" who studied the Greek heritage, and the Ash'arite theologians who denounced them. For the former, Sabra noted:

> the aim of theoretical investigation, whether mathematical, physical or metaphysical, was to ascertain the nature of all things as they are in themselves to the farthest extent possible, and the aim of the investigator was to *gain knowledge of the truth for the sake of knowing the truth.*[53]

We could get a glimpse of this spirit from Ibn Sina, one of the towering Muslim "philosophers" in question. In his autobiography, he writes that he mastered medicine at the very early of age sixteen, and:

> Then, for a year and a half, I devoted myself to study. I resumed the study of logic and all parts of philosophy. During this time I never slept the whole night through and did nothing but study all day long. Whenever I was puzzled by a problem . . . I would go to the mosque, pray, and beg the Creator of All to reveal to me that which was hidden from me and to make easy for me that which was difficult. Then at night I would return home, put a lamp in front of me, and set to work reading and writing. . . . I went on like this until I was firmly grounded in all sciences and mastered them as far as was humanly possible. . . . Thus I mastered logic, physics, and mathematics.[54]

But such a passionate curiosity about the created world was less likely to emerge among the occasionalist Ash'arites, for whom "nature of all things as they are in themselves" simply did not exist. What rather existed were God's "habits," which could be observed, but not as knowledge separate from the knowledge about God. So science could not be something separate, let alone independent, from religion. In al-Ghazali, as Sabra explained, this led to an "instrumentalist view" of science, which meant:

> not only that religious knowledge is higher in rank and more worthy of pursuit than all other forms of knowledge, but also that all other forms of knowledge must be subordinated to it. . . . Thus, among the non-revealed forms of knowledge; medicine is necessary only for the preservation of health; arithmetic for the conduct of daily affairs and for the execution of wills and the division of legacies in accordance with the revealed law; astronomy, a science praiseworthy in itself but blameworthy in some of its implications, is useful in performing an operation legitimated by the holy Qur'an, namely the calculating of celestial movements; and logic is just a tool for weighing arguments in religious as well as non-religious branches of inquiry.[55]

So, science was valuable as long as it was religiously, and immediately, "useful." Thanks to this view, scientific research continued in post-Ghazalian Islam, but, in the words of Sabra, only as confined "to very narrow, and essentially unprogressive areas."[56]

A hadith quoted by al-Ghazali nailed this instrumentalism forever as a religious truism. "O God," the Prophet supposedly said, "I seek refuge in Thee from the knowledge which does not benefit."[57]

Over time, this "instrumentalist" view of knowledge would reject even the ones initially considered beneficial by al-Ghazali.[58] He had appreciated logic, for example, but later Sunni scholars, such as al-Suyuti (d. 1505), shunned it. In fact, "hostility to logic" became "a predominant feature of Sunni thinking, especially during the 13th, 14th, and 15th centuries."[59] Jurists insisted that all Muslims needed to understand God's will was the Arabic grammar, not the universal laws of logic.[60]

Similarly, Ahmad al-Faruqi al-Sirhindi, also known as Imam Rabbani, an early seventeenth-century scholar from India who is largely respected in the Sunni world as *mujaddid,* or "renewer" of Islam, minced no words for "the philosophers" and all their "stupid" disciplines. "Among their codified and systemic sciences is geometry that is totally useless," he wrote. "The sum of three angles in a triangle is two right angles—what benefit does it have?"[61]

What benefit did geometry really have? Soon after Imam Rabbani rhetorically asked this in India, Muslims at the other end of Islamdom, the Ottomans, would find out. The European armies they used to defeat in the past were now much stronger, better organized, and better equipped. Hence, in the early eighteenth century, the Ottoman elite initiated military reforms, but only to realize that they lacked the necessary know-how. In their *madrasas,* or "schools," the "rational and mathematical sciences," which initially existed, had gradually vanished, limiting education only to religious education.[62] So the Ottoman state had to import experts from Europe. Among them was the French officer François Baron de Tott, who supervised the first "House of Geometry" in Istanbul in 1775, also called Ecole de Théorie et de Mathématiques. This first Western-style school in the Ottoman Empire would be followed by others, to raise Western-educated generations to spearhead more reforms. One such Ottoman intellectual was Ziya Gökalp, who had worked hard to include mathematics back in the curricula of Ottoman *madrasas*—a dream realized only in 1910, or about a decade before the empire's collapse in the aftermath of World War I.[63]

Inevitably, the effort to Westernize was going to provoke its resistance. Here were the seeds of what would ultimately become a colossal culture war between the adherents of *alla Franca,* "the style of the Franks," and of *alla Turca,* the style of the Turks.

Today, the Islamists who represent the anti-Western side in this culture war—not just in Turkey, but in much of the Muslim world—claim their own authenticity while condemning the Westernizers as soulless "imitators," if not treacherous sellouts. The Westernists do deserve some criticism for focusing on the superficial expressions of modernity, such as dress codes, and for being often authoritarian in their politics. But Islamists fail to realize that the whole effort to Westernize had begun because of the painful Muslim underdevelopment compared to Western modernity. Unless the root causes of this underdevelopment are addressed, "Islamic" solutions will not promise anything other than emotionally captivating utopias that will prove disastrously disappointing.

REASON, CAUSALITY, AND OTTOMAN REFORM

The late Ottoman Empire is in fact a good place to further observe how occasionalism influenced Muslim minds—regarding not just natural sciences, but also social and political affairs as well.

Ethan L. Menchinger, a British historian focusing on Ottoman intellectual history, offers some little-noticed insights on this matter in an article titled "Free Will, Predestination, and the Fate of the Ottoman Empire."[64] He first reminds us of a known tension in late Ottoman history: from the early eighteenth century onward, some Ottomans pushed for Western-inspired reforms, while others believed in preserving the old ways. What is less known is that this reformist-conservative rift, which certainly involved complex social dynamics, also had something to do with a more or less causal perception of the world.

This perception gap can be detected in the usage of the term *esbab*—the Turkish version of the Arabic *asbab*, literally meaning "causes"—which was a part of the Ottoman religious language. Virtually all Ottomans honored God as the Creator and Sustainer of the world, but the emphasis they made on *esbab* differed.

On the reformist side, a shining figure was Ibrahim Muteferrika, who is famous for introducing the printing press to the Muslim segment of the Ottoman Empire in 1727—with a catastrophic delay of almost three centuries, after the first printing press in 1455 by the German inventor Johannes Gutenberg. Muteferrika's personal journey, as a Hungarian-born Unitarian Christian who later converted to Islam, is an interesting story in itself, but we will not get into that, or the broader Ottoman-Unitarian connection, here.[65] What is relevant to our discussion is that Muteferrika, as one of the "founding fathers" of the "Ottoman Enlightenment," had a worldview in which "causes" were definitive.[66]

This was evident in his 1731 tract titled *The Rational Basis for the Ordering of Nations,* where he called for Ottoman military reform. "Victory, success, and triumph over the enemy depend always and utterly on the Lord God's infinite aid to believers," he first granted, only to add: "However, God has consigned the outward realization of every matter to initiative through causes." Man must operate with this realism, Muteferrika argued, drawing on "an explicitly causal discourse to argue for reform."[67]

Who would disagree with this? We get an answer from Ottoman bureaucrat Ahmed Resmi Efendi (d. 1783), who analyzed the Russo-Ottoman War of 1768–74, which had ended with a terrible defeat for the Ottomans, costing them parts of the Caucasus and Crimea. In Ahmed Resmi's evaluation, this disastrous war had been provoked and prolonged by men who championed precisely the opposite of Muteferrika's view: "that God grants victory through pious zeal alone."[68] Ottoman bureaucrat Canikli Ali Pasha also was describing the same men who displayed unwise bravado, and "when they failed in preparations, they blamed fate."[69]

Another Ottoman bureaucrat of the time was Vasıf Ahmed Efendi (d. 1806), whom Menchinger dubs as "the first of the modern Ottomans."[70] His work provided the intellectual framework for Nizam-i Cedid, or the "New Order"—a reformist program that Sultan Selim III pursued from 1789 to 1807, only to be killed at the end by reactionary soldiers. It was such men, according to Vasıf

Ahmed, who failed to understand that "it is God's custom to create everything as an outcome of secondary causes [*esbab-ı zahire*]."[71] When an earthquake took place in Anatolia in 1784, for example, traditional scholars explained it as "divine punishment for sin and injustice." Vasıf Ahmed, in contrast, took the side of the "philosophers" who explained earthquakes with "vapors within the earth."[72] Also, when a lunar eclipse took place in Istanbul in 1795, Vasıf Ahmed described the incident in astronomical terms while criticizing the traditional religious scholars who took "fright," and who believed in "a divine omnipotence that does not follow general laws."[73]

On the very opposite side of Vasıf Ahmed, there was the popular preacher Fazlızade Ali of the mid-eighteenth century, who agreed that the Ottoman Empire was in decline but found the culprit in impiety, sin, the growing social visibility of women, and the influx of "heretical Persian philosophies."[74] So the solution was in the restoration of piety and authenticity—an argument that still echoes among modern-day Islamists. Quite tellingly, Fazlızade Ali also believed in a theology that eschewed the influence of "causes": "If God wills that there should be a cause, the thing comes about through a cause," he wrote. "What He wills without a cause, comes about without a cause."[75]

Against such irrational minds, who often called for hopeless wars based on a belief in inevitable glory, the reformist Grand Vizier Halil Hamid Pasha (d. 1785) was writing the following words of caution:

> While I have no doubt that God is almighty and powerful and will help the weak and oppressed, it is undeniable that the divine practice is always to create everything through causes. . . . Therefore, to open the gates of war with such potent enemies while secondary causes are entirely lacking, relying on supernatural aid, is like taking mortal poison and trusting blindly in the antidote's unknown efficacy. . . . It would be a disaster for the empire.[76]

Halil Hamid Pasha would pay the price of his sanity with being beheaded by the fanatic war party. Yet still, rational Ottomans never fully lost the control of the empire, and reforms continued in the nineteenth century, leading to new laws and institutions, a liberal constitution, modern schools, and even a feminist movement.[77] But perhaps more could have been achieved, and progress could have begun much earlier, had more Ottomans focused on the "causes," in order to understand, analyze, and change the world in which they were living.

A LEAP OF REASON

Today, the Muslim world does not experience anywhere near the scientific brilliance it had a thousand years ago. Quite the contrary, as Pakistani physicist Abdus Salam (d. 1996), one of the very few Muslim Nobel laureates, once sadly put it, "Of all civilizations on this planet, science is weakest in the lands of Islam."[78]

There are complex historical dynamics that brought us here, but there is also the deep impact of a certain mindset—a mindset that shows limited interest in facts and the causal relations between them, hindering both natural and social sciences. It is rooted in Ash'arism, which, in the words of Turkish theologian Mehmet Evkuran, led to "the loosening of the connection with reality in Muslim societies."[79] Today, in the words of the late Egyptian scholar Nasr Abu Zayd (d. 2010), it comes out in a religious discourse which

posits "God" in the immediate material world, and in the process, automatically excludes humanity. Natural and social "laws" are also denied, and any knowledge is suppressed that doesn't have a basis in religious discourse or that is not based on the authority of the religious scholars.[80]

In popular Muslim culture, this comes out in interpretations of human history as an arena where God grants victory, to Muslims or their enemies, as divine rewards or punishments, rather than the earthly dynamics we mortals can understand—such as hard work, meritocracy, technology, or creativity. It gives Islamist movements unrealistic expectations about their supposedly inevitable glory, which is often deduced simply from a literal reading of a Qur'anic verse or a dubious prophesy in hadiths. Conversely, it interprets military defeats as a result of "departure from the Qur'an and Sunna."[81]

The same mindset also perceives natural disasters as manifestations of divine wrath, rather than causal processes of the earth, the atmosphere, or the oceans. Consequently, it shows little interest in taking rational and scientific precautions. This was revealed in a 2002 survey held in Morocco among earthquake survivors. Many of the respondents stated that "seismic-related forecasting, construction, architectural standards, and/or related education" were not just ineffective but even *haram,* or religious prohibited. The surveyors also found:

> Less educated often stated that Allah protected the devout, and considered most scientific assessment as futile since it was related to forecasting (also *haram*). New construction, building standards were considered as a waste since only the *kafir* (non-Muslim) or *munafiq* (hypocrite) were at risk of death or injury from earthquakes.[82]

None of this means that most modern-day Muslims are decidedly anti-science. Quite the contrary, most of them, including the Islamists, appreciate science, which they understand as the West's big secret, and they only want to have more of it. However, they understand it "as an instrument of power rather than a system of thought with its own epistemological assumptions."[83] In other words, they do want to have iPhones, flat screens, and warplanes, but they are not interested in the mindset that has invented these technological products. Other Muslims, whom we can call apologists, are busy proving that all the achievements of modern science actually came from Islam, and were even foretold in the Qur'an, with arguments that convince only those who are already faithful. Some other Muslims, who borrow from postmodernist literature, argue against adopting "Western science," and call for building some authentic "Islamic science," missing the very fact that Islam's earlier scientific grandeur had come out of not such religious exclusivism but, quite the contrary, cosmopolitanism.[84]

What we still can't fully embrace is what gave rise to modernity in the West: a methodological study of observable facts in nature and society, and an objective effort to figure out the causal links between them—a more rational and scientific view of the world, so to speak.

Cultural criticisms of this kind can spark some knee-jerk accusations of "Orientalism." Hence, it may be helpful to hear the greatest critique of Orientalism. On the question of the intellectual transformation that Muslim societies need, Edward Said (d. 2003), the great Arab intellectual, said the following:

> It isn't knowledge as a product or commodity that we need; nor is it a matter of remedying the situation by having bigger libraries, a greater number of terminals, computers and so forth, but a qualitatively different knowledge based on understanding rather than on authority, uncritical repetition, mechanical reproduction. It is not facts, but how facts are connected to other facts, how they are constructed, whether they relate to hypothesis or theory, how one is to judge the relationship between truth and interest, how to understand reality as history. These are only some of the critical issues we face, which can be summed up in the phrase/question, how to think?[85]

Edward Said was right on point. The question is a very fundamental one: How to think? How to discover facts and connect them to other facts?

Alas, long before Said, there was another Arab intellectual, an even greater one, who had a similar insight. He had warned us, in fact, that if we Muslims sacrifice reason, we would fail to understand the nature of things, and therefore we would inevitably regress. Without reason, he also realized, we can't reinterpret our laws and reform our societies. He had seen the problem coming and did his best to avert it. So, our next chapter will be about him.

A woodcut in Simon Ockley's translation of
Hayy ibn Yaqzan. Under the dome of wisdom,
there are two Muslim philosophers:
Avicenna (Ibn Sina) and Averroes (Ibn Rushd).

THE LAST MAN STANDING: IBN RUSHD

As striking, even as unwarranted as it seems at first glance . . . an early version of the famous eighteenth-century European Enlightenment is to be found in medieval Islamic philosophy, particularly in the writings of . . . Averroës.

—Charles Butterworth, emeritus professor of political philosophy[1]

It is time now to go back to our good old friend, Hayy ibn Yaqzan.

Remember, he was the hero of our first chapter, as well as the hero of a philosophical novel, the first of its kind, that fascinated early modern Europe. He grew up on an island all by himself, with no society, no religion, no scripture. But with his systematic study of the world, he figured out the nature of things. By reason, intuition, observation, and experiment, Hayy discovered the secrets of the universe, as well as moral truths. When he finally met other humans who lived in a society with a traditional religion, he was disappointed with their lack of sophistication. Yet religion, he also realized, preached the same truths that he had reached through reason.

Ibn Tufayl, the Muslim thinker who wrote this novel in the late twelfth century, was trying to do something. Put simply, he was trying to carve out a legitimate place for philosophy in a religious tradition that had become unfriendly to philosophy. Just a few generations before, al-Ghazali had penned his landmark book *The Incoherence of the Philosophers*. Here, the great Ash'arite scholar was not only refuting Muslim philosophers, in particular Ibn Sina, for their absorption of Greek metaphysics, but he was also condemning them for *kufr,* or "infidelity"—adding a brief verdict in the last page of this book that they can be "punished with death."[2] "It is necessary to shut the gate," al-Ghazali also wrote elsewhere:

> so as to keep the general public from reading the books of the misguided as far as possible ... on account of the danger and deception in them. Just as the poor swimmer must be kept from the slippery banks, so must mankind be kept from reading these books; just as the boy must be kept from touching the snake, so must the ears be kept from receiving such utterances.[3]

This harsh condemnation would have a deep impact on the Muslim world, where philosophy became a dirty word. Still today, one can find in Muslim societies popular books that define philosophy as a "disease" to be eradicated, or textbooks that condemn it as "a product of human thought contrary to Islam."[4]

Al-Ghazali had penned his assault on the philosophers in Baghdad, whereas Ibn Tufayl was living in the Western edge of Islamdom—Al-Andulus, or Muslim Spain. Conquered in the eighth century from North Africa, this small kingdom was a gem of its time, where not just Muslims but also Jews and Christians flourished in a high culture and a spirit of *convivencia,* or "coexistence." But it wasn't free from the political and doctrinal tensions that hit the central lands of Islam.

It is interesting that Mu'tazila theology, whose strongholds have been Iraq and Central Asia, never made its way to the Al-Andulus. Yet its spirit came in a different form: philosophy. This was evident in the life of the first Iberian Muslim philosopher, Muhammad ibn Masarra (d. 931), whose father was said to have traveled to the

East and to have been acquainted with Mu'tazilis.[5] Ibn Masarra defended *aql*, or "reason," as a path that "proceeds from the bottom up and discovers the same truth the Prophets have brought down from on high."[6] And he received a typically fideist reaction. "By [supplying us with] clearly-stated rules of conduct," one of his detractors declared, "God has spared us the toil of thinking."[7]

In the year 1031, the central "caliphate" of Al-Andulus collapsed due to a revolt, soon to disintegrate into a patchwork of *taifa*, or little "successor kingdoms." Muslims typically abhor such "disunity," but this political plurality opened new spaces and opportunities for philosophers.[8] One of them was a polymath from Zaragoza named Ibn Bajja (d. 1138), known in Latin as Avempace. His works on astronomy were significant enough that in 2009 his name would be given by the International Astronomical Union to a crater on the Moon.

One of Ibn Bajja's students was none other than Ibn Tufayl, who found a job as the court physician at the palace of Caliph Abu Yusuf Ya'qub al-Mansur, a ruler from the Almohad dynasty who had come from North Africa to take over Al-Andulus. During his time at the court, sometime between 1160 and 1170, Ibn Tufayl penned *Hayy ibn Yaqzan*. He also did something else. To the caliph, who enjoyed intellectual conversations, he introduced young philosophers, one of whom would prove historically significant—so significant that among all Muslims, it would be him who had the greatest impact on "humanity's universal culture."[9] His name was Abu al-Walid Muhammad ibn Ahmad ibn Rushd. The West would also know him as Averroes.

THE RELIGIOUS CASE FOR PHILOSOPHY

Ibn Rushd's introduction to the caliph, sometime around the year 1169, is an interesting story in itself. Accordingly, the young philosopher was brought to the court and was posed a sensitive question: Was the world created, or was it coeternal with God? He was first too scared to give an answer, but then he shared his view, which apparently worked well. Soon, as he told in his memoirs, he got a job offer that he couldn't reject:

> Ibn Tufayl summoned me one day and told me that he had heard the Commander of the Faithful complaining about the disjointedness of Aristotle's mode of expression. . . . He said that if someone took on these books who could summarize them and clarify their aims after first thoroughly understanding them himself, people would have an easier time comprehending them. "If you have the energy," Ibn Tufayl told me, "you do it."[10]

That is how Ibn Rushd began his monumental work, which lasted three decades and produced a three-tiered commentary on the Aristotelian corpus—a short or paraphrased version for beginners, a middle version, and a long version. He also commented on a wide range of subjects, ranging from medicine to politics, from ethics to zoology, with references to Greek, Muslim, and Jewish thinkers that came before him.

Besides all this meticulous study of philosophy, Ibn Rushd set out on a mission to prove its compatibility with Islam. This was the theme of one of his short but powerful texts, *Decisive Treatise Determining the Nature of the Connection Between Religion and Philosophy*. Accordingly, it was none other than the Qur'an that calls Muslims to reflect on created beings and seek knowledge about them. "Do they not observe the camels, how they have been created," the Qur'an asks, "and the sky, how it has been raised up?"[11] Such verses, Ibn Rushd explained, call for "a preliminary study of logic," which "must be learned from the ancient masters," such as Aristotle, "regardless of whether [they] share our religion or not."[12]

While arguing that revelation itself commands philosophy, Ibn Rushd also argued that the findings of philosophy would not contradict the teachings of revelation: "For truth does not oppose truth, but accords with it and bears witness to it."[13] But what if there was an apparent contradiction? Then findings of philosophy would be upheld, and an "allegorical interpretation" of revelation would be sought.

To bolster this case, Ibn Rushd also offered a rare interpretation of a well-known Qur'anic verse, which says that some verses are "definite in meaning" but others are "ambiguous." In its usual translations, this verse concludes, "Only God knows their true meaning. Those firmly grounded in knowledge say, 'We believe in it: it is all from our Lord.'"[14] Ibn Rushd, however, opted for a possibility allowed by the Arabic grammar. The verse could also read, "Only God knows their true meaning, *and* those firmly grounded in knowledge." And who would be "those firmly grounded in knowledge"? They were the philosophers, of course, as "knowledge" referred not just to religious texts but all the wisdom humanity has accumulated over time.

With such arguments, Ibn Rushd was intervening in the ongoing debate on faith and reason. The earliest defender of reason in this drama, the Mu'tazila, was long suppressed. "Their books have not reached us in sufficient number in this Peninsula," Ibn Rushd wrote, referring to Muslim Spain.[15] But when compared with the Ash'arites, he noted, "the Mu'tazilites are generally sounder in their statements."[16]

But if reason was a sound way to find truth, why was religion necessary? Ibn Rushd's answer was that while only a few people had the means to pursue philosophy, everybody could understand the call of religion. That is because religion proclaimed truth in "rhetorical" language that relied on its own forceful proclamation, whereas philosophy used the "demonstrative" method, where logical arguments are built with painstaking evaluations of facts and their relations. Somewhere in the middle, there was also the "dialectical" method of the theologians, where opposite views were compared, which was more refined than "rhetorical," but not as precise as "demonstrative."

This three-layered classification of thinking, and the people who are fit for using it, may sound too elitist to our modern ears. In the Middle Ages, however, when the overwhelming majority of people were illiterate and had little time for anything other than sustenance, the elitism of the intellectual class was just realism. Ash'arite theologians, such as al-Ghazali or al-Razi, had also made a distinction between the *hawas*, or the "elite," and the *awam*, or the "common people."[17]

THE INCOHERENCE OF ASH'ARISM

After al-Ghazali, it was impossible to defend philosophy in Islam without coming to terms with him. Hence, against his damning book *The Incoherence of the Philosophers*, Ibn Rushd wrote a cleverly titled rejoinder: *The Incoherence of the Incoherence*. This was a meticulous rebuttal with pages-long excerpts beginning with the line "Ghazali says," and following with similarly long answers beginning with "I say."

One of Ibn Rushd's concerns was the condemnation of the previous philosophers as apostates who deserved being killed. In return, Ibn Rushd argued that things were more nuanced than what al-Ghazali thought. For example, the big controversy on "the eternity of the world" was in fact a matter of semantics: God certainly preceded the world, but this could have been in the sense of causality, not time, and the Qur'an had verses suggesting that God made the world out of some prior matter.[18] At certain places, Ibn Rushd criticized the philosophers in question, especially Ibn Sina, as well for not getting Aristotle right.

Even more important to us are Ibn Rushd's criticisms to the broader Ash'arite theology, especially in light of the recent chapters of this book. Some of these were directed toward occasionalism. "They denied that fire burns, water quenches thirst and bread satisfies hunger," Ibn Rushd wrote, referring to the Ash'arites.[19] Then he warned that such a worldview is intellectually detrimental:

Denial of cause implies the denial of knowledge, and denial of knowledge implies that nothing in this world can be really known, and that what is supposed to be known is nothing but opinion.[20]

This was a really wise warning against any "post-truth" world, where facts cease to be facts and all objective knowledge collapses into wishful thinking—whether that wish be religious or secular in nature.

Ibn Rushd also realized that belief in such an arbitrary world would lead to an arbitrary God. He would become "like a tyrannical prince who has the highest power, for whom nobody in his dominion can deputize, of whom no standard or custom is known to which reference might be made."[21]

Right from this point, Ibn Rushd challenged the divine command theory. If the Ash'arites are correct, he wrote, "there would be no essential good in the present world but only posited [good], and there would be no essential evil."[22] He found these views "similar to those by Protagoras"—the Greek sophist who had advocated a radical moral relativism.[23] While Protagoras claimed, "Man is the measure of all things," Ash'arism was saying, "God is the measure of all things." Both views were denying the objective meaning of "good" and "bad."

What about miracles? Ibn Rushd did not deny miracles— extremely extraordinary things, such as a staff turning into a snake, as in the story of Moses. But unlike al-Ghazali, who denied the laws of nature in order to justify miracles, he rather defined miracles as "certain rare possibilities hidden in the warp and woof of the cosmic structure."[24]

All in all, Ibn Rushd was trying to save the reality of nature, the laws of nature, and objective ethical norms from the Ash'arite dogma that claimed to be "the arbiter of philosophy, metaphysics and science all at once."[25] And he was doing this not because he wasn't a believer in God, but rather because he believed in a more principled and intelligible God. In the words of Ibrahim Kalın, a Turkish scholar:

> Ibn Rushd's cry is that of a believing "rationalist" who thought it to be an insult against God to describe Him as capable of contradicting Himself, disregarding His own creation and servants, and judging them at will and almost whimsically. For him, this makes justice and accountability, the two tenets of the Islamic faith, practically meaningless, and creates a metaphysical chaos where nobody can know anything for sure.[26]

Ibn Rushd had realized, in other words, that if we lost faith in objective reality, we would also lose reason. And if we lost reason, we would end up believing in a despotic God whose wisdom cannot be understood, let alone be interpreted.

One wonders what would have happened if we had followed Ibn Rushd's way. What would have happened if we kept, as he suggested, a sense of objective reality and ethics, along with a philosophical tradition to study them, apart from religion? How would that have influenced the way we look at religion itself? We will now look into that.

THE PHILOSOPHER'S SHARIA

Most people who have studied Ibn Rushd look at him as a philosopher, which is also at the core of his historical prestige. But in the footsteps of his father and grandfather, he was also a *faqih* and a *qadi*, or a "jurist" and a "judge," whose job was to interpret and implement the Sharia.

The main work that introduces us to this juristic side of Ibn Rushd is his two-volume *Bidayat al-Mujtahid,* or *"The Distinguished Jurist's Primer,"* in which he presented a thematic overview of the opinions of Muslim jurists on various matters. He referred to not just the Maliki school he himself followed, but also the Hanafi,

Shafiʿi, Hanbali, and Zahiri traditions. Instead of sticking faithfully to the immediate judicial precedent, which had become the norm, he went back to the original sources, especially the Qurʾan, to create more room for interpretation. He also showed that there are differing passages in the Qurʾan on the same issue—such as jihad, as we will see closely in a bit--and interpretation depends on which verses one takes as more "general" or more "specific."[27]

Yet still, *The Distinguished Jurist's Primer* does not reveal a big reformism within Islamic law. Based on that, some have suggested that despite his unorthodox place in Islam as a philosopher, Ibn Rushd's work on the Sharia was still "orthodox."[28] However, careful readers of the Muslim philosopher realized that he had much more to say on law, but because of the precariousness of his situation, he only "hinted at them quietly in commentaries."[29]

These commentaries were the philosophical texts in which Ibn Rushd embraced Aristotle's idea of natural law. He wrote, for example:

Laws are of two kinds: some are particular, and others are general. Particular laws are written laws, which we fear would be forgotten unless they were written down; and these [particular laws] are specific to each people or each community. As for the general laws, they are unwritten laws, which are acknowledged by all people such as filial piety and thanking the benefactor.[30]

As we saw in the previous chapters, "thanking the benefactor" was a concept used by the Muʿtazila: it was one of the moral intuitions to which they referred in order to argue that even without religion, people could figure out moral truths. Now Ibn Rushd was using the same concept to make the same case with the Muʿtazila: that the Sharia only "reveals and commands to man what is objectively right."[31] These objective values were established by "unwritten laws," or *sunan ghayr maktuba*, which Ibn Rushd explained as follows:

What I mean by the unwritten laws are those that are in the nature of all people. These are what all people consider just or unjust by nature although they had no explicit stipulation or contract among one another. . . . These laws oftentimes contradict written laws so that they [i.e., unwritten laws] are used to induce persuasion that what was believed to be unjust based on written laws is just.[32]

So the "unwritten laws"—say, universal values—could contradict our written laws, such as the Sharia. In that case, we had to reinterpret the latter.

Ibn Rushd also added that while written laws can be just for a certain time and milieu, they may became unjust in a different setting. The reason, he said, is that "no one can lay down universal and general laws according to all people of all times and all places." This, he added, "sometimes calls for an addition or a subtraction."[33] All this implied that Islam's own written laws—the Sharia—had to be checked according to universal ethical values, and the changing circumstances of the human reality.[34]

How would this look in practice? As an example, we can see what Ibn Rushd thought about a topic that was as important in his time as it is controversial today: jihad.

A REASONABLE VIEW ON JIHAD

"Jihad" comes from an Arabic term that means "struggle." In that linguistic sense, it can refer to any kind of struggle—like a spiritual battle against temptation, or a critical stance against tyranny. However, the main meaning given to "jihad" from the earliest days of Islam has been "military struggle"—to take up arms to fight *fi sabillah,* or "for the sake of God."

That is why "The Book of Jihad," a chapter in Ibn Rushd's *The Distinguished Jurist's Primer,* was about the rules of war. There he tells us that Muslim scholars agree that jihad can be launched on non-Muslims for two reasons: "either for their conversion to Islam or their payment of *jizya*," the latter being the "poll tax" non-Muslims were required to pay under Muslim rule. Muslim scholars also agree, Ibn Rushd notes, "that it is not permitted to slay minors or women, as long as they are not waging war." So noncombatants are not legitimate targets. But what about collateral damage? "The majority of jurists agreed," Ibn Rushd writes, "about the permissibility of attacking fortresses by means of mangonels, irrespective of women or children being in them"— but some other jurists raised concerns. Meanwhile, some jurists argued that captives of war are "not to be executed," but others justified their execution.[35]

All in all, this was a good overview of the medieval doctrine of jihad, which was much more humane than the jihad of the modern-day terrorist groups, such as ISIS or Al-Qaeda, which intentionally target noncombatants. But it was not so humane when compared to the modern rules of war. One major problem is that it justified *aggressive* war—conquest for the sake of forcing people to convert to Islam or to pay taxes to a Muslim state, due to a skewed reading of the Qur'an.[36]

So what was Ibn Rushd's view on this?

He gave a little-noticed yet quite remarkable answer in his *Commentary on Aristotle's Nicomachean Ethics*. There, he used his distinction between unwritten laws and written laws, and the changing circumstances that require the reinterpretation of the written laws, to argue that the jihad doctrine should be revised. He wrote:

> This will be clear from what is laid down on the matter of war in the law of the Muslims, for the command in it regarding war is general, until they uproot and destroy entirely whoever disagrees with them. But regarding this, there are times when peace is more choiceworthy than war. As for [the fact] that the Muslim public requires this generality, despite the impossibility of destroying and uprooting their enemies entirely, they attain

in this great harm; this is ignorance on their part of the intention of the legislator.[37]

This was a complicated but significant statement. Ibn Rushd
was first pointing to the fact that war only brings "great harm."
From this, he was inferring the need to sometimes prefer "peace."
Then he was criticizing the "Muslim public" for understanding the
Sharia's call for war as "general," rather than contextual. This was
coming from "ignorance on their part of the intention of the legislator." God could not have intended this great harm, Ibn Rushd
was implicitly reasoning, and hence religious commandments for
aggressive war had to be revised.[38]

To us modern readers this all may sound like common sense—
and not so extraordinary. But in Ibn Rushd's time, it was not that
common to look at the consequences of religious commandments,
decide that they are harmful, and then to seek reinterpretation. No
wonder Ibn Hazm, a prominent jurist who lived in Ibn Rushd's
hometown, Córdoba, a century before him, had taken the exact
opposite view. He had observed that people have a natural tendency to "abandon the fight against unbelievers," because of the
destruction caused by war. Yet he took this not as a reason to interpret the texts about jihad, but, quite the contrary, to impose them
more rigorously. "The purpose of law and government," Ibn Hazm
argued, was to "keep people's desires (*hawa*) restrained"—and to
keep them fighting.[39]

Ibn Rushd used his "corrective philosophy of law," as contemporary scholar Feriel Bouhafa calls it, on other matters as well,
such as corporal punishments. He praised a ruler who declined to
amputate the hands of a thief, based on the man's state of poverty.
This was a sign of *hilm*, meaning "gentleness or moderation," an
ethical value that should have encompassed the implementation
of the Sharia.[40] He also opposed the intolerance that many jurists
at his time had to the idea of Muslims living under non-Muslim
rule.[41]

That is why George Hourani (d. 1984), a modern expert on Ibn Rushd, sees in his philosophical works a "correction of positive law," based on a belief in "natural right." It is a natural right "to which the Legislator conformed," and "by our direct knowledge of which we may interpret His intentions.[42]

Noah Feldman, who translated Ibn Rushd's *Commentary on Aristotle's Nicomachean Ethics* from Hebrew, also sees his comments on jihad as a "rectification" of the jihad doctrine. By "incorporating the Greek philosophical hermeneutic into normative Islamic legal reasoning," Feldman adds, Ibn Rushd had "engaged in a remarkable intellectual act."[43]

Ibn Rushd, this remarkable intellectual, was even bolder on another topic that he wrote about—a topic that wasn't controversial at his time, but is very much so today: the role of women in Muslim societies.

A PROGRESSIVE TAKE ON WOMEN

Ibn Rushd lived at a time when virtually nobody had a sense of gender equality. Neither Christians nor Muslims saw men and women as equals. Authorities such as al-Ghazali had, in fact, had quite misogynist views. In a chapter on marriage, he defined it as "a form of enslavement"—and he didn't mean this as a critique. "She is his slave," he explained of the wife's status; "she should obey the husband absolutely in everything he demands of her."[44]

The Greek philosophical tradition that Ibn Rushd inherited wasn't necessarily much better. In particular Aristotle, Ibn Rushd's intellectual master, was explicitly in favor of male supremacy. "The courage of a man lies in commanding," he wrote; "a woman's lies in obeying." Despite his towering rationality on most issues, he even falsely believed that women have fewer teeth than men, from which he concluded that the female is an "incomplete male" or "a deformity."[45]

That is why one would not expect Ibn Rushd to have

ground-breakingly progressive views on women. But, well, that is exactly what he had.

That is partly thanks to Plato, who, on the particular issue of women, had more enlightened views than Aristotle, his student. In his *Republic*, Plato had argued, "women and men have the same nature," the only difference between them being in physical strength.[46] In his *Commentary on Plato's Republic*, Ibn Rushd embraced this view and expounded on it. Females have no intellectual deficiency compared to males, he argued, and the only thing that puts them down is social conventions. That is why, he wrote, if women were properly trained, they could be "philosophers and rulers," even clerics. Then Ibn Rushd looked at the Muslim societies of his time and slammed their marginalization of women:

> In these states, however, the ability of women is not known, because they are only taken for procreation there. They are therefore placed at the service of their husbands and [relegated] to the business of procreation, rearing and breast-feeding. But this undoes their [other] activities. Because women in these states are not being fitted for any of the human virtues, it often happens that they resemble plants. That they are a burden upon the men in these states is one of the reasons for the poverty of these states. They are found there in twice the number of men, while at the same time they do not, through training, support any of the necessary activities; except for a few which they undertake mostly at a time when they are obliged to make up their want of funds, like spinning and weaving. All this is self-evident.[47]

Erwin I. J. Rosenthal (d. 1991), who translated the text above from Hebrew, had found "this outspoken criticism of the structure of Islamic society" astonishing, especially from a Muslim scholar who lived under the fundamentalist Almohads and who was "well versed in *fiqh*," or Islamic jurisprudence. This showed, in the words of Rosenthal, how Ibn Rushd "applied to Islamic civilization . . . notions derived from an entirely different outlook and social organization."[48]

What is even more remarkable is the way Ibn Rushd tried to advance this progressive view of women within Islamic jurisprudence. This is evident in *The Distinguished Jurist's Primer*, where he cherry-picks the most women-friendly views in various schools of Islamic thought, often departing from his own Maliki school. For instance, he argues that a woman cannot be forced to marry against her wishes and that she can contract her own marriage independently of a male "guardian." He also says that a wife has a right of divorce equivalent to that of the husband. He does his best to argue that women can lead prayers, at least in a household, and that they can work as judges, clearly in financial matters and perhaps in all matters as well. He takes a bold step against polygamy, arguing that a bridegroom must fulfill the demand imposed by his wife, such as not marrying another woman. As for women's dress code, he advises "modesty" but not the face veil.[49]

Catarina Belo, a contemporary professor of philosophy who has examined all these "undeniably feminist" views of Ibn Rushd, comes to the following conclusion about him, which is worth quoting at length:

> Averroes' considerations on women . . . offer a remarkably original insight. He considers women on a par with men in essence and intellectual ability. His references to women break new ground, and prefigure important debates that would flourish in modern Europe. He urges society, in particular his Muslim contemporaries, to allow women a greater role in public affairs, for the benefit of the entire state. Averroes does not see a contradiction between this and his Muslim faith—as the difference between the genders is at bottom physical. According to him there is nothing precluding women's full participation in society. Underpinning his position is a stark rationalism, namely

the view that reason pervades creation, noticeably in the way God devised and created a universe that is intelligible to human beings. Moreover, rationality is a feature of all human beings, including women. Even the physical differences between men and women do not ultimately detract from that essential identity between the genders, since women, like men, are fully rational.[50]

Belo reminds us that Ibn Rushd's call for "more power and independence" for women was quite revolutionary for his time. In fact, it is quite revolutionary even today. Most mainstream Islamic authorities still have a hard time accepting that women are equal to men in their rational faculties. They rather stick to dubious hadiths that teach that women are "deficient in intelligence and religion."[51] Countries influenced by such teachings, such as Saudi Arabia or Afghanistan, keep downgrading their women. More than eight centuries after Ibn Rushd, in other words, patriarchy keeps being a main reason "for the poverty of these states."

A PRECURSOR TO FREE SPEECH

I spent much of my life in Turkey and got involved with its various Islamic groups. One of the dicta I often heard was *Batılı tasvir saf zihinleri idlaldir,* or "The depiction of falsehood is the seduction of pure minds." It implied that irreligious or heretical ideas should not be discussed or quoted at length, for otherwise "pure minds" could be easily deceived by them. It was better to condemn "falsehood" without giving much airtime to it.

This was indeed just an example of the common attitude to knowledge in most traditional societies: bad ideas had to be suppressed, because people had to be protected from them. (Remember al-Ghazali's analogy to protecting a boy from "touching the snake.") How we know what ideas are good or bad in the first place was rarely asked, as the answer was already determined by authority—not through free, rational inquiry. Someone had established what is right and wrong, and what befell on us was to stick to that precedent.

The writings of Ibn Rushd, however, show a remarkably different approach to knowledge. Whenever he opposes something as falsehood, he doesn't shy away from depicting it. When he makes pages-long quotations from al-Ghazali, he doesn't fear that readers will fall for his opponent's arguments. He rather trusts in the power of his own arguments.

Luckily, this unusual approach to knowledge didn't remain buried in the books of Ibn Rushd; it left a trace on the world's intellectual history. I learned this from the late Jonathan Sacks, the former chief rabbi of Britain and also a prominent public intellectual, whom we lost in late 2020. In one of his books, he pointed out that Ibn Rushd's spirit of fair and open argumentation influenced one of his successors: Rabbi Judah Loewe of Prague (d. 1609), one of the distinguished scholars of Judaism and also a philosopher in his own right. In one of his works, Rabbi Loewe shared a quote from Ibn Rushd: "You should always, when presenting a philosophical argument, cite the views of your opponents. Failure to do so is an implicit acknowledgement of the weakness of your own case."[52] Taking this as an inspiration, the Rabbi went on to argue:

> [Averroës'] words hold true for religion as well. . . . It is not proper that we despise the words [of our adversaries], but rather we must draw them as close as we can. . . . Therefore it is proper, out of love of reason and knowledge, that you should not summarily reject anything that opposes your own ideas, especially so if your adversary does not intend merely to provoke you, but rather to declare his beliefs. Even if such beliefs are opposed to your own faith and religion, do not say [to your opponent], "Speak not, close your mouth." If that happens, there will take place no purification of religion.
>
> On the contrary, you should, at such times, say, "Speak up as much as you want, say whatever you wish, and do not say

later that had you been able to speak you would have replied further." . . . This is the opposite of what some people think, namely, that when you prevent someone from speaking against religion, that strengthens religion. That is not so, because curbing the words of an opponent in religious matters is nothing but the curbing and enfeebling of religion itself.[53]

This was quite a remarkable defense of freedom of speech, which would influence later generations. Rabbi Sacks traces it forward to the English intellectual John Milton (d. 1674), who famously argued, "Let [Truth] and Falsehood grapple . . . in a free and open encounter." Then, two centuries later, there came John Stuart Mill (d. 1873), who made the most rigorous argument for free speech, condemning "the evil of silencing the expression of an opinion." All this progression shows us, in the words of Rabbi Sacks, how "first a Muslim, then a Jew, then a Christian, then a secular humanist come together to agree on the importance of free speech and *making space for dissent.*"[54] It also shows us how that particular Muslim, Ibn Rushd, was ahead of his time.

That is why there are scholars who see Ibn Rushd as a precursor to the whole Enlightenment project. One of them was Paul Kurtz (d. 2012), the late American thinker and champion of "humanism," who said:

> What is significant in reading Averroes is his conviction that man is a rational animal and that freedom of rational investigation needs to be defended. It is this defense of rational objectivity and free inquiry that is of crucial significance . . . it is this principle that is later taken up and defended during the Enlightenment.[55]

Would Ibn Rushd himself espouse the Enlightenment, if he had seen it? The answer, I believe, is nuanced. He probably wouldn't like the anti-religious strain within the Enlightenment that sprouted especially in France—and even later influenced the Muslim world's authoritarian secularists. But he would feel close to what is called the "religious Enlightenment," which harmonized religion with "reasonableness, toleration and natural law."[56] Because, as Charles Butterworth, one of his most astute Western observers, points out, Ibn Rushd always lived, thought, and wrote as a Muslim believer. "His attacks upon the defenders of religion in his own day," Butterworth notes, "were attacks designed to foster both religious belief and freedom, not to subjugate one to the other."[57] Erwin J. Rosenthal agrees. The great philosopher of Al-Andulus was a "sincere, orthodox Muslim," and his work was not about a conflict of "faith versus reason." It was rather about "a contrast between intelligent and naive, unquestioning faith."[58]

A TRAGIC LOSS

In previous pages, you may have noticed that I shared quotes from Ibn Rushd that are translated from Hebrew. Why is that? you may have wondered, as he was an Arab scholar who wrote in Arabic. The answer is a sad one: we don't have the Arabic originals of most of Ibn Rushd's books, for they were burnt publicly, in his hometown, Córdoba, to finish off his "heresy."

This happened around the year 1195, when the new Almohad caliph, Abu Yusuf Yaqub al-Mansur, gave in to the pressures of religious conservatives—unmistakably Ash'aris—who were long disturbed by Ibn Rushd's philosophical writings.[59] Finally, one of them found a pretext to attack him: in one of his manuscripts, Ibn Rushd had quoted a Greek philosopher who treated the planet Venus as a deity. This was presented as evidence that Ibn Rushd himself was a worshipper of Venus, which would make him an apostate to be killed. Soon the caliph condemned Ibn Rushd, and all such "philosophers," who were declared "worse than Christians and Jews."[60] Ibn Rushd's philosophical books were set on fire, while he was publicly disgraced at the Great Mosque of Córdoba, where he was made to stand while attendants passed, damning him and spitting on his face.[61] Then he was banished to Lucena, a small and predominantly Jewish town southeast of Córdoba. A visitor later wrote in his memoirs:

> When I entered the city, I asked about Ibn Rushd and I was told that he was under house arrest on the orders of the caliph Ya'qoob, and no one was allowed to visit him, because of the many strange views that were narrated from him, and the many shunned branches of knowledge that were attributed to him.[62]

Two years later, Ibn Rushd silently returned back to favor and was to called to Morocco to join the caliph's new court on the other side of Gibraltar. But he was already too old and fragile. He died in Marrakesh, in December 1198, at the age of seventy-two.

That is how his own civilization rejected Ibn Rushd. But his philosophical books, which were translated into Hebrew and Latin, moved on and changed the world. The time was the early thirteenth century, when the first great universities were being established in Italy, France, and England. At the University of Paris, a group of philosophers called the "Averroists" began to champion Ibn Rushd's ideas, which they partly misunderstood, to cause an earthquake within the Roman Catholic Church.[63] "They passionately argued that human beings had the right to learn everything they could about the natural world," notes a science historian, "without worrying whether it contradicted Scripture or Church doctrine."[64] Saint Thomas Aquinas opposed the excesses of these Averroists, but he also borrowed many ideas of Ibn Rushd's himself, which he quoted in his own works no less than five hundred times.

In the next three centuries, Ibn Rushd would haunt the European minds as "The Commentator" on Aristotle, whose name had become synonymous with philosophy. The idea that religion and reason are different approaches to the same truth, as argued by Ibn Rushd, proved "revolutionary in a Europe unaccustomed to linking those concepts."[65] Ultimately, this prepared the way "for the complete separation of religion and philosophy, which allowed Western philosophy to develop into its characteristic form of modernity."[66]

Among Jews, Ibn Rushd was understood, and appreciated, more accurately. His thoughts on the relationship between philosophy and religion "inspired a renewed interest in the interpretation of scripture and the Jewish religion."[67] Pivotal Jewish philosophers such as Abraham ibn Ezra (d. 1167) and Moses Narboni (d. 1362) embraced Ibn Rushd's ideas and took them into novel directions. Narboni was also the first person to translate Ibn Tufayl's *Hayy ibn Yaqzan,* which elucidated Ibn Rushd's ideas in literary form, to another language, namely Hebrew. It was this translation that would fascinate Pico della Mirandola, the key philosopher of the Renaissance.

While it had this tectonic impact on Jewish and Christian minds, the Andulusian Muslim philosophy faded away among Muslims themselves. In the world of Islam, Ibn Rushd "became almost immediately after his death a non-person, sometimes referred to with grudging respect, but more usually totally ignored."[68] Until the modern era, very little was known of his work. His name wasn't reputable, his books were lost, and his passion— "philosophy"—was despised.

Only in the modern era, some Muslim intellectuals, shocked with the advent of modernity, rediscovered Ibn Rushd as a lost source of wisdom. One of them was Muhammad Abid al-Jabiri, a Moroccan professor of philosophy and Islamic thought who passed away in 2010. Al-Jabiri penned a monumental three-volume work titled *Naqd al-Fikr al-Arabi,* or *"Critique of Arab Thought."* He argued that the common Arab thinking, which could well be extended to the broader Muslim world, remained in the level of "rhetoric" that Ibn Rushd defined as the lowest level of reason, and never rose up to the higher level of "demonstration." This mindset interpreted the world mainly through *analogy* to known precedents, rather than *analysis*. The result, al-Jabiri argued, was "the resigned mind" that hinders independent thought and shies away from discussing crucial cultural issues. Another important insight of Ibn Rushd—that education must aim for "comprehension rather than memorization"—was also overlooked, and that is why educational systems in Muslim-majority countries, even secular ones like Turkey, are still focused on memorization rather than on critical thinking.[69]

In short, by rejecting Ibn Rushd, and the broader philosophical tradition he represented, we Muslims really harmed ourselves. What we did, in the words of Fazlur Rahman, was nothing short of an "intellectual suicide."[70]

THE JEWISH SECRET

Today if you visit the beautiful city of Córdoba, in the Andalusia region of modern-day Spain, you will probably not miss the magnificent Mezquita-Catedral, or the "Mosque-Cathedral," at the heart of the city. It is called this because it was first built as a mosque in the late eighth century by victorious Muslims, and was converted into a cathedral in the early thirteenth century by victorious Catholics. With its charming courtyard, elegant gates, horseshoe-style arches, and intricate mosaics, it is a breathtakingly beautiful structure whose Christian remake didn't conceal its Islamic past.

There is another gem in Córdoba, though, a much smaller one, that not all tourists catch. In a walking distance from the Mezquita-Catedral is a statue of Ibn Rushd, presenting him as sitting on a pedestal, with a turban on his head, a handsome beard on his face, and a thick volume in his hand. It is a powerful monument that invites you to just sit there and ponder, as I was lucky to have done a few times.

And in the same vicinity, just a few minutes away, there is another statute worth seeing. It is again a man sitting on a pedestal, with a turban on his head, a handsome beard on his face, and a thick volume in his hand. His full name is Rabbi Moshe ben Maimon, and the world knows him in short as Maimonides.

These two outstanding statues in Córdoba seem quite appropriate, because Ibn Rushd and Maimonides were probably the two greatest minds the city has ever raised—one of them Muslim, the other one Jewish. The latter, just like Ibn Rushd, was both a religious scholar and a philosopher. In his masterpiece, *The Guide for the Perplexed,* written around 1190 in Arabic with Hebrew letters, he did for Judaism what Ibn Rushd did for Islam: reconciling philosophy, in particular Aristotelian philosophy, with scripture—in his case, the Torah. The two men were contemporaries, and they had a similar approach to reason and its relation to religion.[71]

Now here is something remarkable: in Judaism, Maimonides has become a highly respected authority, as he is still today. He has even been called the "Second Moses," the first being the Prophet Moses. In contrast, Ibn Rushd, as we have seen, didn't have the same luck in Islam. His rationality rather remained as the road not taken. Could this be the sign of something significant, something fateful?

Maimonides himself can help us a bit here, as he wrote about not just the Jewish approach to reason but also the Muslim approach, and he explained their interaction. In a remarkable passage in *The Guide for the Perplexed,* he first acknowledged the great influence of the "Mohammedan *mutakallimun*," or the "Muslim theologians," on their Jewish counterparts, whose works were "insignificant in comparison with the kindred works of the Mohammedans."[72] However, those Muslims had a rift on the role of reason, Maimonides noted, and the Jews took a side:

It also happened, that at the time when the Mohammedans adopted this method of the Kalam, there arose among them a certain sect, called Mu'tazilah, i.e., Separatists. In certain things our scholars followed the theory and the method of these Mu'tazilah. Although another sect, the Asha'ariyah, with their own peculiar views, was subsequently established amongst the Mohammedans, you will not find any of these views in the writings of our authors.... On the other hand our Andalusian scholars followed the teachings of the philosophers, from whom they accepted those opinions which were not opposed to our own religious principles.[73]

That is why, while the Mu'tazila faded in Islam, the "Jewish Mu'tazila" arose in the tenth century and "dominated Jewish theological thinking for centuries to come."[74] For the same reason, key Ash'ari doctrines—voluntarism, occasionalism, and predestination—did not appear as strong currents in medieval Judaism.[75]

To be sure, there were dogmatists among Jews as well who opposed the philosophical rationalism of Maimonides. One of them, a thirteenth-century Talmudist named Solomon ben Abraham, even instigated the Dominican monks in Southern France to burn *The Guide for the Perplexed*. "You burn your heretics," he kindly said to the Christians, "persecute ours also."[76]

Yet Maimonides was never fully rejected. His *Mishneh Torah*—the compilation of and commentary on Jewish law—became a widely acknowledged classic. More important, the philosophical faith he articulated in *The Guide for the Perplexed* inspired the Haskalah, or the "Jewish Enlightenment," of late-eighteenth- and nineteenth-century Europe. Its main pioneer, Moses Mendelssohn (d. 1786)—whose meticulous study of Maimonides left him with his famously crooked posture—argued that the Jewish faith is based on rational and universal values on which Jews can connect with gentiles.[77] Based on that premise, he called on his coreligionists to fully participate in modern society, sparking an intellectual and cultural flourishing among European Jews. "The age-old Jewish habit of Talmud study" was transferred to "the newly opened-up fields of secular culture."[78] This intellectual energy, combined with the minority talent to "think outside of the box," generated the remarkable Jewish success in arts and sciences.[79]

Today, many Muslims are aware of this Jewish accomplishment in the modern world, which looks painfully tragic when compared to our own record. For example, among the nine hundred Nobel Prize laureates over a century, there are more than two hundred Jews. In contrast, as of 2019, there were only twelve Muslim Nobel laureates. And that is despite there being a hundred times more Muslims than Jews in the world.

How should we explain this dramatic gap? Some Muslims find an answer in the imagined conspiratorial powers of the Jews.[80] But the distinct trajectories reason has followed in Judaism and Islam points to another answer. It points not to a Jewish conspiracy, but a Muslim self-sabotage.

WHY WE LOST REASON, REALLY

A tyrant never fears religious knowledge or knowledge of the After World. . . . But the tyrant would shiver in fear of worldly knowledge such as theoretical wisdom, intellectual philosophy, the rights of nations, civil policy.

—Abd al-Rahman al-Kawakibi, late-nineteenth-century Muslim intellectual[1]

So far, we have seen that a fateful war of ideas took place in early Islam. Muslims who saw reason as a guiding light—first in the form of Mu'tazila theology and then Aristotelian philosophy—accomplished a great intellectual achievement, with impressive consequences in virtually all aspects of civilization. However, Muslims who distrusted reason opposed them, renounced them, and marginalized them. Ultimately, reason faded in the Muslim world, which gradually lost its creativity. In contrast, it flourished in Europe, paving the way to modernity.

But why? Why did this happen? Why did reason fade among Muslims?

Those Muslims who are loyal to the Sunni orthodoxy think that this happened because, thank God, the true faith prevailed against its heresies. For them, both the Mu'tazila and the philosophers were dangerous currents that could harm the *iman,* or "faith,"

of believers. So God protected his religion by sending great scholars like Imam al-Ghazali, who condemned what had to be condemned and kept the religion on the right track. The Ash'arite
theology—with all its ethical voluntarism, occasionalist cosmology, and scriptural literalism—was nothing but "true Islam," which
disgorged what was alien to it.

There is another group of people who would fully agree with
this view, although from a totally opposite perspective. These
are the Islamoskeptics in the West, who believe that Islam, right
from its core, has been an unusually dogmatic religion that lacks
the rationality one can find in its Abrahamic sisters—Judaism and
Christianity. Often combining these two religions into a single
"Judeo-Christian" tradition, the advocates of this skeptical view
single out Islam as the exceptionally rigid and absolutist version
of monotheism.

One of the proponents of this view is American intellectual
Robert R. Reilly, whose notable book *The Closing of the Muslim
Mind* offers, despite missing some important nuances, a powerful critique of the very problem we have examined so far. Reilly,
a Catholic, also admits that all the problematic theological doctrines in Islam—voluntarism, occasionalism, fatalism—emerged
in Christianity as well. However, he says, what really made the big
difference is the biblical teaching that man is "made in the image
and likeness of God." This notion, he reminds us, doesn't exist in
the Qur'an, and that is why the "rationality, free will, and sovereignty" of man, which flourished in the West, did not flourish in
Islam.[2]

However, while the Qur'an indeed does not define humans as
created in the "image of God," it does describe them, repeatedly,
as God's "vicegerents" on earth.[3] It also tells that God commanded
angels to bow down before Adam, and that the latter received a
"divine trust" given to no other creature.[4] From such Qur'anic precepts one can infer a view of human dignity. That was precisely

what the Mu'tazila and the philosophers did, in fact, as we saw in the previous chapters.

In my view, there is an elephant in the room that orthodox Sunni Muslims and Islamoskeptics are both missing: the Islamic tradition did not develop in a vacuum. Since its very birth, Islam has been under the thumb of powerful states that had political goals and ambitions of their own. These states had their hands in the making of the Islamic orthodoxy, as they suppressed certain schools and established others. (The real difference with Judaism and Christianity may well be here: their association with the state has not been as permanent and definitive as it was in Islam.)

We already had a glimpse of this political hand in Islam: the Umayyad dynasty, which captured the caliphate some thirty years after the Prophet Muhammad and dominated it for almost a century, suppressed the doctrine of free will and instead promoted "Compulsionism," or predestination; for the latter doctrine instilled a culture of blind obedience that served despotic rule.

Could a similar political hand have sealed the fates of the Mu'tazila and the philosophers as well? Or, conversely speaking, could Ash'arism have dominated Sunni Islam thanks to its political use, rather than its theological merit?

Let's have a look.

"CANCEL CULTURE" BACK IN THE DAY

In fact, when you look at the history of political intrusions into Islamic theology, especially in the formative centuries, the first episode you may notice will show the Mu'tazila theology as the state-imposed doctrine. This is the *mihna,* or "trial," that the early Abbasid caliph al-Ma'mun established in 813 in order to impose the "createdness of the Qur'an" doctrine, which was one of the tenets of the Mu'tazila.

The *mihna* was certainly wrong, unwise, and disastrous.[5]

However it lasted for only sixteen years.[6] Soon after that, things turned upside down—and not for a short period, but forever. With the rule of Caliph al-Mutawakkil (r. 847–861), the "uncreatedness of the Qur'an" became the official dogma, while the Mu'tazila became the new outcasts to be purged, lashed, and jailed.[7] "Now the reign of innovators ended," a poet recited, "because they had become weak and collapsed."[8]

In the early eleventh century, the late Abbasid caliph al-Qadir, a Hanbali himself, further sealed orthodoxy by promulgating what is known as the "Qadiri Creed," in two subsequent edicts. First, in 1017, all Mu'tazila scholars were ordered to publicly retract their "heresy" and to desist from any public or private teaching of any Mu'tazila ideas. Otherwise, they would face corporal punishments and exile.[9] A year later, a second edict took a tougher line: "He who says the Qur'an is created is an infidel, whose blood may legitimately be shed."[10] Read out loud in the caliph's court, in the presence of religious scholars, the document concluded, "This is the profession of faith of the Muslims; he who is opposed to it is a transgressor of the law and an infidel."[11] This state-imposed orthodoxy did not remain in Baghdad, the capital, but was implemented in the four corners of the Muslim world. Scholars were forced to publicly retract their views, and those who resisted were jailed, while their "heresies" were condemned at mosque pulpits.[12]

This is how earthly power defined mainstream Islam. For "Sunnism as understood today," in the words of contemporary scholar Ziauddin Sardar, "is the Qadiri Creed all but in name."[13]

Now here is something interesting: when you read the Sunni literature about the history of theology in Islam, you will not miss the *mihna*. It is told and retold to emphasize how the terrible Mu'tazila oppressed true believers like the great Imam ibn Hanbal. But you probably will never read about the Qadiri Creed, which was a much more extensive and effective case of state-imposed orthodoxy. (Similarly, you will never read about the earlier execution of proto-Mutazilites—the defenders of free will—under Ummayad rule as well.) In fact, the Qadiri Creed was virtually unknown until the early twentieth century, when German academic Adam Metz (d. 1917) discovered it in "its only known source"—a manuscript by the twelfth-century Hanbali scholar Ibn al-Jawzi.[14] Other scholars from the same era, however, were conspicuously silent on the Qadiri Creed. The winners of Muslim history, apparently, didn't choose to highlight their own tyranny.

The caliphate not only imposed an orthodoxy but also ingrained it with education. In the late eleventh century, the Seljuk Empire, the Muslim superpower of the time, established an unprecedented system of state-sponsored madrasas under the leadership of the powerful vizier Nizam al-Mulk, whose honorific name means the "Order of the Realm." First founded in Baghdad and later extended to other major cities, these schools, which would operate for over four centuries, were formed "for the propagation of state-approved Islamic thought."[15] And this thought was nothing but Ash'arism.

At this time, there were tensions between Hanbalis and Ash'aris as well, but they were soon reconciled. In the thirteenth century, the Mamluk Sultanate, which took control of Egypt, Hejaz, and Syria, imposed a "Sunni unity" minimizing the differences between these two theological camps and the big four jurisprudential schools. It also turned the common tenets of Hanbalism and Ash'arism into a common and simple *aqidah,* or "creed," marginalizing the very notion of *kalam,* or "theology."[16] From that point on, Sunni Muslims would only hear about "*what* to believe, but not *how* or *why.*"[17]

And Muslim rulers kept imposing their favored orthodoxy. Writing in the fifteenth century, the famous Egyptian historian al-Maqrizi was noting how the "theology of al-Ash'ari" became the status quo in Egypt, broader North Africa, Syria, and the Arabian Peninsula, thanks to sultans making it "a necessary requirement" in all madrasas. "This theology became so predominant in these lands that whoever opposed it would have had his neck cut off," he wrote. "And this remains the case until our times."[18]

In this environment, the Mu'tazila tradition lived only in the shadows. Ibn Battuta (d. 1377), who has been called the "Muslim Marco Polo," had given a glimpse of that when he reported about a "group of prominent people" he met in Khwarazm, a region in Central Asia, around the year 1334. These people were convinced by Mu'tazila doctrine, but "they did not openly profess it," due to their fear of the "orthodox Sunni" ruler.[19]

In addition to the Mu'tazila, the philosophers were condemned as well, often only more passionately. A century after al-Ghazali, Ibn al-Salah (d. 1245), a Shafi'i hadith scholar, was not only declaring them as under the grip of Satan, but also calling on the Sultans to finish them off:

> Those who meddle in philosophy, either as teachers or students, will meet disappointment and deprivation and will fall into the grip of Satan. The sultan has a duty to protect believers from the evil of these inauspicious people, expelling them from schools and exiling them, punishing those who practice their art and offering those who believe the doctrines of the philosophers a choice between the sword and Islam, so that their fire will die out and all traces of it, and of them, will be obliterated.[20]

It was this zealous purge—whose milder version is called "cancel culture" today—that made Ash'arite theology the Sunni orthodoxy. It won the day not because of its merits, but because of the dictates of the states that ruled the medieval Muslim world. The fact that these states had sweeping powers unchecked by the constraints in Europe—such as landed aristocracy, city-states, and natural boundaries—made their decisions more effective, influential, and everlasting.[21]

But a question still remains: Why did Muslim states opt for Ash'arism? Why did they prefer it to its rationalist alternatives?

To seek an answer, we need to look at something about the Mu'tazilites and the Ash'arites that we haven't checked so far: their attitude toward political authority.

THE "ANARCHY" OF THE MU'TAZILA

In Islam, the very first political authority was the Prophet Muhammad. No Muslim ever doubted that. But what should happen after the Prophet turned out to be a big challenge. There was an ever-expanding state to run, and most Muslims agreed that it should be led by a "caliph," or an "imam," as he was also called. But who was the rightful imam, what were the limits to his authority, and what would happen if he proved to be a tyrant? These questions led to assassinations, massacres, and civil wars. Ultimately, the dynastic despotism of the Umayyads prevailed, later to be replaced by that of the Abbasids. They made the Sunni mainstream.

In return, two significant strains of dissent emerged. The first was that of the Shiites. They refused to accept the legitimacy of the existing Sunni imamate, but only because they aspired to the imamate of Ali and his descendants—a fixation that made them a disillusioned minority with messianic hopes. The second was that of the fanatic Kharijites, or "Dissenters." They not only condemned the existing imamate but also the Muslims who gave them allegiance, making the Kharijites an extremely militant faction.

Then there was a third strain of dissent, which was none other than that of the Mu'tazila. As a testimony to their rationalism, they asked the magical question that did not occur to most Muslims: Is the imamate really necessary? Do Muslims, in other words, really need a state? Some Mu'tazila scholars—such as al-Asamm (d. ca. 816), al-Nazzam (d. ca. 840), or Hisham al-Fuwat (d. 840)—gave a negative answer: no, the state wasn't necessary. The law was certainly necessary, but the law could exist without a state.

Patricia Crone (d. 2015), a Western historian of Islam, called these scholars "Muʿtazila anarchists."[22] They were "anarchists" only "in the simple sense of believers in an-archy, 'no government.'" They were not "communists, social reformers, revolutionaries or terrorists," but "merely thinkers who held that Muslim society could function without what we would call the state."[23] This makes them an unusual phenomenon in world history, Crone added, as it is difficult to find anarchism "outside the Western tradition."[24]

The Muʿtazila anarchists' skepticism of the state came from experience. "Since imams kept turning into kings," or despots, they reasoned, "the best solution was not to set them up in the first place."[25] But how could the society function, then? Various answers were given, including, "provincial imams in federation, or local imams elected for a term, or with executive committees, or simply with the leaders of households and tribes as they were, or with straightforward self-help."[26]

Other Muʿtazila scholars weren't anarchists, as they accepted the need for a state. But still, they made an important distinction: the necessity of the state came from reason, not religion. So the structure of the state could be rationally discussed, allowing some Muʿtazila scholars to propose an "extreme decentralization" of power, such as establishing "several, semi-independent imams."[27] Or a single imam could be temporarily appointed to fight an enemy that invaded Muslim lands, and he could later be deposed when the war was over.[28]

All in all, the Muʿtazila political thought was unhelpful to Muslim despots, who aspired for absolute power, often in the name of God. In the words of Crone:

> One way or the other [the Muʿtazila] all denied that the imamate was God-given. In other words, they all desacralized it: it did not reflect the absolute; it was just a fallible human institution like any other.... Given that the imamate was simply a human convention, one could have it or not as one saw fit:

people had had it in the past, and it had worked very well, but nowadays it was preferable, or even necessary, to do without it. In short, they cut the link between the imamate and the law on which Islamic society rested.[29]

In light of this political theology, it shouldn't be surprising that besides the short-lived exception under Caliph al-Ma'mun, whose fascination with reason and philosophy seems to have made him pro-Mu'tazila, the caliphate didn't like the Mu'tazila. The latter's theology just wasn't helpful to power.

"POLITICAL SCIENCE" OF THE PHILOSOPHERS

The second wave of rational thought in early Islam, as we have seen, was the *falasifa*, the philosophers who were influenced by Greek thought. In their work, we do not see any anarchism, perhaps partly because these handful of thinkers needed the patronage of the state to survive. Yet they introduced into Islam a novelty that we can call "political science," which included a critique of tyranny.

The origin of this political science went back to Plato, who didn't actually offer a good start. For Plato is notorious for opposing the Athenian democracy in which he lived and, rather, proposing an aristocracy ruled by a "philosopher king." In contrast, Aristotle offered a more neutral observation of the various political systems of his time and also introduced the notion of rule of law, to be developed later by Montesquieu. Yet Aristotle's most definitive political book, *Politics,* never made its way to the medieval Islamic civilization. Hence, his greatest Muslim student, Ibn Rushd, would regret that "it has not yet fallen into our hands."[30]

What fell into Muslim hands were Plato's two seminal books, *The Republic* and *The Laws,* and the Muslim philosophers would try to make their best out of them. The first of these philosophers

was al-Farabi, whose *Book of the Political Regime* followed Plato
in idealizing a "virtuous city" run by a "philosopher king." For al-
Farabi and others who would follow him, this was an irresistible
template fitting neatly into the ideal early Muslim society led by
the Prophet Muhammad.

But what were the alternatives to this "virtuous city"? Plato
had listed several imperfect models, ranking the "despotic city"
as the worst, while also devaluing the "democratic city" as the
second worst. Here, al-Farabi had a crucial divergence from
Plato that is often missed: he did not disparage the "democratic
city" as the second-worst model—he rather praised it as the
second-best model. This was a city where all people had *hurri-
yah,* or "freedom," al-Farabi wrote, so that "everybody loves it
and loves to reside in it, because there is no human wish or desire that this city does not satisfy." This very freedom, he added,
allows "philosophers, rhetoricians, and poets" to thrive in the
democratic city, which would also help raise "virtuous men." In
other words, instead of seeing political freedom as a stepping
stone to corruption, as Plato did, al-Farabi rather saw it as a basis
for cultivating virtue.[31]

This was a significant political outlook, which, in the words of
contemporary philosopher Anthony Booth, "makes [al-Farabi] an
advocate of liberalism."[32]

No wonder al-Farabi despised "despotism," or *taghallub.* The
Arabic term literally means "winning by force," and it referred
to any regime that was built on sheer power. Ibn Sina, who came
about a century after al-Farabi and followed his footsteps, was so
radically against *taghallub* that he justified armed rebellion against
despots.[33] If a ruler captures power only "by virtue of power," he
even wrote, "it becomes the duty of every citizen to fight and kill
him."[34]

When we come to Ibn Rushd, who brought Muslim philosophical tradition to maturity, we again see a denunciation of *taghallub.*

In a remarkable passage in his commentary on Plato's *Republic*, we also see a denunciation of oligarchy:

> Men will be of two categories: a category called the masses, and another called the mighty, as is the case of the people in Persia and in many of our own states. In such a situation, the masses will be plundered by the mighty. The mighty commit excesses by seizing property from them, until this leads them at times to tyranny, just as happens in our own time and our own state.[35]

This criticism, especially of "our own time and our own state," was "unusually strong language."[36] Some even argued that it could be a real reason behind Ibn Rushd's public disgrace by the Almohad caliphate.[37]

Another interesting insight of Ibn Rushd's was that despotism could grow even under a ruler who claims to uphold the law. He noted this by reference to Plato, whose concept of *nomos,* or "law," was the counterpart to the Muslim Sharia:

> Plato says that it is characteristic of this individual [the tyrant] that he subdues all humans and arouses them to hold fast to the nomos so that it might be thought that he is not tyrannizing, and that he intends the guidance and direction of the citizens [with a view] to dividing property and goods among them, and that he has no other intention than the care of the association and the improvement of the city.[38]

So one had to beware of tyrants who claimed they were only caring for the people. The fact that they "hold fast to the nomos" could also be a mere facade. With these remarks, Ibn Rushd was warning against "the use of the Shariah to strengthen tyrants," an insight that would be "largely lacking in Islamic political thought."[39] And the very notion of "political science" would remain almost nonexistent in the Islamic world until the modern era.[40]

One of those who studied this intellectual history was the late great scholar Franz Rosenthal (d. 2003). "Freedom's greatness and vulnerability" was noticed by Muslim thinkers, he wrote, but to remain only in theory. "Certain philosophers, such as Ibn Rushd, may have dreamed of, or even worked at, convincing their rulers of the desirability of a practical test," he added. "But they never got very far."[41]

IBN KHALDUN, STATES, AND TAXES

Ibn Rushd was the last great philosopher of classical Islam, as his passing closed the Aristotelian chapter in Muslim thought. However, about two centuries later, there came another towering Muslim thinker who stood away from the dangerous territory of philosophy, but he advanced rationality on what we would call "social sciences" today. His name was Ibn Khaldun

Born in Tunisia in 1332, Ibn Khaldun observed the social and political dynamics of North Africa, which he expounded in his magnum opus, *Muqaddimah,* or "Prolegomena," the long introduction to his larger book of history. Here he explained the rise and fall of subsequent dynasties by "cause and effect," rather than divine blessing and curse, which "was an unusual thing for an Islamic historian to do."[42]

One interesting insight of Ibn Khaldun's was the relation between prosperity and economic liberty. He observed that as dynasties stay more and more in power, they grow opulent; employ bigger armies and bureaucracies; and impose "forced labor," "forced sales and purchases," and heavy taxation to finance all of these assets. But these dictates, he noted, "weigh heavily upon the subjects and overburden them." As a result:

> Business falls off, because all hopes (of profit) are destroyed, permitting the dissolution of civilization and reflecting upon

(the status of) the dynasty. This (situation) becomes more and more aggravated, until the dynasty disintegrates.[43]

In contrast, when rulers act with "kindness, reverence, humility, respect for the property of other people, and disinclination to appropriate," Ibn Khaldun observed, things got better for all:

When tax assessments and imposts upon the subjects are low, the latter have the energy and desire to do things. Cultural enterprises grow and increase, because the low taxes bring satisfaction. When cultural enterprises grow, the number of individual imposts and assessments mounts. In consequence, the tax revenue, which is the sum total of (the individual assessments), increases.[44]

Such views of Ibn Khaldun's influenced a few Muslim thinkers that immediately followed him. One was his student al-Maqrizi, who criticized the Mamluk rule in Egypt, under which "the only thing we are allowed to do without paying tax is breathe."[45] Another contemporary scholar from Syria, al-Asadi, also criticized the Mamluks, whose taxes had extended to natural resources such as salt, natron, pastures, and fisheries. "The income derived in this way is apparently considered as supporting and strengthening the ruler," al-Asadi wrote, "but in fact it is weakening the very foundation of the sultanate."[46]

Ibn Khaldun also influenced a few Ottoman reformists in the seventeenth century, such as the official historian Mustafa Na'ima, who had observed, "the success of the infidel rulers depend upon rational politics."[47] These include, he wrote, "increasing the efficiency of tax collection rather than increasing the tax rate" and using the tax revenues effectively.[48] However, despite such calls, until Western influences in the nineteenth century, Ottoman economic thought focused on state-managed provisionism—a "proto-quasi-socialism"— and lacked the two key insights of Ibn Khaldun: a limited state and entrepreneurial dynamism.[49]

Meanwhile, in the Arab world, Ibn Khaldun proved "all but forgotten."[50] His ambition to study society for its own sake was unpopular even in his own time. He was denounced by the hadith scholar al-Sakhawi (d. 1497), because for the latter "history was ancillary to the religious sciences and . . . its chief purpose was to test the reliability of chains of hadith transmitters."[51] In the late nineteenth century, when arch-reformist Muhammad Abduh (d. 1905) realized the importance of *Muqaddimah* and tried to introduce it to the curriculum of the prominent Al-Azhar University, he was told that it was "against the tradition of teaching at al-Azhar."[52]

Ibn Khaldun won the fame he deserved only in the twentieth century, in part thanks to some Westerners who found his work intriguing. His argument for low taxation (and against government involvement in production) inspired the defenders of free-market economics. Among them was Arthur Laffer, whose famous "Laffer Curve" about optimal tax rates clearly goes back to Ibn Khaldun.[53] Another one was Ronald Reagan, the fortieth president of the United States, who, first in a press conference in 1981 and later in a *New York Times* op-ed in 1993, quoted Ibn Khaldun's key observation: "At the beginning of the empire, the tax rates were low and the revenues were high. At the end of the empire, the tax rates were high and the revenues were low."[54]

THE ASH'ARI LENIENCY TO DESPOTISM

So far in this chapter, we have seen the "anarchism" of the Mu'tazila, and the critical opinions of Muslim philosophers against tyranny. We have also seen Ibn Khaldun's economic argument for a limited government. Although these views represent different strains in Islamic thought, they all had the merit of defining politics as a rational realm where arguments could be made based on empirical observations or theoretical models sometimes borrowed from other civilizations—such as the Greeks. And they all had the unfortunate fate of being sidelined and neglected, if not condemned and suppressed.

In the meantime, mainstream Islamic politics was defined by Ash'ari theology, which saw politics not as a rational but a religious realm. The thirteenth-century Shafi'i jurist al-Nawawi explained this view of theirs, and its contrast with that of the Mu'tazila, quite clearly:

> There is consensus among our companions [Shafi'i-Ash'aris] that the appointment of a caliph is an obligation and that this obligation is [established] by revelation, not reason. Some have disagreed . . . say[ing] that the appointment of a caliph is not an obligation altogether, while some of the Mu'tazila who disagree say that it is an obligation, but by reason, not by revelation. Both of these latter opinions are false.[55]

The Ash'arites had inferred their view from a Qur'anic verse: "O you who have believed, obey Allah and obey the Prophet and *those in authority among you*."[56] The latter could be merely the commanders that the Prophet appointed during his lifetime—as some early exegetes thought.[57] Or they could be anybody "in authority among you" anytime, anywhere. The Ash'aris accepted the latter view. Moreover, they accepted hadiths that commanded obedience to almost any kind of Muslim ruler. "You will be ruled after me by some who are benign, and some who are depraved," one such hadith read. "Listen to them and obey them in all that is right."[58]

Ibn Hanbal put this submissiveness even more bluntly in his *Aqida*, or "Credo," agreed upon by ninety prominent like-minded scholars of his time. "The Jihad is valid with the imams, whether they act justly or evilly," he wrote, adding that the sultans must be obeyed, "even if they are not upright, just and pious." Similarly, taxes should be paid to the commanders, the *umara*, "whether they deal justly or wickedly."[59]

This unmistakable complacency to despotism was criticized by none other than the Mu'tazila. "It is a part of their doctrine," a Mu'tazila scholar wrote in the early ninth century:

that they will treat as imam in every age whoever has established control over the domain (of Islam), provided that he is a man who formally professes the religion, and they deem it obligatory to pray behind him, and conduct holy war under him, and allow him to apply the hudud (punishments).[60]

Another Mu'tazila scholar had also slammed the *hashwiyya*—a derogatory term for literalists, often implying the Hanbalis—for showing "obedience to whoever wins, even if he is an oppressor."[61] Al-Jahiz similarly slammed them for teaching: "to speak against bad government is tantamount to civil war, and that to curse tyrants is tantamount to heresy."[62]

This submissive doctrine took its most articulate form in the hands of Abu al-Hasan al-Mawardi (d. 1058), whose book *The Ordinances of Government and Religious Offices* became the standard text of Sunni political thought. He argued that the best way to elect a caliph would be election by prominent Muslims ("those who loose and bind"), but he also justified *imarat al-istila,* or "amirate by usurpation"—a far cry from the philosopher's condemnations of *taghallub*. He also coined the term *haqq al-sultana*, or "rights of the ruler," which included brutal punishments, in addition to the two sets of "rights" known to classical Muslims: "rights of God" and "rights of men."[63]

Two centuries later, another influential Ash'ari theologian, Adud al-Din al-Iji, whose objection to natural astronomy we have already seen, further elevated the status of the Muslim ruler, coming close to divine ordination. "Rather than arguing for the right of the Community to elect one of them as their representative," his argument implied, "the Sunni imam is chosen directly by God."[64]

Why were the Ash'arites so inclined to empower the rulers? Did this have something to do with their epistemology—their theory of knowledge? This question, which is "seldom treated in modern scholarship," is scrutinized by Ovamir Anjum, a contemporary Muslim academic, in his book *Politics, Law, and Community in*

Islamic Thought. Anjum first notes that, in the formative centuries of Islam, spanning from the seventh to the twelfth, there were two distinct political visions. One was the "community-centered vision," which assumed that political power was trusted by God to the hands of the Muslim community that held the right to elect a political leader and also to depose him if he went astray. But the second vision, namely "caliphate-centered vision," considered the ruler as an appointee of God, whose "appointment" could merely be his usurpation of power by brute force.

The crucial point here is that the "community-centered vision" flourished among those who considered the imamate as a "rational" matter—such as the Mu'tazila—whereas the "caliphate-centered vision" was "underpinned by theological cynicism toward reason."[65] This, according to Anjum, was no accident:

> The institution of the caliphate/imamate required by revelation was different [from the rational view] in that it remained an obligation even if it did not furnish its rational benefit. This fits well with the Ash'ari theological insistence that God's commandments need to have no purpose, and that He may oblige humans to perform acts that are rationally unjustified or even downright impossible.[66]

In other words, the theology of a God whose wisdom is beyond question was well fit for the politics of a ruler whose wisdom, likewise, was beyond question.

THE DIVINE RIGHTS OF MUSLIM KINGS

That is all why Ash'arite theology, "intentionally or unintentionally," led to the "dominance of the political absolute." Hence it has remained, "from its very inception, the winning doctrine of authority."[67] That is also why, Abd al-Raziq (d. 1966), the seminal critic of the politicization of Islam, found the Ash'ari doctrine of politics reminiscent of the European notion of "divine rights of kings." In contrast, Abd al-Raziq argued, the Mu'tazila doctrine was similar to the social contract theory of John Locke.[68]

This was not because of some cynical sycophancy on behalf of Ash'ari scholars. Quite the contrary, they, too, were concerned by tyranny, and their insistence that the rulers must obey the Sharia has at times served as a constraint on power.[69] But their solution to tyranny didn't go beyond moral counseling to the ruler, and it fell short of offering any mechanism against the abuse of power, as Rashid Rida (d. 1935) would rightly criticize.[70] Even their moral counseling was limited by hadiths that are too conspicuously lenient to rulers. Al-Ghazali quotes two of them in his magnum opus, *Revival of the Religious Sciences*. One of them reads:

> If one has something to advise a ruler with, he should not talk to him in public, but rather he should be alone with him and talk to him: if he accepts it, this is good, otherwise, he will have fulfilled what is incumbent upon him.[71]

"He who disgraces a ruler," the other hadith reads, "will be disgraced by Allah on earth."[72]

This marriage between fideist theology and absolute power proved quite fateful for the Muslim world. As political scientist Ahmet Kuru demonstrates in *Islam, Authoritarianism, and Underdevelopment*, it led to an "ulema-state alliance" that established and sustained political authoritarianism. This alliance marginalized not just independent thought (by rational theologians and philosophers), but also trivialized the status of merchants. Consequently, Kuru argues, the two main forces that spearheaded liberalism in Europe—the intellectuals and the bourgeoisie—remained feeble in Islam.[73]

Also remaining feeble was the idea that rulers must be constrained. Muhammad Abduh had seen the problem in his native Egypt in the late nineteenth century. "I was among those persons who called upon the Egyptian population to recognize their right over their ruler," he wrote, adding that this notion "had not occurred to them for over twenty centuries."[74]

Today, the "ulema-state alliance" is still effective in Muslim dictatorships, of which there is no shortage, where many religious scholars are happy to justify autocratic rulers as long as the latter pose as the defenders of the faith. The first rule in this scheme is not to question how the ruler came to power. A contemporary Saudi text puts this quite nonchalantly: "The existence of the ruler in the Muslim community is one of the important duties of religion," it argues, "*regardless of the method by which he came into power*."[75] The second rule, the same text notes, is to be "obedient and loyal" to the ruler, "in everything that does not contradict the Islamic Sharia."[76] And since what contradicts the Sharia is defined only by religious scholars, ordinary citizens have no right to raise their voices.

In this worldview, any act of opposition to the ruler—from a public demonstration to a mere tweet—can be criminalized as *fitna,* or "sedition." Opposition becomes legitimate only when the ruler can be condemned as an "apostate" who deserves to be killed. The result is a political culture of "despotism tempered by assassination."[77] A political culture, in other words, that one can easily trace in the history of the Middle East.

FROM EARTHLY DESPOTS TO HEAVENLY GOD

On top of all this nexus between Islamic theology and Muslim politics, there is one more layer to add: Ashʿarism didn't merely justify earthly despots. It also projected, arguably, the traits of those earthly despots onto God.[78]

To see what this means, let's recall the kind of God that Ashʿarites envisioned. It was a God of absolute power, with no limits to His whimsical authority. He could punish and reward His creatures at will, and nobody could ask, "Why?" There were no laws, rules, or principles that obliged Him. His will, rather, was the basis of every law, rule, and principle. It was a God that acted on the age-old maxim of power, "Might makes right."

Alas, this was also the very definition of a despotic ruler, who also respected no laws, no rules, and no principles. Remarkably enough, this analogy between such an earthly despot and the heavenly God was drawn by none other than the Ash'arites themselves. As al-Ash'ari himself put it:

> The proof that whatever [God] does it is for Him to do is that *He is the king, not subject to anyone.* There is no one above Him who can . . . fix boundaries for Him. If this is so, nothing can ever be morally bad for Him.[79]

Another argument Ash'arites used while defining the justice of God—which, for the Mu'tazila, is His key attribute—was also quite telling. "No injustice or tyranny can be imaginable on His part," one of them noted, adding:

> Should He (Glorious is He!) destroy all His creatures in the blink of an eye, He would be neither unjust or tyrannous to them, for *they are His dominion and His slaves.* He has the right to do as He pleases in His dominion.[80]

So, since God was acting in His own domination—the very universe He created—none of His acts could be wrong. This was, again, an allusion to a despotic ruler whose power over his dominion was also unquestionable.

Ash'aris referred to earthly despots also to illustrate occasionalism—that there are no laws of nature but only the "habits" of God. An interesting source which tells us about this is Maimonides, who, while criticizing the Ash'arites, notes the following:

They say that the thing which exists with certain constant and permanent forms, dimensions, and properties, only follows the direction of habit, *just as the king generally rides on horseback through the streets of the city,* and is never found departing from this habit; but reason does not find it impossible that he should walk on foot through the place.[81]

"On this foundation," Maimonides added, "their whole fabric is constructed."[82]

None of this implies that Ash'arites were intentionally mischaracterizing God with some cynical purpose. We are not speaking of a conspiracy here. We are rather speaking about the influence of sociopolitical conditions on the conceptualizations of theology. Since God, the ultimate authority, is always invisible and unreachable, people tend to imagine Him in the way they imagine the earthly authorities around them—such as the father, the king, the sultan. This was, in fact, established in the Islamic tradition itself with the notion of *qiyas al-shahid ala al-ghayb,* or "analogy from the seen to the unseen."

That is why in cultures where relationships with the earthly authority have become less hierarchical, beliefs about God also have turned less slavish. This transformation has happened in Western Christianity, where the predestinarian views of the past—which also posited a despotic God—have been largely replaced with "libertarian" views that accept free will. Derk Pereboom, a contemporary philosopher of religion, both observes this interesting change and offers an explanation:

Theological determinism [predestinarianism] appears to have been in a steady decline since the eighteenth century, at least among Christians. Why this change? An intriguing hypothesis is that it matches an alteration in how people conceive of their relationship with God. The eighteenth and nineteenth centuries featured a trend toward viewing one's relationship with God as an intimate personal relationship, on analogy with the interpersonal human paradigm. Arguably, this model requires conceiving of the participants as freely responding to each other. This replaces viewing one's relationship with God on analogy with a relationship with an authority, such as a king or a lord, which is compatible with theological determination and a delimited variety of free will.[83]

Of course, one may want to grasp the true nature of God, and the ultimately correct theology, regardless of such changing sociopolitical conditions. But we mortals can never get out of our earthly reality, so we may never fully grasp the ultimate truth. At the very least, however, we can realize that what has come down to us as our religious tradition carries the residues of the sociopolitical conditions of its time. In Islam, this means that the mainstream religious tradition, defined by Ash'arism, carries the residues of premodern culture, including its political despotism.

This also means that we modern-day Muslims do not need to see Ash'arism as sacrosanct. It doesn't mean that we have to fully— let alone dogmatically—accept alternative strains in early Islam, such as the Mu'tazila and the philosophers, but we can benefit from their insights. With such a broader source of wisdom, we can have a new theology that defines a more reasonable and intelligible God, along with a more empowered and dignified human nature. And on this basis, we can develop a new jurisprudence that is fit for our times.

How to exactly do that is a giant endeavor that would go beyond the reach of this book—but I have already highlighted some contours. We Muslims need to develop an ethical philosophy of "good" and "bad," according to which we should reinterpret our transmitted religious tradition. To reinterpret the Sharia, in particular, we need to focus on the divine "intentions" behind commandments, rather than their literal wording. We also need a more scientific view of the world, which explains phenomena according to objective facts and laws, not the presuppositions in our minds. And to be able to do all this, we should break our self-containment and connect with the rest of humanity so that we can learn from its achievements while also contributing to them.

We should even go back to the very core of our faith—the Qur'an—and reconsider the way we understand it. No Muslim would deny the divine source of the Qur'an, otherwise he or she would not be a Muslim. But one can read the Qur'an with a mind-set built by Ash'ari theology, which is the mainstream way of reading it, or a mindset offered by the Mu'tazila theology. In the next chapter, we will do the latter—and we will see what difference it makes.

BACK TO MECCA

The first essential step . . . is for the Muslim to distinguish
clearly between normative Islam and historical Islam.

—Fazlur Rahman (d. 1988), Islamic scholar[1]

Toward the end of the Qur'an, in its traditional arrangement, there
is a very short sura, or chapter, about a man named Abu Lahab.
"May the hands of Abu Lahab be ruined," it condemns. "May he be
ruined too." Then it tells us that both he and his wife will burn in
hell, as a severe punishment from God.[2]

Why this wrath on Abu Lahab? Muslim sources tell us that he
was one of the most powerful men in Mecca at the dawn of Islam.
He was also an uncle of the Prophet Muhammad, only to become
one of his fiercest enemies. When the Prophet began publicly
preaching against idolatry, with just a few dozen believers around
him, both Abu Lahab and his wife proved venomous. They not
only verbally insulted but also physically abused Muhammad. In
fact, "May your hands be ruined" was a condemnation that Abu
Lahab himself used against the Prophet. The Qur'an, one could
say, turned his own ire against him.[3]

Today, Muslims recite the verses about Abu Lahab quite often,
as the sura is one of the ten short ones commonly used in daily
prayers. Very few Muslims, however, stop for a moment and

consider the theological conundrum this sura presents in the face of a mainstream Islamic doctrine established by Ash'arism and Hanbalism: that the Qur'an is an "uncreated" text which existed with God even before the beginning of time.

Here is the conundrum: If the Qur'an is really "uncreated," then God must have condemned Abu Lahab long before he was even born. This also means that the wickedness and the verdict of this seventh-century Arab man must have been preordained by God— not just "known in advance," but rather decreed in eternity. But why, in that case, would Abu Lahab be responsible? If God both predestined his deeds and also condemned him to hellfire for the same deeds, wouldn't this be an unjust thing to do?

As far as we know, these questions were raised in the second century of Islam by a scholar named Amr ibn Ubayd whose theological affiliation you may guess—the Mu'tazila. He was a student of Hasan al-Basri, whose letter about free will we saw in chapter 2. Against those who championed the "uncreated Qur'an" doctrine, Ibn Ubayd pointed to the condemnation of Abu Lahab and other hostile infidels in the Qur'an. God could not have issued their condemnation before creating them, he reasoned, for otherwise "God would have no arguments against them."[4]

In return, those who defended the "uncreated Qur'an" often relied on a verse that says the Qur'an is written on Lawh Mahfuz, or "Preserved Tablet."[5] Exegetes often equated this mysterious tablet with the "Mother of the Book," which the Qur'an describes as residing with God.[6] This led many to think that the Qur'an we have in our hand today was fully preexistent before its revelation to Prophet Muhammad. However, in a careful reading, the Mother of the Book seems to be not the Qur'an itself, but "the knowledge, wisdom and the sovereignty of God," from which the Qur'an, as well as the former Scriptures, are derived.[7] No wonder Jews and Christians are called the "People of the Book," not the "People of the Books."

The early conflict between those who held the Qur'an as

"created" or "uncreated" lasted for a few centuries, only to end with the victory of the latter, for reasons we have seen. So today the uncreated Qur'an doctrine is the official view in Sunni Islam. But we don't have to accept it blindly as an article of faith. And when we consider reading the Qur'an rather as a "created" text, as we will do in this chapter, not just the Abu Lahab story but many other themes in it begin to make more sense.

A CONTEXTUAL SCRIPTURE

Many of those who read the Qur'an for the first time, especially from outside the Muslim culture, find it puzzling. One reason is that this is not a linear book: it jumps from one topic to another, from one story to the next. That is especially true for the common ordering of the suras, which go from longest to shortest, rather than following a chronology.

However, a lack of chronology is not the only complication here. The real complication is that the Qur'an is the compilation of divine messages the Prophet Muhammad received at various points in his twenty-three-year-long prophetic mission. When you are reading the text, you are seeing the divine messages, but you are not seeing what exactly they are talking about. You hear, for example, God declaring an ultimatum against "those of the idol-aters with whom you made a treaty."[8] But you get no idea of what that "treaty" was, what its conditions were, or what brought it to an end. Or you read a verse that says, "Remember when you were on the near side of the valley," but you can't really "remember" that event, because you weren't in it. While the *immediate addressees of the Qur'an*—the Prophet and his companions—had no problem in understanding all these references to their lived experience, you, who are reading the same verses many centuries later, are in the dark.

Luckily, the Islamic tradition developed a literature called *asbab-al nuzul,* or "occasions of revelation," which gives us a sense

of the background of some Qur'anic verses. But this literature appeared a few centuries after the Qur'an, was far from accurate,
and offered "occasions" only for less than 10 percent of all verses.[9]
Moreover, many jurists believed that these "occasions" of revelation do not limit the verses to their original context—that they
were occasions *of,* not occasions *for.*[10] Hence came the juridical
dictum *al-ibra fi umum al-lafz la husus al-sabab,* or "consideration
is given to the generality of the words, not the specificity of their
occasion."[11] Some Ash'ari scholars even assumed that all the occasions were "a human reality deliberately created with the purpose of serving as a *post eventum* justification for revealing these
texts."[12] No wonder the doctrines of the uncreated Qur'an and human predestination were closely linked.[13]

This is still the common view among Sunni Muslims. It decon-
textualizes the Qur'an, and implies that all its commandments are
fully valid and applicable in all times and all places.

However, there are commandments of the Qur'an that are
clearly inapplicable today. Consider, for example, those about observing "the forbidden months."[14] For the immediate addressees of
the Qur'an, these months and their significance were all too clear:
Arab tribes lived through constant battles and raids, but four of the
twelve months of their lunar calendar were designated as "forbidden," as a time of peace, so people could safely travel for pilgrimage.
Hence, when the Qur'an said, "A forbidden month for a forbidden
month," its immediate addressees clearly knew what that meant.[15]
Yet today, say that to a Swede, a Guatemalan, or an Inuit, and they
will simply have no idea.

Or consider the Qur'anic verse telling Muslims that their children should "ask your permission to come in at three times of day:
before the dawn prayer, when you lay your garments aside in the
midday heat, and after the evening prayer."[16] This verse clearly referred to a local Arab custom in which people went indoors and
got undressed due to extreme heat in the midday. Again, tell that

today to an Inuit or Swede, and they will not find it relevant to their own reality.

Even more strikingly contextual are the Qur'an's repeated references to "those whom your right hands possess."[17] The term was a reference to slaves, the owning of which was normal and common in seventh-century Arabia—in fact, in almost the whole world. As a result, many of the Qur'an's immediate addressees were slave owners, so the Qur'an spoke to them about their reality. It advised, notably, a compassionate treatment of the slaves, with commandments like: "Be good . . . to your slaves"; "Give them some of the wealth God has given you"; or "Do not force your slave-girls into prostitution."[18] It also allowed slaves to buy their freedom and encouraged their manumission as a charitable act.[19]

Here the crucial question is: Does the Qur'an's reference to slaves mean that in an ideal Muslim society, there should be slaves? Similarly, should all Muslims "lay your garments aside in the midday heat," in order to follow God's decrees? Or should they seek to establish a tradition of "forbidden months," in societies that have no trace of it, and no need for it as well?

DEALING WITH ARAB PATRIARCHY

Today most Muslims would answer the above questions negatively, for the absurdity of universalizing the Qur'anic context is all too obvious in these cases. However, the same absurdity is applied in other cases, such as universalizing the patriarchal culture of seventh-century Arabia—a context within which the Qur'an spoke, only, in the words of Asma Barlas, to "offer remedy for the injustices of seventh-century *jahili* [pre-Islamic] misogyny."[20]

For example, when the Qur'an told Muslim men to treat women fairly "when you divorce them," it was addressing a society in which divorce was always decided upon by men.[21] But most traditional scholars took this as the enaction of a universal norm.[22]

They ruled, in other words, that the husband can divorce the wife at will, while the wife's right to divorce is only "exceptional."[23] Similarly, polygamy, which was justified—in fact, required—by the shortage of men caused by constant warfare, was blessed as a universally valid form of marriage. Likewise, the Qur'anic phrase "Men are maintainers of women" could be merely *descriptive*, explaining how seventh-century Arab society was. Yet virtually all classical commentators took it as *prescriptive*, establishing a patriarchal template for humanity.[24]

In the long run, this literalist approach often led to the sacrifice of ethical intentions behind Qur'anic commandments. One dramatic case is the divorce law that developed out of the verse: "Divorce is two times." "If a husband redivorces his wife after the second divorce," accordingly, "she will not be lawful for him until she has taken another husband."[25]

This was quite a peculiar rule, but it had a good reason: pre-Islamic Arabs held that once a man divorced his wife, the latter should still wait for a period of three months, called *iddah*, to see if she was pregnant or not. In the meantime, the couple could reunite at any moment. In itself, the custom made sense as a precaution against hasty breakups—and no wonder the Qur'an continued it.[26] However, some Arab men were using the custom abusively. We learn this from Aisha, one of the Prophet's wives, who reportedly said:

> The people were such that a man would divorce his wife . . . a hundred times, or even more.
>
> Such that a man could say to his wife: "I will neither divorce you irrevocably, nor give you residence ever!"
>
> She would say: "And how is that?"
>
> He would say: "I will divorce you, and whenever your *iddah* is just about to end, I will take you back."[27]

Such an abused woman came to Aisha asking for help. The latter told the story to the Prophet, who soon received the revelation:

"Divorce is two times; after that, retain her on reasonable terms or release her with kindness."[28] So no man could divorce a wife "a hundred times," just to "keep her hanging."[29] A terrible practice was ended with a practical solution.

However, a new problem emerged over time: some couples were divorcing three times, but then they were genuinely desiring to reunite. Yet jurists, who upheld the letter of the law, never allowed them to do that. Instead, some tolerated a terrible solution: a short-term marriage with another man, which, according to most jurists, had to include consummation.[30] It was called a marriage of *tahlil,* which made it *halal,* or "permissible," for the woman to go back to her original husband.

As one can imagine, this tradition has traumatized many Muslim couples over the centuries and led to an understandably critical literature in modern times.[31] Yet it is still alive today, even in Europe. In 2017, BBC journalists exposed a number of online services in the United Kingdom that offer *tahlil* marriages to triple-divorced Muslim women. The latter had to pay thousands of pounds to "marry, have sex with and then divorce a stranger, so they can get back with their first husbands."[32]

Some jurists even exacerbated the problem by ruling that a "triple divorce" can take place in only one instance—when a husband merely says, "I divorce you," three times. In the recent decades, such "instant triple divorces" have taken place even via email or texting. The practice is most common among the Muslims of India, where a nationwide ban on triple divorce was introduced in 2019. According to Muslim feminist Zakia Soman, the practice had persisted so long because many Muslim men believed it was "approved by the Qur'an."[33] And that is because they totally lacked a contextual understanding of the Qur'an.

What we need to understand is that the immediate addressees of the Qur'an, the first Muslims, and us, Muslims of the twenty-first century, are two very different peoples. So we can't take all the divine commandments given to the first Muslims, in their very peculiar contexts, as literally applicable in our very different societies.

What we ultimately need is Fazlur Rahman's method of "double movement": first going back to the context of the Qur'an in order to understand the divine *intentions* behind laws, and then coming back to the modern context to formulate new laws to serve those intentions.[34] With that perspective, the verses about forbidden months could teach us about chivalry, the verse about "asking permission at three times of day" could educate us about privacy, and the verses that regulate women's affairs could give us a vision to improve the female condition in any given society.

AN INTERACTIVE SCRIPTURE

A careful reading of the Qur'an, in fact, suggests that it is not only a contextual but also an interactive text—that it has been partly formed by the experience of its immediate addressees.

The first among these addressees was naturally the Prophet Muhammad. Hundreds of verses dealt with his doubts and insecurities, regulated his personal affairs such as marriages, or gave him tactics in winning battles or establishing peace. Other verses reflected his conversations with his companions. "God has heard the words of the woman who disputed with you about her husband and complained to God," a verse read.[35] The woman was complaining from *zihar*, another patriarchal Arab tradition, where men could instantly divorce their wives by declaring, "You are like my mother." In return, God supported the woman, and rebuked the husband.[36]

The Qur'an's engagement with its immediate addressees included the latter's questions to the Prophet, which are quoted in several verses:

"They ask you about fighting in the prohibited month . . ."
"They ask you what they should give [as alms] . . ."

"They ask you about orphans . . ."
"They ask you about menstruation . . ."

In all these "They ask you" verses, the Qur'an gives answers to questions posed by mortal beings, reflecting, in the words of the late Egyptian scholar Nasr Abu Zayd, "the dialogical nature of the Qur'an with the human interest."[37]

This suggests that if people around the Prophet Muhammad asked different questions, then we would have a slightly different Qur'an. The Qur'an itself, in fact, makes this clear:

> You who believe, do not ask about matters which, if made known to you, might make things difficult for you. *If you ask about them while the Qur'an is being revealed, they will be made known to you.*[38]

The dialogical nature of the Qur'an extended to the enemies of Islam as well—as certain verses came as *jawaban li-qawlihim,* or "answers to their words," as traditional exegetes had noted. Abu Lahab, who we mentioned earlier, was one of them. Others are not noted by name, but their arguments are quoted and answered. Here is an example:

> We know very well that they say, "It is a man who teaches him," but the language of the person they allude to is foreign, while this revelation is in clear Arabic.[39]

It we take the Qur'an to be "uncreated," then we have to assume the Meccan polytheists who made the accusation above, the man they referred to, the whole social setting, and in fact the Arabic language itself must be predestined. To make the unfolding of history fit into the prewritten Qur'an, we actually have to assume that the whole human history is predestined. Or we can take the Qur'an as "created," spoken by God in time, in a dialogical relationship with the temporal human reality. That is perhaps what the Qur'an means by its own *nuzul,* or "descent"—a descent of the divine to the level of the mortal.

You may wonder why this distinction is so important. It is important because the human reality to which the Qur'an responded includes not only conversations of the Prophet, the questions of the first believers, or accusations of the unbelievers. It includes raids and battles. It includes power and conquest. And whether we see them as normative Islam preordained by God, or historical Islam partly shaped by human history makes a big difference.

WHAT ISLAM INITIALLY ASKED FOR

Let's go back and recall the course of events during the Prophet Muhammad's time. As we Muslims believe, he received the first revelation in the year 610. In the first three years, he shared his message only secretly, gaining just a few dozen converts. Then came a command for public preaching. This infuriated the notables of Quraysh, the Arab tribe that ruled Mecca, which initiated a policy of persecution that would last for the next nine years.

What was it about Islam that alarmed Quraysh so much? Were the tiny group of Muslims threatening their security by acts of violence? Were they building a militia to conquer the city by force? Or were they asking from Mecca to accept Muhammad as its ruler?

The answers to these questions are simply "no," as we clearly understand from the Qur'an. The new faith propagated by Muhammad was emphatically nonviolent and noncoercive. Muslims were preaching monotheism and defying the idols as false gods, but they were not attempting to win anyone by force. One of the short suras titled "Kafirun," or "Disbelievers," made this quite clear:

> Say: "Disbelievers: I do not worship what you worship, you do not worship what I worship, I will never worship what you

worship, you will never worship what I worship. *You have your religion and I have mine.*"⁴⁰

The word "Say," with which the above sura begins, also exists in the beginning of more than three hundred verses. It is a directive from God to Muhammad to say something to certain people. With the same style, another Meccan verse reads: "Say, 'Now the truth has come from your Lord: let those who wish to believe in it do so, and *let those who wish to reject it do so.*'"⁴¹

The rest of the verse above, like various other passages in the Qur'an, threatened unbelievers with hellfire, or supernatural disasters, but not with any earthly punishment by Muslims themselves, because only God had the authority to punish people. Muhammad himself was only a "warner"—a term repeated more than twenty times in the Qur'an—as well as a "witness" and a "bearer of good news."⁴² Another Meccan revelation said to the Prophet:

> Now clear proof has come to you from your Lord: if anyone sees it, that will be to his advantage; if anyone is blind to it, that will be to his loss. [Say], *"I am not your guardian."*⁴³

There was also a theological rationale to this preach-but-let-live attitude. "Had your Lord willed, all the people on earth would have believed," a verse read, "so can you compel people to believe?"⁴⁴ This point was repeatedly made by God to curb His own messenger's passion to convert the people of Mecca: "God could bring them all to guidance if it were His will, so do not join the ignorant."⁴⁵ Yes, the idol worshippers of Mecca were in deep error, but, "if it had been God's will, they would not have done so."⁴⁶

The Qur'an even embraced the "turn the other cheek" attitude of Jesus, which is reported in the New Testament but often criticized by Islamists as too meek.⁴⁷ "Repel evil with what is better," a verse advised, "and your enemy will become as close as a warm friend."⁴⁸

In other words, in Mecca, nascent Islam was a theologically ambitious but politically peaceful movement. The first Muslims, to draw an analogy, were like religious preachers in modern-day open societies who show up in a public space to proclaim, "Fear God," "The End is Near," or "Repent." They were also condemning societal evils such as infanticide, the exploitation of orphans, or the mistreatment of women and slaves. But they were not doing anything more than that.

So what was the problem, then? Why did polytheist Mecca not tolerate Islam?

Some have found the answer in the economy, arguing that nascent Islam threatened Meccan trade. But the Quraysh's own accounts suggest that the real answer was in culture—that Mecca was not an open society.[49] Muslims were preaching a new religion that defined the established religion as a delusion. One of the early revelations named the three major Arab idols—al-Lat, al-Uzza, and Manat—only to assert, "These are nothing but names you have invented yourselves, you and your forefathers."[50] For the arrogant notables of Quraysh, this was an unacceptable insult, as we see in the ultimatum they gave to Abu Talib, the protective uncle of the Prophet:

> Your nephew has cursed our gods, insulted our religion, mocked our way of life and accused our forefathers of error. [So] either you stop him or you let us get at him.[51]

In other words, in today's terms, early Islam was guilty of "offensive speech" and "blasphemy."[52] (So what an irony, one must note, that today it is often Muslims who are most eager to ban "offensive speech" and "blasphemy.")

Mecca's wrath against Muslims turned growingly bitter. In 615, Sumayyah bint Khayyat, a female slave and the seventh convert to Islam, was tortured to death by her owner. Another slave, Bilal ibn Rabah, the black Ethiopian who would later be the first person to recite the call to prayer, was also tortured. Free people from powerful tribes, including the Prophet himself, were protected from such wanton violence, but none of them felt safe. Hence the most vulnerable fled to Ethiopia, whose Christian king was seen as—and would prove to be—a savior. Those who remained faced a boycott, cutting them off from all business and marriage ties. In an instance, a group of pagans came close to lynching the Prophet, as his close companion Abu Bakr cried, "Woe to you! Do you slay a man just for he says that my Lord is Allah?"[53] Finally, in 622, Meccan tribes united for a plot to assassinate Muhammad, which is why he finally fled his hometown. This was his historic *hijra*, or "emigration," to Medina, a city in which Islam would establish a political order and a military force.

One wonders how things could have progressed if Mecca had accepted the Qur'an's sensible call: "You have your religion and I have mine." What could have happened, in other words, if Meccans accepted what we would today call "freedom of speech" and "freedom of religion"?

Only God would know. Yet we can hypothesize that, in that case, there would have been no *hijra* to Medina. Prophet Muhammad and his followers would have continued to live in Mecca, to practice and preach their faith, without being a "guardian" over others. Probably the appeal of monotheism and the moral imperative of the Qur'an would attract more and more people, and Islam would gradually grow, perhaps to ultimately win over the whole city. But this would be a totally peaceful conquest—just like Christianity's gradual conquest of Rome. And in that case, the Qur'an we would have in our hands would be a totally nonviolent and noncoercive text.

The human history of early seventh-century Arabia, however, took a different direction.

THE SHIFT IN MEDINA

When the Prophet Muhammad arrived in Medina in June 622, he and his fellow *muhajirun*, or "immigrants," finally found peace. Yet their homes and properties, which they'd left behind, were soon raided and plundered by Meccan pagans. They had the moral right to take all this persecution as a legitimate cause of war. Hence, soon the Qur'an gave them a new permission:

> Those who have been attacked are permitted to take up arms because they have been wronged, God has the power to help them. [They are] those who have been driven unjustly from their homes only for saying, "Our Lord is God."[54]

This was the beginning of the whole notion of military jihad, or struggle, which has been one of the most controversial aspects of Islam to date. As we will see, it has been disputably extended to justify imperial conquest. But we should not forget that it was born as a reaction to persecution.

With this divine permission to take up arms, the new Muslim polity in Medina began targeting Meccan caravans with *ghazwa,* or "raids," a custom that "permeated the whole Bedouin society, its social and economic life, and its folk literature."[55] One of these raids took Muslims to their first big military conflict with the Meccans: the Battle of Badr, which Muslims decisively won. This led to two consequent attempts for revenge by the Meccans. Finally, after a short-lived peace treaty, there came the Muslim conquest of Mecca—a basically bloodless affair—which was followed by the Battle of Hunayn with the polytheist tribes that militarily threatened the growing Muslim power. There was even a conflict with Byzantine forces in the Battle of Mu'tah. Muslims had founded an armed state, and they kept fighting for its survival, doing whatever was "necessary if the Islamic state was to survive"[56]

Today, the Qur'an has more than a hundred verses that address these conflicts that took place in the latter phase of Prophet Muhammad's mission—the Medinan phase. They include commandments like, "Slay the pagans wherever you find them," or "Strike above their necks and strike all their fingertips."[57] To read them

out of context is a big mistake, done intentionally or unintentionally, either by militant Muslims who seek justification for violence
or anti-Islam polemicists who seek ammunition for propaganda.
These verses must be rather understood as temporary commandments given in a specific context of war—similar to the militant
passages one can also read in the Hebrew Bible.

Speaking of Hebrews, with whom Muslims actually share a lot
of common theology and practice, the Medinan phase included
an encounter with them as well. That is because in early seventh-
century Medina, there were several Jewish tribes, three of which
were prominent: Banu Nadir, Banu Qaynuqa, and Banu Qurayza.
When the Prophet came to the city, he signed a historic agreement
with at least some of these tribes, which some today call the "Constitution of Medina." It had a liberal clause that reflected the noncoercive spirit of Mecca: "The Jews have their religion and the
believers have theirs."[58] However the constitution soon collapsed—
not because of religion, one must note, but politics. The Jews' sus-
pected collaboration with Meccan pagans led to their expulsion
from Medina—and, in the case of Banu Qurayza, even a massacre
of all men, although there is some doubt about this grim story.[59]

So in the Qur'an, there are also verses that reflect conflicts with
those Jewish tribes in Medina. A verse, for example, blames them
for conspiring for war: "Whenever they kindle the fire of war, God
will put it out."[60] The "they" here was probably Banu Nadir, as one
of its prominent members reportedly urged the Meccan pagans
to attack back on Muslims after the defeat at the Battle of Badr.[61]
Yet today, quite a few Muslims read such verses not as historical
reports but universal definitions. So they take the phrase, "they
kindle the fire of war," to bolster anti-Semitic tropes about how
"the Jews" are behind every conflict in the world. It is with this
mindset that Hamas, the Palestinian Islamic Resistance Movement, explains both world wars as a Jewish conspiracy. "There is
no war going on anywhere," its charter asserts, "without them
having their finger in it."[62]

In the Medinan phase of his mission, Prophet Muhammad not only led an army but also ruled a state—a state that needed some basic laws. So the Qur'an issued those basic laws, giving us about a hundred verses of legal content. One of them reiterated the biblical principle of *lex talionis,* or the law of retaliation: "a life for a life, an eye for an eye, a nose for a nose, an ear for an ear, a tooth for a tooth, an equal wound for a wound."[63] It also added an encouragement for forgiveness: "If anyone forgoes this out of charity, it will serve as atonement for his bad deeds."[64]

Legal verses of the Qur'an also included punishments for a few specific crimes: amputation of a hand for theft; "death, crucifixion, the amputation of an alternate hand and foot, or banishment from the land" for violent robbery; a hundred lashes for adultery; and eighty lashes for the false accusation of adultery.[65] These punishments have been sanctified in Islamic law as the *hudud,* or "boundaries," of God. Today, they are in the laws of more than a dozen Muslim-majority states, while Islamist movements elsewhere are also eager to implement them literally, as corporal punishments.

If we have a contextual sense of the Qur'an, however, we can understand these punishments less literally. First of all, they were not novelties introduced by Islam. Amputating a hand for theft was exactly how the Arab polytheists punished theft, as we know from Muslim historian Ibn Qutayba (d. 889).[66] Amputation of an alternate hand and foot was also known in the ancient world, as we see in the Qur'an itself, in the threats of the Egyptian pharaoh.[67] Second, in that time and milieu, there was a very good reason to decree corporal punishments: there was no other way. Muhammad Abid al-Jabiri explains why:

> In a Bedouin society, where the people move about with their tents and camels in search of pasture, it was not possible to penalize the thief by imprisonment. There are no walls or prisons in the desert, and no authorities to guard the prisoner and

provide him with food, drink and clothing. Therefore, the only alternative was corporal punishment.[68]

It is no surprise then that there were no formal prisons in Medina under the rule of the Prophet.[69] Only years later, when the Muslim state became more established, Caliph Umar bought a house in the city and converted it into a prison.[70]

From all this, we can understand that the Qur'anic commandment for amputating the hand of a thief was probably contextual. Then, by following Fazlur Rahman's method of "double movement," we can come back to today and employ other means to punish theft—means such as imprisonment, which is gradable and retractable, and also allows a normal life after the punishment.

Conservative Muslims are often not comfortable with such reinterpretative approaches to the Qur'an. However, there are Qur'anic commandments that even they do not understand and implement literally. One is the verse that tells Muslims to prepare for war, with "whatever forces you can muster, including war-horses."[71] No Muslim army today takes this commandment literally by really raising "warhorses." They rather intuitively interpret the term as a reference to modern military equipment. Yet they just stop there and do not consider the significance of the step they have just taken.

THE STATIZATION OF ISLAM

In June 632, at the age of sixty-two, Prophet Muhammad passed away in Medina. An amazing saga had unfolded from the first revelation in Mecca. Muslims had begun their historic journey as a small persecuted sect, only to end up as a victorious state commanding almost the whole Arabian Peninsula. But how much of this historic journey amounted to the divine essence of Islam, how much of it was mere human history?

There were no ready answers to this question, so the answer would be given in a new historic journey—that of Muslim life after the Prophet. After some consultations, and disputes, prominent members of the Muslim community elected one of the Prophet's closest companions, Abu Bakr, as the "caliph," or successor to Muhammad. This made him the political ruler of the Medina-based Muslim state. But did this mean that Islam was now identified with that state?

This was the question underlying the key controversy during Abu Bakr's two-year-long reign: the issue of zakat, or alms, one of the obligations the Qur'an brought on Muslims. Meccan verses suggested that zakat should be given to the poor and the needy, while a Medinan verse added "those who administer them," who were appointed by the Prophet.[72] But now, since the Prophet was gone, could Muslims deal with their zakat as they deemed fit?

Some of them, certain tribes outside of Medina, thought so. So, they ceased paying zakat to Medina, without renouncing their faith in Islam. They referred to the early Qur'anic verses about zakat as charity, evoking "the voluntary system of the community's beginnings in Mecca."[73]

In return, there emerged a dispute in Medina. Caliph Abu Bakr claimed that he would fight all the tribes who refused to pay "even a camel's rope which they used to pay to the Prophet."[74] But Umar, his second-in-command, disagreed. Despite his usual tempestuousness, Umar argued that no one who declares, "There is no god but God," should be fought. He also advised moderation to the caliph: "Join people in love and be kind to them."[75] There are reports telling that most companions of the Prophet agreed with Umar on this issue.[76] Later, prominent jurist Malik ibn Anas (d. 795) would also support this view, noting that the Qur'anic commandment to collect zakat only addressed the Prophet.[77] If these lenient views prevailed at that fateful moment, we could have had a very different history of Islam.

Yet Abu Bakr stuck with his decision—advising Umar not to

be "violent in *jahiliyya* [pre-Islam], and weak when you have embraced Islam."[78] So he launched what is known as wars on *ridda*, which later became the Islamic term for "apostasy." In fact, the matter was political rebellion instead of religious apostasy, but the two got conflated, as Abu Bakr's view of "religion" also included "legislation, authority, public order and government."[79] This fateful step would forever blur the distinction between religion and politics, between believing in Islam and obeying a state, between voluntary piety and imposed piety. Later jurists would use this precedent to further justify compulsion in religion.[80]

In short, with the *ridda* wars, Islam's marriage with power was consolidated—not as a temporary adaption in Medina due to extraordinary circumstances, but as a permanent system—a system that would prove, frankly put, both aggressive and coercive.

It was aggressive because despite the Qur'an's emphasis on the defensive nature of war, the caliphate justified, and engaged in, offensive war. According to the jihad doctrine, whose details would be perfected over time, Muslims had the right to conquer any non-Muslim territory by giving its inhabitants three choices: either convert to Islam and join the caliphate as full citizens; or preserve your religion (unless it is Arab polytheism) but accept Muslim supremacy by paying the *jizya*, or "poll tax"; or face the sword, with consequences such as death, slavery, and expropriation. It was with this doctrine that Muslim armies, in a century after the Prophet, conquered a vast territory stretching from Spain to India.

The caliphate system also turned coercive because it made the practice of Islam not a matter of voluntary piety but rather a collective obligation imposed by both the state and the community. So, just like paying the zakat, keeping the daily prayers or fasting during Ramadan became public laws, the breaking of which put one in serious trouble. We will see more of that in the next three chapters.

In a sense, there was nothing so shocking about Muslims using violence and coercion to advance their faith, because that is what virtually everybody did at the time. Christianity was defined by the "Constantinian revolution," which similarly employed "state power to promote right belief and purge wrong belief."[81] The Sasanian Empire of Persia, whose political culture seems to have influenced that of Islam, also saw "kingship and religion" as "twins."[82] The problem in Islam, however, is that statization became an integral part of the religious tradition that has lived on to date—captured in the motto that Islam is both *din wa dawlah,* or "religion and state." That is why when finally a reformist like the Egyptian scholar Abd al-Raziq wrote a book in 1925 declaring Islam "a religion, not a state; a message, not a government," he was furiously contested.[83]

Since then, the idea of separating Islam from power has progressed to some extent but is still bitterly opposed by Islamists and even many conservatives. Among the former was the Pakistani arch-Islamist Mawdudi, who chided the Muslims who believed in "preaching alone." True Muslims, he wrote, would rather "take power and use it on God's behalf."[84] A contemporary Turkish Islamist put it more poetically: "Islam is a jealous religion," he wrote, proudly. "Wherever it appears, it doesn't allow the appearance of others—the falsehood—and it doesn't share its power, its hegemony."[85]

THE ABROGATION OF MECCA

You may wonder, at this point, what had happened to the Qur'anic message in Mecca that the Prophet is nobody's "guardian," that he is only a "warner," and that "those who wish to reject" Islam could freely do so? What happened, really, to that nonviolent and noncoercive message?

Well, that message is still in the Qur'an and is still highlighted by the more liberal-minded Muslims. But the aggressive and coercive tradition that took shape under the caliphate found a way to get rid of it. It, literally and officially, "abrogated" it.

The abrogation doctrine, which I also touched upon in the Introduction, began to take form under the Umayyad caliphate and took its most definitive form under al-Shafi'i, who built the principles of Sunni jurisprudence. Accordingly, earlier verses of the Qur'an could be rendered ineffective by later verses with a different tone. Scholars would never fully agree on exactly which verses were abrogated, but there emerged a common list of 137 verses.[86] Most crucially, as noted by Asma Afsaruddin, a contemporary professor of Islamic studies, the list reflected a "certain pattern":

First of all, almost all the [abrogated] verses are Meccan to early Medinan, according to traditional chronology. Second, all the abrogating verses tend to promote a narrower, privileged definition of being Muslim at the expense of "others." Third, without the meditation of the "abrogated verses," the abrogating verses may be understood to set up antagonistic, binary relationships—primarily between Muslims and non-Muslims.[87]

The most crucial abrogators were the "verses of the sword."[88] These include 9:5, which reads, "Wherever, you encounter the idolaters, kill them." They also include 9:29, which reads, "Fight those of the People of the Book . . . until they pay the *jizya* [poll tax] and agree to submit." By taking such commandments as universally definitive, rather than as specific to certain episodes in the Prophet's mission, jurists canceled out many verses that called for "negotiation, patience, peace, compassion, and mercy."[89]

Yet there were dissenters. One of the earliest among them was Medinan scholar Ata ibn Abi Rabah (d. 732), who argued that the verses about fighting non-Muslims "were prescribed only during the time of the Prophet and his Companions," while universally it is "never permissible to fight those who do not fight."[90] Asma Afsaruddin sketches such early views about jihad and abrogation, and shows that the most militant views conspicuously came from scholars serving the Umayyad caliphate, which had its own earthly ambitions for imperial conquest.[91]

How dare Muslim scholars cancel out hundreds of verses in the Book of God? Admittedly, they found a basis in the Qur'an itself, a verse that reads, "We do not abrogate a verse or cause it to be forgotten except that We bring forth [one] better than it or similar to it."[92] Yet they disregarded a key nuance: the verse refers to God, not humans, as "the abrogating agent."[93] Despite this, and despite their customary aversion to any rational interpretation of the Qur'an, virtually all Ash'arite and Hanbali scholars accepted the theory of abrogation. It is remarkable that despite their usual aversion to *hawa*, or "whimsical desire," they did not see any trace of it in a jihad doctrine tailored for imperial conquest.

THE USES AND ABUSES OF *FITNA*

In the classical era, we know of only one scholar who forcefully argued against the overall theory of abrogation: Abu Muslim al-Isfahani (d. 1066), who was, unsurprisingly, a Mu'tazilite. He argued that divergent verses of the Qur'an do not abrogate each other, but indicate *takhsis,* or "specification." Accordingly, the war-like Medinan verses did not cancel out the peaceful Meccan ones but only "addressed a different society," a different context.[94] Yet his work never survived, and we know his arguments only from secondary sources that argued against him.[95]

The debate was reopened in the modern era, where scholars with reformist tendencies—broadly called "Islamic modernists"—began questioning the abrogation doctrine, hoping to revive the more liberal spirit of the Meccan verses. One of them, the Sudanese scholar Mahmoud Mohammed Taha, went as far as turning the doctrine upside down: the universal message of Islam is in the Meccan verses, he argued, while the militarization and legislation in Medina was time-bound. In return, the ascendant Islamist movement in Sudan, which found the idea detrimental to its own ideology, got Mahmoud Mohammed Taha arrested in January 1985. After a brief trial, the seventy-five-year-old Muslim scholar was executed by hanging in public.[96]

Mohammed Taha was sentenced for *fitna,* a vague term that Muslim tyrants have used and abused for centuries to criminalize any dissent. In the Qur'an, it is used several times, but often to mean "temptation" or "trial of faith."[97] When the first civil wars broke out soon after the Prophet, Muslims called these *fitna* as well, giving the term a political meaning of "disturbance." But soon even peaceful schisms got labeled in the same way. Hence, today one can find frequent rants among conservatives about "*fitna* of the Mu'tazila," "*fitna* of philosophy," or "*fitna* of feminism."

The vagueness of the term even helped justify aggressive war. The Qur'an, in two separate verses, told Muslims to "fight them [polytheists] until there is no more *fitna.*" Today most modern translations define the word as "persecution."[98] In this case, the Qur'an seems to order a limited war to end persecution. However, most classical exegetes defined the word as "disbelief" or "polytheism."[99] In that case, the Qur'an seems to order a universal war against other creeds.

Such subtle shifts in the meaning of words had dramatic consequences. Another example is an important sentence repeated three times in the Qur'an: "It is He who has sent His messenger with guidance and the religion of truth, that he may *proclaim it over all religion.*"[100] The Arabic term here is *yuzhirahu,* which means making something "manifest." In this sense, and in the Yusuf Ali translation I just quoted, the verse heralds that Islam will be manifested over all religions, so that everyone will hear its message. However, the overwhelming majority of scholars, even today, translate *yuzhirahu* with more supremacist words such as "conquer," "overcome," "prevail," or "become superior."[101] The Islamist Mawdudi happily embraced this view, adding that Islam is destined to be "dominant over all the other ways and systems of life."[102]

Luckily, all this supremacist attitude, well established in the tradition and still championed by the Islamists, has been questioned in the modern era. As a result, the idea of taking over the whole world with military conquests is now widely seen as a utopia of radicals, if not wild-eyed terrorists.

However, much of the liberal spirit of the Meccan Qur'an still remains "abrogated" in mainstream Islamic jurisprudence, thought, and culture. Due to the fourteen-century-long statization of Islam, many Muslims still see their religion not as an individual belief and practice followed by voluntary choice, but rather as a social order imposed by power. So, for example, when they say, "Islam bans alcohol," they don't mean voluntary abstinence by individual believers. They rather mean a legal ban on all society.

In the rest of this book, we will focus on the two key values that this coercive tradition has largely overshadowed in the Islamic tradition—values to which I have been repeatedly alluding since the beginning. The first and foremost one is freedom.

FREEDOM MATTERS I: *HISBAH*

Only free conduct is moral conduct. By negating freedom,
and thus the possibility of choice, a dictatorship contains
in its premises the negation of morality. To that extent,
regardless of all historical apparitions, dictatorship and
religion are mutually exclusive.

—Alija Izetbegović, Bosnian intellectual & statesman[1]

What is freedom? What does it mean?

If you ask this question to a conservative Muslim scholar or an
Islamist intellectual, it is quite probable that you will get an answer
like this:

> We must first define *real freedom,* as taught by Islam. It is not
> the freedom of the materialist West where it means license to
> follow your selfish ambitions and carnal desires. This false free-
> dom makes people slaves to money, sex, fame, and other human
> beings. No, real freedom is being saved from the yoke of all
> these created things, and to seek refuge in only the Creator.
> Real freedom, therefore, is slavery to Allah.[2]

The last verdict above, "Real freedom is slavery to Allah," is
in fact a motto one comes across often in the Muslim universe.
In Turkey, it was the topic of a 2017 sermon given in all mosques

across the nation.³ It is endlessly repeated on the internet and social media.

There is certainly some truth to this view, because "slavery to Allah," in the sense of voluntary submission to God, can really save a human being from the weight of worldly fears and anxieties. Relying on God, or *tawakkul*, gives a sense of relief against the ups and downs of life, while belief in the afterlife makes death less frightening. Religious practice also helps self-discipline, guarding one against obsessions and addictions. Therefore, true believers in Islam really may achieve a sense of "real freedom."

It is not just Islam, though. Other religious traditions offer a similar bliss to their believers. Christians, especially those who have a "personal relationship with Christ," also feel liberated, as their faith offers "freedom from sin, from law, from corruption and death."⁴ No wonder a devout Christian author defines "real freedom," as "being a servant to Jesus Christ."⁵ Meanwhile, Buddhism also preaches its own "real freedom," which is "freedom from thinking, freedom from all attachments."⁶ Buddhist monks pursue that peculiar freedom by living a life of absolute poverty.

Now imagine a devout Muslim, devout Christian, and devout Buddhist living happily in a neighborhood, all enjoying their "real freedoms." Also imagine, though, that the neighborhood is targeted by an authoritarian government, which is paranoid about sedition, and arrests these three people based on their political remarks on social media. While rotting in jail, these believers may still retain their subjective "real freedoms" in their hearts and minds. But they will have certainly lost a more tangible freedom: the right to move around freely, to speak their minds without persecution.

What this example illustrates is that there are two kinds of freedom—"inner" and "outer."⁷ The religious believers who claim to have found "real freedom" in their worship are in fact referring to inner freedom. That is, of course, a very important ideal, but it is a matter of spirituality, and it is also very subjective as it depends on what one believes in.

Meanwhile outer freedom—the freedom from external constraints—is not only a very important ideal as well, but it is also an objective value on which we can build principles and rules. In other words, in the story above, we can't make laws to bring more inner freedom to the Muslim, the Christian, and the Buddhist—that is their own spiritual struggle—but we can make free-speech laws to keep them out of prison.

That is why, as a universal value, what really matters is outer freedom. It is the kind of freedom, as philosopher Friedrich A. Hayek put it, that "refers solely to a relation of men to other men, and the only infringement on it is coercion by men."[8]

So, by this measure, how does our Islamic tradition fare?

On the one hand, it fares well—according to the standards of its own time. This was acknowledged by a scholar no less critical than the late Bernard Lewis, who noted: "The medieval Islamic world . . . offered vastly more freedom than any of its predecessors, its contemporaries and most of its successors."[9] This was mainly thanks to the Sharia, which established a rule of law, protecting the lives and properties of individuals.[10] Thanks to the Sharia, for example, Muslims could devote their wealth to charitable foundations that rulers could not dare to confiscate. This allowed the rise of a robust civil society, with schools, hospitals, and charities operated by merchants, guilds, and Sufi orders.[11]

On the other hand, though, the Sharia itself imposed serious limitations on freedom, all somehow aiming to serve these three broad objectives:

1. Keeping Muslims observant of religion—by banning sin
2. Keeping Muslims within the religion and its orthodoxy—by banning apostasy and heresy
3. Making non-Muslims respect the religion—by banning blasphemy

In this chapter and the next two, we will take a closer look at these coercive measures, question their origins, and see how they have become extremely detrimental, for Muslims and others, in the world we now live in.

HOW TO BEAT SLACKERS AND POUR WINE

In the mid-2010s, the terrorist army that called itself the "Islamic State of Iraq and Syria" (ISIS) took control of large parts of Iraq and Syria. While shocking the world with its monstrous violence against non-Muslims, Shiites, and even fellow Sunnis who merely dissented, it also established a totalitarian regime under its self-declared "caliphate." A key function of this regime was the imposition of the practice of Islam according to the ISIS's extremely strict definitions. Ordinary people would find themselves in jail and even face torture for failing to perform their daily prayers or keeping the fast of Ramadan. Consuming alcohol or smoking tobacco would lead to public floggings. Militants would patrol the streets in vans, and shout out to people, "It's prayer time! Go to mosque! Hurry up! Shut your business. You, woman, cover your face!"[12]

The ISIS department that carried out all this zealous religious policing had a name: al-Hisbah. But the Arabic term *hisbah*, which roughly means "accountability," is a concept that goes beyond ISIS. Other Islamic states—such as Saudi Arabia, Iran, Sudan, parts of Afghanistan under the Taliban, the Aceh province of Indonesia, or the Kano state in Nigeria—also have police forces devoted to *hisbah*. Compared to ISIS, they are often milder, but they follow the same idea: Muslims should be prevented from committing sin, at least publicly. The Malaysian religion police, which arrested me for merely giving a public lecture (see Introduction), is also a *hisbah* force that patrols the streets to "prevent indecent behavior among Muslims."[13]

Unfortunately, all this religious policing goes back to authoritative texts from classical Islam. One of them is *The Ordinances of Government* penned by the eleventh-century Ash'ari scholar al-Mawardi whom we already met in our discussion of Sunni political thought. "The task of *hisbah* is one of the fundamental matters of the *deen*," or "religion," he wrote in a long chapter devoted to the duty. He also listed the crimes that must be pursued, which includes "not performing the obligatory prayer until after its time." He then explained the views on punishment:

> If the person abandons [the prayer], claiming that it is not an obligation, then he is a nonbeliever; and the same ruling as that governing the renegade applies—that is, he is killed for his denial, unless he turns for forgiveness. If he has not done it because he claims it is too difficult to do, but while acknowledging its obligation, then the *fuqaha* [jurists] differ as to the ruling: Abu Hanifa considers that he should be beaten at the time of every prayer, but that he is not killed; Ahmad ibn Hanbal and a group of his later followers say that he becomes a kafir by his abandoning it, and is killed for this denial. . . , Al-Shafi'i considers . . . he is not put to death until he has been asked to turn in *tawbah* [repentance]. . . . If he refuses to make tawbah, and does not accept to do the prayer; then he is killed for abandoning it—immediately, according to some, after three days, according to others. He is killed in cold blood by the sword, although Abu' Abbas ibn Surayj says that he is beaten with a wooden stick until he dies.[14]

Soon after al-Mawardi, al-Ghazali also wrote a long chapter about *hisbah* in his landmark book *Revival of the Religious Sciences*. He explained it as a duty of every Muslim to prevent sins with "direct acts," such as "breaking the musical instruments, spilling over the wine and snatching the silk garment from him who is wearing it."[15] (Music was banned because it "incites to the drinking of wine," and it would bring together all the "dissolute people."[16] Silk was banned, for men, as it seemed indulgent.) Hanbalites would expand the list of banned items with chess and backgammon.

The only space that offered freedom from this strict social control was the home, whose privacy was guarded by a Qur'anic directive: "Do not enter houses other than your own, until you have asked permission."[17] However, al-Ghazali explained, even household privacy had its limits:

> If the voices rise and become so high to hear from outside the house, the hearer has the right to enter it and break the musical instruments. Similarly, if the voices of the drunk rise and become audible to those walking in the street, *hisbah* becomes obligatory. The same is true of the smell.[18]

Not just al-Mawardi or al-Ghazali, but countless other classical jurists defined such religious policing as a part of Islam.[19] They only disagreed on whether *hisbah* was a duty for all ordinary Muslims or only appointed officials—the *muhtasib,* which literally means "the one that does *hisbah.*" They seem to have taken for granted that the duty was established by both the Qur'an and the Prophet. However, both sources are in fact much more ambiguous, leaving us room to reinterpret what *hisbah* should mean today.

THE EVOLUTION OF THE *MUHTASIB*

Let's begin with the Prophet. One of his important qualities, which is rare among the founders of religions in world history, was that he was a longtime merchant, which gave him a good sense of commerce. Hence, soon after he established himself in Medina, he founded a new marketplace in the city. "This is your market," he said reportedly; "let it not be narrowed, and let no tax be taken on it."[20] He also began frequenting it. On one visit, a narration tells us, he found out that a vendor had watered his grain to make it weigh heavier. On this occasion, the Qur'anic sura "Mutaffifin," or the "Defrauders," was reportedly revealed, which read:

Woe to those who give short measure, who demand of other people full measure for themselves, but give less than they should when it is they who weigh or measure for others! Do these people not realize that they will be raised up on a mighty Day—a Day when everyone will stand before the Lord of the Worlds?[21]

So fraud in business was a major sin that God would punish on Judgment Day. But since it was also a crime that wronged people in this world, the Prophet appointed someone to oversee the market and to prevent any possible fraud. Interestingly enough, at least one source tells us that this official was a woman named Samra bint Nuhayk al-Asadiyya.[22] (One theory is that maybe she had jurisdiction only over the women's section of the market.[23]) A few decades later, Caliph Umar also appointed a women, al-Sifa bint Abd Allah, in addition to three men, to oversee the Medinan market.[24]

In this first century of Islam, these inspectors were often called *amil al-suq,* or "overseer of the market." In Muslim Spain, they were also called *sahib al-suq,* or "the master of the market." The functions of the latter were described by the Córdoban scholar Yahya ibn Umar (d. 901), who only wrote about "the orderly running of the market place, particularly with regard to weights, measures and scales."[25] Remarkably, the market overseer he described had "no religious connotations nor concern[ed] itself with censure of public morals."[26] Other reports, too, defined the job of market overseers as checking the quality of the products, the accuracy of weights and measurements, the genuineness of coins, in addition to the safety of buildings and the cleanness of the streets and the water supply.[27] Some scholars have pointed to the parallels with the *agoranomos,* or "market inspector," of Ancient Greece and the Byzantine Empire.[28]

However, as time went by, the functions of the Muslim market inspector expanded, assuming a "wider duty" of the "ordering of social life."[29] These new functions included what al-Mawardi and al-Ghazali speak about: enforcing prayer or fasting, pouring out wine, silencing music, or banning free mixing of the sexes in streets. In the meantime, the term *amil al-suq* was conspicuously replaced by *muhtasib*—the one that does *hisbah*. That is why, in the words of Tunisian historian Yassine Essid:

> In reading the different treatises devoted to the *hisbah* we discover two categories of responsibilities, or rather, we find ourselves looking at two different figures: the censor of morals who breaks musical instruments, pours out wine, beats the libertine and tears off his silken clothing, and the modest market provost, a man who controls weights and measures, inspects the quality of the foods on sale, ensures that the markets are well supplied, and occasionally sets the prices of goods.[30]

As time went farther on, moral policing became the primal duty of the *muhtasib,* whereas market supervising turned trivial. This was unmistakable in *Nisab al-Ihtisab*, a book in which fourteenth-century Indian jurist al-Sunami described *hisbah* mainly as correcting "moral and religious behavior which is contradictory to the correct teaching of Islam," while addressing market supervision "only on some occasions."[31]

In short, what eventually turned into religious policing seems to have begun under the Prophet Muhammad merely as market inspection—something that every society would need and appreciate.

Besides market inspection, did the Prophet go strictly after sinners? One answer is that he didn't need to, because all his companions were fervent believers who followed all Qur'anic injunctions willingly—an exceptional experience that may not be replicated in any modern society. Yet still, there are a few reports of punishing personal sin, most particularly drinking wine. After the Qur'an banned wine, we read in the hadith literature, the Prophet ordered

forty lashes to a man who was caught drunk—an incident that became a precedent for all the later punishments for alcohol consumption.[32] However, there are reasons to think that the goal here
was not mere piety but public order. "There were things that happened [in Medina] due to the consumption of intoxicants, before
they were made unlawful," as we read in the literature on the occasions of revelation.[33] In one case, a group of drunken Muslims had
a fight in which one of them had his nose broken. In another case,
the Prophet's own uncle, the legendary Hamza ibn Abdul-Muttalib,
got drunk and slaughtered and mutilated someone else's camels.[34]
No wonder the verse that soon banned wine also noted that with
it, along with gambling, "the Satan seeks only to incite enmity and
hatred among you."[35] This may give an idea about the rationale
behind both the religious ban on wine and its public enforcement—
a rationale that still outlaws "public intoxication" in many secular
democracies, including the United States.

A MATTER OF "RIGHT AND WRONG"

The duty of *hisbah* is based not merely on the hadiths, though. It is
also based on a Qur'anic concept: "commanding the right and forbidding the wrong." Several verses define this duty as incumbent
on the prophet and ordinary Muslims as well. One of these verses
even calls for a specific group to carry out the duty: "Let there arise
out of you a band of people inviting to all that is good, enjoining
what is right, and forbidding what is wrong: they are the ones to
attain felicity."[36]

This is why the religion police in Saudi Arabia call themselves
the "Committee for the Promotion of Virtue and the Prevention of
Vice." The one operated by the Taliban has a similar name.

However, what the Qur'an means by "commanding the right and
forbidding the wrong" is much less clear than what these religion
police forces believe. We can see this in the writings of the earliest
commentators of the Qur'an. One of them was Abu al-Aliya (d. 712),

who was among the *tabiun,* or the first generation after the Prophet, who described the duty as "calling people from polytheism to Islam and . . . forbidding the worship of idols and devils."[37] A little later, Muqatil ibn Sulayman (d. 767), whose three-volume book is considered the oldest commentary on the Qur'an, also defined the duty in minimal terms. For him, "commanding the right" meant "enjoining belief in the unity of God," whereas forbidding wrong meant "forbidding polytheism."[38]

Meanwhile, a political interpretation of "commanding the right and forbidding the wrong" also emerged in the first century of Islam. Accordingly, the duty primarily implied standing up to tyrants—by either moderate or radical ways. The moderate way was what we today call "speaking truth to power." It was supported by a hadith that defined the highest form of jihad as "speaking out in the presence of an unjust ruler"—"and being killed for it," as some versions added.[39] The radical way was armed rebellion against an unjust ruler. While the Kharijites took this license to the extreme, the Zaydis and Mu'tazilites defined it more sensibly.[40]

However, what ultimately defined the meaning of "commanding the right and forbidding the wrong" is the Sunni mainstream, which equated "right and wrong" with all the commandments of the Sharia. The third-century Qur'anic exegete al-Tabari was stressing this point when he wrote, "'commanding right' refers to *all* that God and His Prophet have commanded, and 'forbidding wrong' to *all* that they have forbidden."[41] So, since God commanded daily prayers and forbade wine, all Muslims had to command prayer and forbid wine to each other. The transformation of the *muhtasib* from market inspector to religion police seems to have been underpinned by this totalist approach to "commanding the right and forbidding the wrong."

What if people disagreed on what "right" and "wrong" mean? Al-Ghazali addressed this question and answered it by granting some legal pluralism. "The Hanifites have no right to disapprove

Shafiites for eating mastigure," he wrote, "nor do the Shafiites have the right to disapprove the Hanifites for drinking the *nabidh*."[42] (The latter refers to alcoholic drinks made out of dates or barley, which Hanafis, considering it different from wine, allowed in nonintoxicating amounts—an interesting fact unknown to many Hanafis today.[43]) But al-Ghazali limited this nice pluralism to the four Sunni schools, whereas he condemned all other interpretations of Islam as heretical "innovations." The latter could not define *hisbah*. Quite the contrary, *hisbah* was needed against them—a *hisbah* "more important than against all the other evildoings."[44]

But who could guarantee that al-Ghazali's own interpretation of Islam was not an "innovation"? What if someone tried to purge this interpretation with a counter *hisbah*—as it happened indeed under the *mihna*, or "trial," of Caliph al-Ma'mun? This was the first blind spot in the classical *hisbah* theory.

The second blind spot was that neither al-Ghazali nor al-Mawardi nor others saw a contradiction between coercion and another value they believed in: sincerity of intentions behind religious acts. Al-Ghazali has a whole chapter devoted to this matter, where he warns Muslims not to pray, fast, or give charity with ungodly intentions, such as showing off to people, "to be recognized for it," or even just to feel good about themselves.[45] "Sincerity," he keeps insisting, is to worship God "in such a way that there is no motive other than it."[46] Yet he never considers that coercing someone to observance would also generate a motive other than worship.

The blindness here may be related to the fact that the Ash'arites did not see human freedom as a precondition for moral responsibility—unlike the Mu'tazila, who did.[47] For example, the great Mu'tazila scholar Abd al-Jabbar wrote: "An agent deserves praise only when he could have done something other than what he did. . . . This is not possible in the case of compulsion."[48] In contrast, the Ash'arites, undervaluing human freedom, only emphasized *fahm*, or the "capacity to understand speech," as a precondition for moral responsibility.[49] And while this gap between the two sides was about human freedom vis-à-vis God, it could be also applied to human freedom vis-à-vis other humans.[50]

THE COSTS OF IMPOSED RELIGION

Now, if we fast forward from the time of al-Ghazali to today, and look at contemporary examples of *hisbah,* we will see that the two blind spots in the tradition devolved into big black holes.

One is the imposition of one interpretation of Islam on all other Muslims. In Saudi Arabia, this interpretation is Wahhabism, and hence, Shiites can be "savagely beaten" for holding Shiite-style prayers.[51] In Iran, it is the opposite: Shiite Islam is the official religion, and Sunnis can be banned from holding Eid prayers.[52] Even al-Ghazali's limited legal pluralism can't work anymore, for all modern states are centralized entities with a standard law of the land. Meanwhile, Muslim-majority societies have become only more diverse, with new "modernist" interpretations of Islam, along with nonpracticing Muslims and other minorites. Any attempt at religious policing is nothing other than the imposition of the Islam of whomever has power in any given territory. What is imposed is not "God's law," in other words, but the law of Wahhabi clerics, Shiite ayatollahs, or Shafi'i jurists.

The other, and even darker, black hole is the unintended consequences of religious policing: hypocrisy and resentment. Both are quite visible in Iran, where forty years of religious policing by the Islamic Republic made Iranian society not more pious but only less so. The policy of *gozinesh,* or "choosing," which means promoting state employees according to their religious observance rather than professional competence, only made people "pretend to be religious."[53] In wider society, the ban on alcohol only boosted homemade production, which led to many incidents of death.[54] Meanwhile, the oppression of the "Islamic" regime made many dissidents despise not just the regime but also Islam. As a result, many Iranians left the religion, converting to Christianity or atheism.[55]

Some Iranians have seen the disastrous impact of all these dictates. Among them was the exceptionally liberal Ayatollah Montazeri, who warned in 2008 that "mandating the performance of the Sharia" only causes "the evasion of religion and hostility towards religiosity."[56] Yet still, as I was writing this book, Iranian authorities were chasing women on the streets to make them cover their heads, and to punish thousands who defied their rule.

Is there a way out of this blind insistence on religious policing?

Yes, there is, and that is to revisit what "commanding the right and forbidding the wrong" means. As I noted above, the mainstream Islamic tradition—both Sunni and Shia—turned this into religious policing because they equated "right" and "wrong" with the commandments of the Sharia. Behind this, there was an epistemology—a theory of knowledge—which al-Ghazali notes in passing in his *Revival of the Religious Sciences*. Preventing evildoing is the goal, he says, but the "condition is that *its being evildoing should be learnt without reasoning.*"[57] The things that Muslims should "command" and "forbid," in other words, should not be defined by reason. Wine, for example, should be banned not on the basis of a rationale such as public order (which can be discussed), but on the basis that it is *haram,* or "religiously forbidden."

But the Mu'tazila had a different view. They said that "right" and "wrong" are known not merely by revelation, but by "both revelation and reason." Examples of the latter included injustice (*zulm*) or lying, or "someone being pained by the evil act of another."[58]

The Mu'tazila was on to something here, because the term that we keep translating as "right" in "commanding the right" is the mysterious term that we met before: *ma'ruf,* which literally means "the known." It is not *ma'ruf bi-l-shar,* or "known by the Sharia," but just "known."[59] This can well be, in the words of Shiite scholar

Tabatabai (d. 1981), what "people know by insight as earned by experience in social life" or what they grasp "intuitively."[60] In other words, it can be a wisdom not specific to Islam and Muslims, but accessed by all human beings.

And this distinction can allow us Muslims to reinterpret the duty of "commanding the right and forbidding the wrong." First we can separate between what is known merely by religion and what is known by reason. The latter is something on which we can build laws, as all people may agree, through "public reason," that murder or theft should be "forbidden," or stopping at a red light should be "commanded." But truths known merely by religion—all the rituals, commandments, and prohibitions of any religion—are subjective. So their implementation should be left to individuals and communities who have agreed to live by them.

But wait. Can people really agree, or not agree, to live by religion? Can they choose, in other words, what religion, if any, they will follow?

For an answer, we need another chapter.

FREEDOM MATTERS II: APOSTASY

The individual [has] one important right against the community: the right to leave the community. If there are any fundamental rights, this has to be that right. It is an inalienable right, and one which holds regardless of whether the community recognizes it as such.

—Chandran Kukathas, liberal political theorist[1]

In a TV interview in 2006, Yusuf al-Qaradawi, one of the most prominent Sunni scholars in the Arab world, said something that proved more viral than what he probably expected. "If they left apostasy alone [free], there wouldn't have been any Islam," he said. "Islam would have been finished right after the death of the Prophet."[2] To his Muslim audience, he was trying to explain why apostasy—the abandonment of Islam—is indeed a grave crime that should be punished with death. To some others, however, he was only confessing that Islam has survived to date thanks to violent coercion.

This matter, the punishment of apostasy, is the zenith of the coercive tradition within Islamic law. Accordingly, if a Muslim openly renounces his faith, to adopt another religion or no religion, he must be seized and asked to recant. If he doesn't recant, he must be executed. All the four Sunni schools of jurisprudence, along with their Shiite counterparts, unanimously agree on this grim verdict. They only differ in minor details. Hanafis and Shafi'is think that the apostate must be given three days to recant before execution. Malikis allow up to ten days. For Hanbalites, no waiting period is necessary. Hanafis and Shiites also accept a minor leniency for female apostates: instead of being executed, they must be imprisoned and beaten in regular intervals so maybe they can see the light and come back to Islam.[3]

Worse, these verdicts do not remain buried in classical books of jurisprudence but shape the laws of more than a dozen contemporary Muslim states. As of 2020, these included Saudi Arabia, Iran, Sudan, Afghanistan, Brunei, Mauritania, Maldives, parts of Nigeria, Somalia, Qatar, United Arab Emirates, and Yemen, all of which criminalized apostasy as a capital offense. In milder cases, such as Malaysia, Jordan, Kuwait, and Oman, there were no direct laws in the penal code, but still Islamic courts could decree prison sentences, enforce "rehabilitation," or annulment of marriages—as apostates don't have the right to be married to Muslims. Meanwhile, even in countries where apostasy isn't banned by law, there can be vigilante violence against apostates—real or purported. Grim cases of such violence have occurred in Egypt, Pakistan, and Bangladesh.

The harsh verdict on apostasy is also one of the key justifications of terrorism in the name of Islam, because terror groups like ISIS and Al-Qaeda kill fellow Muslims by declaring them as apostates first. Luckily, mainstream scholars condemn these terrorists as "extremists," saying that the latter have no right to declare other Muslims as apostates. But they rarely question whether *any apostate* really deserves to be targeted.

In short, the *umma,* the global Muslim community, has a big problem here. Killing somebody for his or her lack of belief in Islam—or even a specific interpretation of Islam—is not only a gross violation of human freedom, but it is also absurd. For by threatening, "Believe in Islam again, as I define it, or I will kill you," what can you really achieve other than hypocrisy and resentment?

This would have been quite obvious to all Muslims, if they all followed the Qur'an, and nothing else, for religious instruction.

For the Qur'an, which discusses apostasy in no less than twenty-one separate verses, decrees no earthly punishment for it. It does have several verses that threaten apostates with God's wrath in the afterlife, but that is the afterlife, not this life.[4] Moreover, the Qur'an has verses that one can use against the punishment on apostasy—such as the famous phrase "There is no compulsion in religion."[5]

But, as we have seen before, the mainstream Islamic tradition "abrogated" or limited such verses more than a millennium ago. That is why, again as we have seen, some modern translators of the Qur'an insert a few words into the no-compulsion phrase that dramatically reduce its scope: "There shall be no compulsion in religion (in becoming a Muslim)."[6] You are free to become a Muslim, that means, but you are not free to become an ex-Muslim.

TWO SUSPICIOUS HADITHS

Like almost all other coercive elements in Islamic law, the punishment for apostasy comes from not the Qur'an, but the hadiths. As I noted before, while many Muslims take these narrations as binding, there are good reasons to be cautious of them. First of all, they were canonized about two centuries after the Prophet, before spreading as oral traditions and mixing with many hearsays and forgeries. The scholars who collected and classified them—Ahmad ibn Hanbal, Muhammad al-Bukhari, Muslim ibn al-Hajjaj, and others—claimed to have figured out all the "authentic" ones, but we can never rule out their shortcomings and biases. In fact, their own writings show these scholars knowingly accepted many "unreliable" hadiths, given that these hadiths supported the doctrines they already believed to be true.[7]

With that general caveat in mind, let's have a look at the two hadiths on which the apostasy ban is based. Both are in the all-authoritative *Sahih al-Bukhari*. The first one plainly reads, "Whoever changes his religion, then kill him."[8] The second one repeats the same verdict while listing first two other reasons for the death penalty: "The blood of a Muslim . . . is not lawful to shed unless he be one of three:

a married adulterer, someone killed in retaliation for killing another, or someone who abandons his religion and the Muslim community."[9]

Now, while all hadiths may be questioned, there are some specific reasons to suspect these two. First of all, even by their collectors, they were classified as *ahad*, which means having a single source, in comparison to *mutawatir*, which means coming from multiple sources and being much more reliable. Also, the narrator of the first hadith, Ikrima, is a controversial figure even by the standards of classical hadith collectors.[10]

Secondly, both hadiths are suspiciously devoid of any context. We hear the Prophet ordering the killing of apostates, but there is no detail on where and when he said this or what really happened after that. Other narrations do not present us any story that can match these verdicts. Quite the contrary, they tell us about instances when the Prophet in fact did *not* go after apostates. One is a Bedouin who came to Medina, asked the Prophet, "Cancel my pledge," meaning religious allegiance, and left the scene without anyone following him.[11] Another instance, reported in the Qur'an, is a group "from the people of the book" who said to each other, "At the beginning of the day, believe in what has been revealed to these believers [Muslims] then at the end of the day reject it."[12] This seems to be not even mere apostasy, but apostasy with the clear intention of confusing Muslims. Yet still, the Qur'an only ordered a mild verbal response—to say, "True guidance is the guidance of God"—and we have no narration that the Prophet did anything different.[13]

Third, there is something more bizarre about the apostasy hadiths: we don't hear them being quoted in the key disputes in early Islam in which apostasy was the burning issue. The first of these was the major incident during the rule of the first caliph, Abu Bakr—*ridda*, or the refusal of some Arab tribes to pay tribute to the Muslim state in Medina. As we have noted, the incident provoked controversy in Medina, where the caliph favored a hawkish response, whereas others such as Umar pleaded for leniency. The curious point is that the caliph is on the record for asserting his own opinion, but not for quoting any hadith. That is strange, because he would have most likely referred to the apostasy hadiths if they were really known at that point.[14]

Another incident from early Islam is one of the most outrageous exploitations of the verdict on apostasy: the execution of Ghaylan al-Dimashqi, whose story we touched upon in chapter 2. The pious Syrian theologian was not an apostate at all, but merely a defender of the doctrine of free will, which refuted the contradictory doctrine of predestination that the Umayyad dynasty promoted to justify its despotism. His brutal execution took place after a show trial, which included a fatwa by Abd al-Rahman al-Awza'i (d. 774), who was a Sunni jurist, a zealous enemy of free will, and a minion of the throne. Al-Awza'i's justification of political murder was no big surprise, but it is remarkable that his fatwa doesn't include any of the apostasy hadiths.[15]

These all suggest that the hadiths about the execution of apostates may not have been around until the late second century after the Prophet Muhammad, when hadith collections such as *Sahih al-Bukhari* were not yet written. That is probably why, writing at this time, early jurists such as al-Nakha'i (d. 713) and al-Thawri (d. 778) could write that the apostate "should forever be asked to recant"—not asked for a few days before being killed, as later *ijma,* or "consensus," decreed.[16]

All this makes it quite possible that the grim verdict on apostasy didn't come from the Prophet but rather was projected back onto him by Muslims who found the verdict necessary.

And why would early Muslims find it necessary to punish apostasy? There are two answers, one being somewhat innocent, the other less so.

THE USES OF KILLING APOSTATES

The more innocent answer is that "apostasy" had a more alarming meaning in the premodern world, as the very concept of "religion" was more comprehensive than what we think of today. It was not just a belief, but also communal belonging and political allegiance. The apostate would be renouncing all these loyalties and also perhaps joining a deadly enemy. That is why the Christian Byzantine Empire, too, had no sense of religious freedom. According the Justinian Code of AD 534, all citizens were forced to profess Christianity, while those who stayed true to Hellenic paganism—"the heathens"—were stripped of property and at times killed and crucified.[17] "Not by their own free choice but under compulsion of the law," wrote Byzantine chronicler Procopius (d. 570), "they had changed the beliefs of their fathers."[18] Islam was born into such an oppressive world, and Muslims seem to have adopted its norms.

The second and more cynical use of the apostasy ban was that it was a great tool to silence any Muslim dissident. The Umayyad's murder of the defenders of free will—Ghaylan al-Dimashqi and Mabad al-Juhani—were the first stark examples. Then came al-Ghazali's verdict on "the philosophers." Then came the whole literature on "the words of disbelief," or utterances that would make a Muslim immediately an apostate deserving death. In a long list of such lethal words, Hanafi scholar Shaikhzadeh (d. 1667) included things like "to assert the createdness of the Qur'an" or "to assert one's belief in transmigration or in the uncreatedness of the world."[19] These were unmistakable references to the views of the Mu'tazila and the philosophers. Words of disbelief even included "to ridicule scholars" and "to address scholars in a derisive manner," unabashedly serving the very scholars who came up with these harsh verdicts.[20]

Today, the Justinian Code is long gone, along with other dark chapters in Christian history in which faith was dictated by brute power. Yet the Muslim ban on apostasy is still present, both in theory and practice. This leads to gross human rights violations, as ex-Muslims can be threatened, jailed, tortured, and executed.[21] The more cynical use of the verdict is also at play. Muslim scholars and intellectuals who merely have critical ideas, some of whom have been quoted in this book, can be condemned as "apostates" and then be targeted. Consequently, Muslim societies can't even begin to discuss their burning problems regarding the interpretation of religious texts.

ACCEPTING THE GOLDEN RULE

Scholars who defend all this oppression have implausible arguments. Yusuf al-Qaradawi, for example, argues, "every community in this world has basic foundations that are to be kept inviolable," and therefore "no community accepts that a member thereof changes its identity."[22] That is clearly untrue, as people in the modern world in fact can freely change their religion or, if they can, their nationality. A Vietnamese Buddhist doesn't face the death penalty, or any penalty, when he turns himself into, say, a Canadian Christian—or vice versa.

To be fair, al-Qaradawi at least makes a distinction between "major" and "minor" apostasy, which has become the typical "moderate" position on the matter. Accordingly, minor apostasy is a mere loss of faith, which in itself doesn't constitute a crime. In major apostasy, though, the ex-Muslim also "wages war on Islam and Muslims," and that is why he deserves death. But what is "war on Islam and Muslims"? If that means bombing mosques and slaughtering people, sure, that is a grave crime, irrespective of the attacker's beliefs. Yet by "war on Islam and Muslims" what al-Qaradawi means is merely "proclaiming" the apostasy and "openly calling for it in speech or writing."[23] That, he says, justifies the death penalty. Others make the same argument—that apostates deserve to be killed once they "start championing and spreading their spiritual and intellectual disorders to others."[24]

To see what is wrong here, we Muslims should consider a universal rule of ethics: the Golden Rule, which says, "Treat others as you would like others to treat you." Many people from other faith traditions freely and openly convert to Islam, and some of these new Muslims criticize their old faiths as well. How would we feel if their former coreligionists condemned them for apostasy and decide to kill them? If that would be outrageous, then our apostasy laws are outrageous, too. Asking for an exception for Islam because it is the "true religion" would not work as well, because every religion is true to its believers, and none can claim universal rules favoring only itself.

A contemporary Muslim thinker who has grasped and articulated the point here is Rached Ghannouchi, the prominent Tunisian scholar and politician whose moderation helped his country prove the only good outcome of the Arab Spring of the 2010s. In his 1993 book *Public Freedoms in the Islamic State*, he said the following:

> If it is the right, indeed the duty, of a Muslim to address his message (*dawa*) to his non-Muslim compatriot, then the latter also has the same right. And if there is any fear for the faith of the Muslims, then there is no other solution for them but to grow deeper in their faith. . . . Antithetical viewpoints will reach Muslims by any means, and the only means of protection against any discussion is to offer another discussion, this one better, more intelligent, and more cogent.[25]

So Ghannouchi was making a case for not just freedom of religion but also freedom of speech: that Muslims could hear speech that goes against their faith, but their right response would be to offer better speech.

But what if speech against Islam comes across as "insult"? What if people mock God and His Prophet? What should Muslims do to such blasphemers? That question, too, requires a new chapter.

FREEDOM MATTERS III: BLASPHEMY

If all of the six billion human inhabitants of this earth . . .
were blasphemous . . . it would not have the slightest effect upon His greatness.

—Indonesian Muslim scholar K. H. Mustofa Bisri, in his
poem "Allahu Akbar," or "God Is Greatest"[1]

When I was working on this book, Pakistan was going through
turmoil over Asia Bibi, a poor Christian woman who had seen hell
on earth. Until June 2009, Bibi, a mother of four, worked on a farm
in Punjab. But on a fateful day, she had a quarrel with Muslim co-
workers, one of whom soon went to the police and complained that
she "insulted the Prophet Muhammad." Soon she was arrested, put
on trial, and was sentenced to death by hanging. She spent the next
eight years on death row and in solitary confinement, only to be
released thanks to the Pakistan Supreme Court, which found her
innocent. Yet angry Islamist groups still wanted to see her dead, so
she saved her life only by silently fleeing to Canada in May 2019.

While I watched this whole Asia Bibi incident with sadness, I
was also intrigued by a curious detail in it. The Pakistani press ran
many articles on the case, but they never explicitly said what the
blasphemy in question was. In its fifty-six-page-long decision that
saved Bibi, the Supreme Court, too, only referred to the alleged

"derogatory remarks against the Holy Prophet," but never quoted those remarks.[2]

Apparently there was a reason for this silence, which Pakistani novelist Mohammed Hanif explained, with a hint of humor, in an article in *The New York Times*: "We can never know what she may or may not have said," Hanif wrote, referring to the incident that put Asia Bibi in jail. "Because repeating blasphemy is also blasphemy, and writing it down may be even greater blasphemy. So let's not go there."[3]

When I read this, I paused for a second. "Alas," I said to myself, "with this logic, the Pakistanis must ban the Qur'an as well." Because, with this logic, the Qur'an is also full of blasphemy. In fact, outrageous blasphemy.

HOW THE QUR'AN COUNTERS BLASPHEMY

What I am referring to are the Qur'anic verses that reflect the polemics between the Prophet Muhammad and the polytheists of Mecca with whom he was trying to share the message of Islam, only to get hostile reactions. We hear these people saying, for example, "Receiver of this Qur'an! *You are definitely mad.* Why do you not bring us the angels, if you are telling the truth?"[4] Another Qur'anic verse also quotes the polytheists, whose offensive words go uncensored:

> When Our revelations are recited to them in all their clarity, the disbelievers say of the Truth that has reached them, "*This is clearly sorcery,*" or they say, "*He has invented it himself.*"[5]

The Qur'an also quotes a "stubbornly hostile" man who condemns the Qur'an by saying, "*This is just old sorcery,* just the talk of a mortal."[6] A group of unbelievers who dismiss the revelation are also quoted in full: "We have heard all this before, we could say something like this if we wanted, *this is nothing but ancient fables.*"[7] Blasphemous depictions of God are also quoted in the Qur'an as the words of the misguided: "God is tight-fisted"; "God has a child"; or "God has begotten."[8]

When the Qur'an quotes these offensive statements, it often answers them with counterarguments. To those who said, "God is tight-fisted," it responds, "Truly, God's hands are open wide: He gives as He pleases."[9] Against polytheists, it defends monotheism with reasoning: "If there had been in the heavens or earth any gods but Him, both heavens and earth would be in ruins."[10] And to those who claim that the Prophet Muhammad himself made up the Qur'an, it presents an intellectual challenge: "Then produce a sura [chapter] like it, and call on anyone you can beside God if you are telling the truth."[11]

In other words, when the Qur'an encounters blasphemy, it responds to it with sensible arguments. At most, it threatens blasphemers with God's wrath in the afterlife, but it decrees no punishment in this life. It certainly doesn't decree that blasphemers should be jailed and killed, or even that their words should be censored.

What if the blasphemy in question is not something you can reason with, but sheer insult? In that case, too, the Qur'an doesn't order any violent or coercive response. "When you come across people who speak with scorn about Our revelations," reads a verse, "turn away from them until they move on to another topic."[12] This is in the Meccan sura "An'am," so, by those who are fond of abrogation, it may be explained away as a temporary restraint due to lack of power. But the Medinan sura "Nisa" repeats the same commandment with a reference to the earlier one:

> As He has already revealed to you in the Scripture, if you hear people denying and ridiculing God's revelation, do not sit with them unless they start to talk of other things, or else you yourselves will become like them.[13]

Another Medinan verse also tells Muslims that insult is a "test," which they should bear:

You are sure to hear much that is hurtful from those who were given the Scripture before you and from those who associate others with God. If you are steadfast and mindful of God, that is the best course.[14]

Commenting on this verse, Fakhr al-Din al-Razi, the great thirteenth-century exegete, wrote that while some jurists consider it as "abrogated," others, including himself, don't think so.[15] He also supported it with other verses of the same spirit: "Tell the believers to forgive those who do not fear God's days."[16] These believers are also described by the Qur'an as "The servants of the Lord of Mercy . . . who walk humbly on the earth, and who, when the foolish address them, reply, 'Peace.'"[17]

Despite this tolerant spirit in the Qur'an, Islamic jurisprudence developed a harsh verdict for blasphemy—in particular, blasphemy against Prophet Muhammad, called *sabb* or *shatm al-rasul*. Hanafis conflated it with apostasy, which means they took it as a capital offense, while leaving room for repentance. Shafi'is took a similar position, whereas Malikis allowed repentance for only women, and Hanbalites allowed it to no one. The latter's severity was embellished by Ibn Taymiyya in his treatise *The Unsheathed Sword Against the One Who Insults the Messenger*, which has proven highly influential even among non-Hanbalis.[18] Accordingly, anyone who insulted the Prophet would be killed, even if he repented and asked for mercy.

Today, this medieval jurisprudential tradition is still influential, as it underlies the blasphemy laws that are in practice in some thirty Muslim-majority countries. (Some of these laws, such as in Pakistan, are leftovers of European colonialism, but the passion to preserve, extend, and implement them is unmistakably religious.[19]) Worse, at the hands of militants, blasphemy laws turn into vigilante violence against "those who insult Islam," real or perceived, from author Salman Rushdie to Asia Bibi, to the French magazine *Charlie Hebdo*.

A "DEAD POETS SOCIETY"?

If the Qur'an doesn't support all this severity, though, where does it come from? Like in the case of apostasy, the source is certain narrations about the Prophet Muhammad. This time we don't have any clear hadiths ordering violence against acts of blasphemy. We rather have stories in the books of *Al-Sira al-Nabawiyya*, or "Prophetic Biography," written down by Muslim chroniclers about a century or so after the Prophet. These stories tell us about the targeted killing of several individuals who wrote hostile poems against the Prophet and his message. These stories have inspired militant Muslims and also led some anti-Islam polemicists to joke about "Muhammad's Dead Poets Society."[20] Both sides, however, seem to miss an important nuance.

For that nuance, we should look at the most iconic figure among these "dead poets": Ka'b ibn al-Ashraf. He was a leader of Banu Nadir, a Jewish tribe in Medina that may have signed the "constitution" with the Prophet Muhammad soon after the latter's arrival in the city. The early Muslim chronicler al-Waqidi tells us what happened afterward: "When the Messenger of God arrived in Medina he desired to establish peace for them and he reconciled with all of them," including the "polytheists and Jews." Some of the latter "hurt the Prophet and his companions grievously" with their bitter words, "but God most high commanded His prophet and the Muslims to be patient and forgiving."[21] Yet still, Ibn al-Ashraf proved growingly hostile. After the Battle of Badr, where Medinan Muslims defeated Meccan pagans, he not only protested the victory but also vowed, "I will go out to the Quraysh and incite them."[22] Then he really went to Mecca, met with polytheist leaders, and wept with them for their dead. His anti-Muslim rhymes reached a wide circulation there, rousing the Meccans "to grief and anger and the desire for revenge."[23] There are also reports that Ibn al-Ashraf tore up a tent the Prophet set up in the Medina market, and even plotted with a group of his kinsmen to kill the Prophet.[24]

Only after all this, Ibn al-Ashraf was reportedly assassinated by a group of Muslims acting on the order of the Prophet. Was he an offensive poet? Yes. But apparently he was also more than that.

Most of the other "dead poets" seem to have combined their offensive words with their active enmity. One was Nadr ibn al-Harith, who was one of the two captives executed after the Battle of Badr, while others were unharmed. The reason, told to his face, was "you said thus and thus about the Book of God," and "you tortured [the Prophet's] companions."[25] Another was Abu Rafi, "who used to hurt Allah's Messenger, and help his enemies against him."[26] Others were targeted after the conquest of Mecca, when the victorious Muhammad announced general amnesty to his former prosecutors, but with the exception of ten individuals. One was Abdullah ibn Khatal, who "used to recite verses abusing the prophet," but also murdered an innocent slave, and who was actually targeted for "retribution for the slave's death."[27] Another one was Huwayrith ibn Nafidh, who had attacked the Prophet's two daughters when they were fleeing Medina.[28]

Here is a point that may explain the murkiness in these stories: In early seventh-century Arabia, poetry wasn't just poetry. There was a specific genre called *hija'*, or "invective poetry," where "the poet could lead his people into battle, hurling his verses as he would hurl a spear."[29] In other words there were no clear lines between verbal denigration and physical aggression, and Muslims might have conflated the two.

On the other hand, there are also incidents in Prophet Muhamad's life where he did *not* punish blasphemous words when they were just words. According to a narration in *Sahih al-Bukhari*, a Jew in Medina used a play on words while greeting the Prophet. Instead of *as-salamu alaika,* or "peace be upon you," he said,

as-samu alaika, or "death be upon you." Hearing this, some companions lost their nerve and asked, "O God's Apostle! Shall we kill
him?" The Prophet said "no," and told them to only respond by
saying *wa alaikum,* or "on you, too."[30] In another version of the
same story, the Prophet also said, "Be gentle and calm . . . as Allah
likes gentleness in all affairs."[31]

In a similar incident, another Medinan named Finhas mocked
a Qur'anic verse calling for alms, saying, "Muhammad's Lord is
in need." The ever-fiery Umar unsheathed his sword, yet he was
stopped by not just the Prophet himself but also a new verse from
God: "Tell the believers to forgive those who do not fear God's
days." Umar complied, promising the Prophet, "You will see no
more anger on my face."[32] In yet another incident, a man named
Dhu'l-Khuwaisira publicly blamed the Prophet for committing
injustice. Umar, again zealous to protect the latter's honor, asked
permission "to strike his neck." The Prophet, again, stopped Umar,
saying, "leave him." (A contemporary Salafi website narrates this
incident, adding: "Such words would undoubtedly deserve execution, if anyone were to say them *today.*" In other words, it admits
that today's Muslims can be much less lenient than the Prophet.)[33]

What this all means is that the "dead poets" from the time of the
Prophet Muhammad cannot justify violence against blasphemy, as
the prominent Hanafi scholar Badr al-Din al-Ayni (d. 1453) had
also argued. "[They] were not killed merely for their insults [of the
Prophet]," he wrote, "but rather it was surely because they aided
[the enemy] against him, and joined with those who fought wars
against him."[34] Seven centuries before him, the very founder of the
Hanafi school, the ever-sensible Abu Hanifa, had made a similar
point. Non-Muslims who insult the Prophet are not to be killed, he
wrote, "because their [overall] unbelief is worse," but they are not
targeted for unbelief.[35]

It is also quite telling that the verdict on killing blasphemers
appeared at quite a late stage in Islamic law—as late as the early
tenth century, or three centuries after the death of the Prophet.

Also telling is that it grew among Malikis, whose geographic positioning in Spain and North Africa put them in close contact, and conflict, with Christians. The first big application was the notorious incident of "martyrs of Córdoba," where some forty-eight Christians were publicly decapitated between 850 and 859 for denigrating the Prophet Muhammad.[36] This Christian defiance seems to have catalyzed the crystallization of the verdict on blasphemy, which used to be unclear.[37]

Therefore, today, Muslims who are eager to punish or silence blasphemy should know that, jurisprudentially speaking, they are on shaky grounds. Rationally speaking, they are out of their minds. By their threats and dictates, they are only confirming the common accusation against Islam—that it is an intolerant and violent religion. They are also provoking only more blasphemy against Islam, because their zeal to silence critics only makes the latter more agitated. Meanwhile, they are enfeebling Muslim societies, which do not learn how to respond to criticism with reason and civility. That is why, like the case in Pakistan, they can't even bear to hear offensive words—unlike the Qur'an, which quotes such words and reasons with them.

NO COMPULSION IN RELIGION—SERIOUSLY

In the past three chapters, we have seen the three genres of coercion present in the mainstream Islamic tradition: coercion to keep Muslims pious, coercion to keep Muslims within the religion and its orthodoxy, and coercion to make non-Muslims respect the religion. We have seen that these genres have no basis in the Qur'an, and their bases in the post-Qur'anic literature is questionable. We have also noted that their impact in the actual world is grave. All this coercion only breeds hypocrisy, resentment, and intellectual poverty among Muslims, while it builds contempt, not respect, among non-Muslims.

It is quite remarkable that with all these coercive measures, mainstream Islamic tradition has turned the Qur'anic maxim "no compulsion in religion" upside down, because in this tradition there are all sorts of compulsion *in* the religion, whereas "no compulsion" can be found only *outside*: only if you are not a Muslim will you not be forced to practice the religion or be loyal to it. And only if you are outside of the reach of Muslims will you be able to freely speak against it.

In the face of this grim freedom deficit, it is no surprise that Muslims who value freedom sometimes distance themselves from the faith. Some totally abandon it. As I explained in a 2020 article, in various Muslims societies, there is now a growing trend of atheism, deism, or conversion to Christianity, precisely because narrow interpretations of Islam are imposed on people by Islamist regimes or groups, only to create a backlash.[38]

The big remedy we need—call it a great "reform" or "renewal"—is really having "no compulsion in religion." It is, in other words, *giving up coercive power in the name of Islam*. This means no more religious and moral policing, no threats to apostates and "innovators," no blasphemy laws, no public floggings or stoning for sinners, and no violence or intimidation in the family. It means accepting that "religion is advice" as one of the better hadiths in *Sahih al-Bukhari* reads, and advancing Islam only with advisory means, such as preaching, counseling, exemplifying, and educating.[39] Quite a few Muslims are already doing that—as minorities in the West, or as majorities in secular states ranging from Bosnia and Herzegovina to Indonesia—and their experience presents a much brighter story than those in coercive states such as Saudi Arabia or Iran.[40]

Having no compulsion in religion will also require a new Muslimhood—not as collectively disciplined communities, but rather self-disciplined individuals. The latter notion, quite tellingly, was downplayed in the Islamic tradition. A proverb, promoted by the Umayyads, even warned, "Satan is with the individual . . . [so] adhere to the community."[41] This communitarian spirit has lived on for centuries, and it is still powerful today. That is why, as a

Muslim author recently observed, one can often hear about "the Arab Nation, the Islamic Ummah, the Rightly Guided People," but almost never "the Muslim individual."[42] For the same reason, when Muslims from conservative societies find themselves as individuals, in a free medium such as the West, they can turn disoriented if not indulgent, as they are not used to restraining and disciplining themselves.[43]

The solution is not tightening up communitarianism, which is a losing strategy in the modern world. It is, rather, building the character of the Muslim individual, who will follow not the dictates of others, but the dictates of his or her own moral compass.

We would not be the first major world religion to have this transformation—although we may be the last. Christians, in particular, used coercive power for centuries, but European Catholics now recall the Inquisition with embarrassment, in the same way American Protestants remember the witch hunts in the Massachusetts Bay Colony. They outgrew those dark phases thanks to the rational realization that coercion is absurd, and the scriptural realization that it is unnecessary. We, too, have the same resources to make the same leap forward, as we have seen in the previous chapters.

Yet still, there is one final piece missing in this picture: you can't embrace freedom if you see too many intolerable things around you. And quite a few Muslims indeed believe there are too many intolerable things around them. Their tolerance deficit is the final padlock on Muslim minds that we will now address.

THE THEOLOGY OF TOLERANCE

Sincere and consistent doubt is the source of tolerance.

—Peter Berger and Anton Zijderveld, modern sociologists[1]

I believe that my opinions are correct, but I am cognizant of the fact that my opinions may be wrong.

—Abu Hanifa, early Sunni jurist[2]

ISIS, the terror army that has done unspeakable evils in the name of Islam, used to have a magazine called *Dabiq.* The pages of this monthly dose of venom were filled mostly with propaganda against a wide range of enemies, including the West, Christians, Jews, Shiites, and even various Sunni groups. The March 2015 issue, however, targeted a theological doctrine that most Muslims may never have heard of: Irja. This, according to a seventeen-page-long article, was "the most dangerous *bid'ah,*" or "heresy," that Islam has ever seen. No wonder "the scholars of the Salaf," or early generations, had "warned severely against" it. It was so bad, because it "diluted the religion of the Muslims," and made "major sins and even *kufr* [disbelief] appear as something trivial."[3]

When I read these lines, I was impressed, because I knew what Irja is, and I only had great sympathy for it. The fact that ISIS saw it as "the most dangerous" idea in Islam only seemed to confirm my convictions.

So what really is Irja, a concept that we have not yet met in this book?

It is a political and theological doctrine that emerged in the very first century of Islam, in order to find a remedy to the bloody conflicts that tore Muslims apart. At the root of the problem was the parochial rivalry between the two prominent clans of the tribe of Quraysh: the Hashemites, the very clan of the Prophet Muhammad, and the Umayyads, the clan of his uncles. The twelve-year reign of the third caliph, Uthman ibn Affan (d. 656), an Umayyad, awakened this old rivalry, as his nepotism created widespread discontent, which ultimately led to his murder by a group of rebels. The caliphate was then claimed by Ali ibn Abi Talib (d. 661), who was a Hashemite, in addition to being the very cousin and son-in-law of the Prophet. Yet Ali's reluctance to avenge the murder of Uthman, which would be politically risky, angered the Umayyads. This tension soon led to two bloody battles, in which thousands of Muslims killed each other as partisans of either Uthman or Ali. (The very term "Shia" comes from here—the "partisans," or *shia*, of Ali.)

As if all this bloodshed wasn't enough, a fanatic group within Ali's ranks condemned him as well, supposedly for violating "the judgment of Allah" by accepting human arbitration, creating the faction called Kharijites, or "Dissenters." In their eyes, both Uthman and Ali, along with their supporters, had committed "grave sins," which made them "infidels," deserving to be killed. That is why they tried to assassinate both Ali and Muawiyah, succeeding only with the former, inadvertently consolidating the rule of the latter.

It is in this terrible scene that the idea of Irja emerged. Its proponents refused to give any verdict on either Uthman or Ali. If these fellow Muslims have really committed "grave sins," they said, it would be up to God to judge. So the controversy had to be "postponed" to Judgment Day, where God would make things straight. The term "postponement," or *irja,* became their motto, probably with an inspiration from a Qur'anic verse that speaks of people who are "postponed to God's judgment."[4] They became known as the Murji'a—or "Murji'ites"—meaning "Postponers." Some also called them *shukkak,* or "doubters," as they doubted taking a side in the conflict.[5]

THE WISDOM IN "DOUBTING" AND "POSTPONING"

Irja was first a political stance, but it gradually evolved into a theological doctrine. At its heart was leniency on "grave sins"—things such as polytheism, adultery, usury, drinking wine, or abandoning prayer. All Muslims agreed that God would judge these sins in the afterlife, but what should happen in this life, besides the criminal punishments decreed by the Sharia? The Kharijites' answer was that grave sins made Muslims infidels, who must be killed for apostasy. The Mu'tazila, whose rationalism I have often embraced in the previous chapters, were milder than the Kharijites, but only to some extent. They considered the grave sinner neither an infidel nor a full believer, but rather somewhere in between as a *fasiq,* or a Muslim gone astray, who would lose some social rights, such as giving testimonies at courts.[6]

The Murji'ites, as the exact opposite of the Kharijites, argued that "grave sins" do not harm one's belief and social status as Muslim. That was because they separated "faith" from "acts," arguing that one's faith will still be intact even if one's acts were sinful. Even a fully nonobservant Muslim, in this view, was still a Muslim.

For the ruling Umayyads, this mild doctrine was preferable to ferocious opposition, so they often tolerated the Murji'ites, giving the latter a bad name as "loyalist supporters of the Umayyads and as apolitical quietists."[7] However, a careful look shows that this view may be mistaken. Murji'ites refrained from condemning the rulers as infidels, but they were still ready to condemn them as wrongdoers. Meanwhile, "their insistence on their right to criticize the injustice of the rulers" actually put them at odds with the Umayyads.[8] Some Murji'ites even actively joined the big Iraqi revolt against the ruthless Umayyad governor al-Hajjaj (d. 714).[9] Salafi sources that still condemn the Murji'ites because "they do not believe that obedience is due to the ruler" seem to echo that legacy.[10]

Who exactly were these Murji'ites? They were urban and educated Muslims, including theologians, jurists, and poets, who had a "predominantly intellectualist-rationalist tendency."[11] Among them was Hasan ibn Muhammad ibn al-Hanafiyyah (d. 719), a grandson of Caliph Ali, whose *Book of Irja* became a key document that spread the doctrine. Yet the most prominent Murji'ite, although he didn't explicitly self-identify as such, was Abu Hanifa, the founder of the Hanafi school of jurisprudence. "We do not consider anyone to be an infidel on account of sin," his credo read, "nor do we deny his faith."[12] Abu Hanifa also made a crucial distinction between religion (*din*) and law (*sharia*). All prophets brought the same religion, he argued, but promulged different laws. So one would not be abandoning religion by abandoning the law.[13]

Abu Hanifa's influence introduced the spirit of Irja into the newly forming Sunni Islam, in particular the Maturidi school of theology. The idea found a silent acceptance among the Ash'aris as well.[14] Yet there was also opposition to Irja, among the ever-rigid Ahl al-Hadith. While Abu Hanifa had defined faith as "belief in the heart and affirmation of the tongue," the Ahl al-Hadith, just like the Kharijites, added "the acts of the limbs."[15] An important voice in this camp was Ibn Taymiyya (d. 1328), who condemned the newly Islamized Mongols as "infidels" by judging their acts— that they didn't fully implement the Sharia. Not too surprisingly, Ibn Taymiyya also wrote a long polemic against the Murji'ites.[16]

This avowedly anti-Murji'ite strain in Sunni Islam would have an unexpected revival in the late eighteenth century, in the middle of the Arabian Desert, under the leadership of a fierce cleric named

Muhammad ibn Abd al-Wahhab (d. 1792). His followers called themselves Muwahhidun, or "Monotheists"—as if other Muslims aren't monotheists. Outsiders gave them a more appropriate name: Wahhabis. They began condemning all other Muslims as infidels, only to attack them ruthlessly. In 1801, they sacked the Ottoman city of Karbala, massacred thousands of Shiites, including women and children, and looted all their wealth. In the twentieth century, when they established a state called Saudi Arabia, they restrained their ferocity, but their radical offshoots would soon revive the violent tradition. The world would hear their name first as Al-Qaeda, and then as ISIS.

"PREACHERS, NOT JUDGES"

The anti-Murji'ite strain in Sunni Islam had another revival in the 1960s, in Egypt, with the writings of Sayyid Qutb. In his landmark book *Milestones*, he argued that contemporary Muslim societies were not really Muslim but *jahili*, or un-Islamic. He had come to this verdict by judging their "acts" with a highly politicized interpretation of Islam that he himself formulated. Accordingly, the meaning of being a Muslim was to accept God as the only lawgiver. So anyone who accepted a legal system other than the Sharia was an infidel, despite the faith that he or she may have in heart.

Qutb was affiliated with Egypt's main Islamist movement: the Muslim Brotherhood. But only a small faction within that movement followed his extremism, soon creating a splinter group called Jamaat al-Muslimin, or "Community of Muslims," implying that only they themselves are Muslims. Others called them al-Takfir wal-Hijra, or "Excommunication and Flight." A like-minded group called Al-Jihad assassinated the Egyptian president Anwar al-Sadat in 1981. One of their members was Ayman al-Zawahiri, who would later become first the ideologue and then the leader of Al-Qaeda.

These jihadists had all broken away from the Muslim

Brotherhood because the latter kept the moderate line defined by Hasan al-Hudaybi, who led the organization from 1951 to 1973 and who also wrote a notable book, *Preachers, Not Judges.* The title was the summary of what good Muslims should do: preach, but not judge. In the words of al-Hudaybi, the right path was "to persuade others to adhere more closely to Islam, and not to judge others as apostates, foment revolt, or apply the Sharia through force."[17]

In return, al-Hudaybi was condemned by jihadists as—guess what?—a modern-day Murji'ite.[18] One of them, Tariq Abd al-Halim, in *The Book of the Truth of Faith,* renounced the idea that faith is just "acts of the heart," insisting that it is also "acts of the limbs."[19] He identified the first argument with the Murji'ites and passionately argued against it.[20] Years later, Abu Muhammad al-Maqdisi, who has been called the "godfather" of both Al-Qaeda and ISIS, made the same argument in a prolixly titled book, *The Penetrating Look into Unmasking the Spurious Arguments of the Modern-Day Murji'ites.*[21] It is this narrative that seems to have gone all the way to the pages of *Dabiq.*

For all these militants, what is the exact problem with the Murji'a? Shaikh Abdullah Faisal, a militant Salafi preacher who was convicted in the United Kingdom in 2003 for incitement to violence, once put it well in a sermon titled "Murji'a: The Devil's Deception": "A Murji'a is a liberal," he explained, "who refuses to make *takfir* [condemning a Muslim as *kafir*] even if the text is clear." The same liberal also "gives hope to people who are perpetrators of major sins, claiming only Allah should do that [judge them]."[22]

That is quite a helpful description of the Irja doctrine, I must say, and that is why it is brilliant. It allows Muslims to tolerate things that they disapprove, not because they don't care about religion, but rather because they leave its judgment to God. That is, put simply, a very godly act.

Punishing people in the name of God—like the old Kharijites did, and their modern-day reincarnations do—may also look like a godly act. But deep down, it is a very arrogant and self-serving act, because it gives legitimacy only to a certain group, which claims to know the exact truth of Islam and also grants itself the authority to punish, and thus dominate, all others. While they claim to be serving God, what such fanatics really do is make God serve themselves.

A wise man who grasped the nuance between these two ways was Abraham Lincoln, the sixteenth president of the United States, who led the North during the Civil War. When one of his supporters told him, as an assurance, "God is on our side," he famously replied, "Sir, my concern is not whether God is on our side. My greatest concern is to be on God's side."[23] He realized, in other words, that a believer must not confuse certainty in God's correctness with certainty in his own correctness. A healthy dose of doubt about the latter is what separates the wise from the fanatic, and the truly righteous from the arrogantly self-righteous.

THE MYTH OF THE "SAVED SECT"

The Kharijites were a marginal force in early Islam, as are the violent jihadists of today. However, the self-righteousness that has motivated them—the claim to be the only true manifestation of Islam—unfortunately has a broader appeal. It is still shared by various groups in the Muslim world, most of whom do not engage in violence yet still look down upon other Muslims as the misguided and the deviant, often to justify their marginalization, if not oppression.

The bulk of this problem is within Sunnism, which, as the dominant majority, has a long history of seeing itself as Islam proper. We have seen in the previous chapters how this exclusivism led to the suppression of the Mu'tazila. After that, the only major rival to Sunnis turned out to be, as they still are, the Shia. They were often denigrated as the Rafida, or "Rejectors," meaning that they reject the legitimate rule of the first three caliphs. For mainstream Sunnis, this made the Shia Ahl al-Bidah, or "People of Innovation," implying that they are erroneous but still Muslim. Hard-core Salafis went further, claiming, "The Shia are *kafir*." That is the ideology behind the savage attacks against Shia mosques and shrines we have seen in the past few decades in the Middle East, Pakistan, and Afghanistan.

The self-righteous zealotry here is not just about judging "acts" in order to question "faith." It is also about classifying the faith itself into one true branch versus many heresies. It goes back to the famous hadith of the "seventy-three sects," which reads:

> My ummah [people] will split into seventy-three sects. All of them are in the Fire except one sect. [They asked]: "And which is it, O Messenger of Allah?" He said: "What I am upon and my companions."[24]

This hadith, which is narrated in various hadith collections with minor variations, was accepted as "authentic" by most traditional scholars, who only disagreed on the designation of *al-firqa al-najiya*, or "the saved sect." Quite amusingly, they all had an easy answer: the saved sect was, of course, theirs. They did this by adding "an explanatory ending" to the hadith or "rewording it in suggestive ways."[25] Toward the end of the Umayyad period, this rewording even included an unabashedly sycophantic version: "This community consists of 73 sects, 72 are lost," it read, adding, "they all hate the ruler; saved is the one that is on the side of the ruler."[26]

In the early Abbasid period, the Murji'ites, who were then surviving under the banner of Hanafism, tried to put a brake on this sectarianism by arguing that "the saved sect" includes "all those who believe," which is the "overwhelming majority."[27] They also used an umbrella term for all Muslims, Ahl al-Qibla, or "Those Who Pray Toward Mecca," wishing for all of them divine forgiveness.[28]

Yet the tougher line within Sunnism, spearheaded by Ibn Hanbal, kicked back. For him, "the saved sect" was nothing but his own

Ahl al-Hadith, and the most deviant ones were those who pursued reason. So a new version of the hadith of the "seventy-three sects" began to circulate among the Hanbalis. "My community will split into some seventy groups," it read, "but the greatest danger will arise from those among them who judge things according to their own free reasoning [ra'y]."[29]

If Muslims had doubted these conspicuously partisan narrations and focused on the Qur'an, they would have done better. Because the Qur'an not only has nothing to say about "the saved sect," but it also warns Muslims precisely against such self-righteous sectarianism. After calling them to piety, it commands them, "Do not join those who ascribe partners to God; *those who divide their religion into sects, with each party rejoicing in their own.*"[30] Exegetes often thought that this criticism was directed at Christians—who, at the time of the Qur'an, indeed had bitter schisms—but today it seems most relevant to Muslims themselves. Muslims are divided into self-venerating groups, and as a contemporary scholar of the Middle East observes, this exacerbates their bitter political conflicts:

> The plague in the Middle East . . . is that all players in the violent conflict claim to have a monopoly on religious truth. Whose Islam is it? Is it that of the Salafist, who wants to return to how he says Islam was practiced during the time of the Prophet Mohammad 1,400 years ago? Or that of the banned Muslim Brotherhood leader in Egypt? Or the leader of a Shia militia in Iraq? Or the Islamic State of Iraq and Syria (ISIS), the Islamic State? Each party believes its religious knowledge is sacred and true.[31]

The remedy to these toxic divisions is not in the endless calls to "unite" all Muslims on "true Islam," the definition of which is the source of all tension. The remedy is rather in the Murji'ite solution: let all Muslims follow their own traditions and persuasions, "postpone" their unresolved disputes to the afterlife, and respect each other as Ahl al-Qibla.

Also, all Muslims should ask themselves why they are really Sunni, Salafi, Shiite, Alevi, Ahmadi, or from some other expression of Islam. Unless they have done some serious questioning and soul-searching, which is rare, the answer will be that they are a part of the family and community into which they are born. If one is born in Tehran, he or she will probably grow up as Shiite. If one is born in Cairo, he or she will probably be a Sunni. Why would God condemn one to hell, and welcome the other one to heaven? That would be a tribal deity, not the God of humanity that the Qur'an speaks about.

This reasoning will only invite another question, though: What about the fate of people who are born in Buenos Aires, Kansas City, Mumbai, or Tel Aviv? If they do what most Muslims do, which is to follow the faith of their families, they will not be Muslim. Should this make them somehow guilty? This question takes us to another discussion, namely the status of non-Muslims in Muslim eyes.

NON-MUSLIMS IN MUSLIM EYES

We Muslims, in fact, can be proud of our historical record on this matter. Because the premodern Islamic civilization did something that its main rival, Christendom, did not do: accept preexisting religious communities as "People of the Book," with the right to practice their faith. That is why "non-Muslim communities living under Islam experienced far less expulsions and persecutions than Jews, or 'deviant' Christians, living under medieval Christendom."[32] That is also why there are still Christian minorities in the Muslim Middle East, while no Muslim minority remained in Spain soon after the Christian Reconquista.

However, from the modern point of view, the premodern Islamic system of toleration had an important shortcoming: non-Muslims, as *dhimmis,* were "protected" but also "subdued." In other words, they had fewer rights. The notion of equal rights came only with Western liberalism, which had its first impact on the Ottoman Empire in the mid-nineteenth century. The latter's acceptance of *musavat,* or equality—first implicitly with the Tanzimat Edict of 1839, followed by the Islahat Edict of 1856, and finally the Constitution of 1876—was a significant milestone in the history of the Islamic civilization. However, the push for equality also provoked a reaction of "Muslim supremacism." The latter, in conflict with rising nationalism among Christians, led to the horrific intercommunal violence in the last three decades of the empire, ending with the expulsion or destruction of most Anatolian Christians.[33]

Today, almost two centuries after the first Ottoman reforms, it is hard to argue that equal citizenship is fully established in the Muslim world. While there are brighter spots, such as Bosnia, Morocco, or Tunisia, most majority-Muslim states discriminate, either explicitly or implicitly, against their non-Muslim citizens, whereas some Islamists openly advocate restoring the *dhimmi* system. That is why progressive initiatives, such as the Marrakesh Declaration of 2016, signed by hundreds of Islamic scholars, feel the need to oppose "religious bigotry, vilification, and denigration," and to call upon Muslim scholars and intellectuals "to develop a jurisprudence of the concept of citizenship."[34]

This is indeed a matter of Islamic jurisprudence as well as secular law. But it is also a matter of theology, which instills a certain disposition among Muslims toward non-Muslims. At its core, there is the common belief that the latter are all *kuffar*—the plural of *kafir,* which is roughly equivalent to the Christian term "infidel"—who deny the supposedly obvious truth of Islam. Because of this, the same belief holds, while God will reward all Muslims with heaven, immediately or eventually, He will punish all non-Muslims with eternal hellfire.

To be sure, one may still tolerate people on earth while thinking they are damned in the afterlife. However, that is not what classical Muslim jurists seem to have thought. One of them was al-Mawardi, whom we met before. He first referred to a Qur'anic verse: "Not equal are the companions of the fire and the companions of heaven."[35] From this eschatological inequality, he inferred an earthly inequality. Accordingly, non-Muslims could not be allowed to build new houses of worship, where they would "congregate . . . to perpetuate disbelief."[36] In Muslim lands, al-Mawardi argued, only Islam should be visible.[37]

Such medieval verdicts are still influential in Muslim-majority societies, where it is not easy for non-Muslims to erect new houses of worship or even repair existing ones. Meanwhile, there are popular narratives, often amplified with political grievances, that depict the non-Muslims as morally defective and politically treacherous. As Aan Anshori, an Indonesian Muslim, critically observes:

> While we are indoctrinated to believe that there is no salvation outside Islam, likewise we are taught that non-Muslims are different from us and also aim to put Muslims worldwide in misery. Their appearance as upstanding individuals, we are taught, masks their actual desire to conquer Islam and Muslims.[38]

This narrative includes fatwas on why and how Muslims should be careful not to "imitate" non-Muslims or "befriend" them. A fatwa on Islamweb.net, a popular Salafi site, even specifies how one should write to them:

> If someone writes a letter to a Kafir, he has to start with a general meaning. . . . It is not permissible to start the letter by writing anything that could mean the glorification of a Kafir by the Muslim, like the title "Sir" or "Dear" and the like. He is not your "master" or "dear" while he is declaring Allah to be his enemy.[39]

Declaring Allah an enemy? Are the non-Muslims of the world really doing that? Not really, as anyone who observes the real world can see. Most non-Muslims are rather doing what most Muslims do—following their family traditions. Their lack of belief in Islam, in other words, is not rooted in any "enmity." Similarly, they are not conspiring against Muslims day and night. Quite the contrary, some may be worrying —reasonably or unreasonably— about Muslim enmity against themselves.

In other words, there seems to be a dissonance between some Muslim presuppositions about non-Muslims and the latter's reality. Why could that be?

WHO THE *KAFIR* REALLY IS

To find an answer, we should revisit what *kafir* really means. Etymologically, it comes from the root *k-f-r,* which means "to cover." It implies that a *kafir* sees the truth but still "covers" it. The term also indicates "ingratitude" along with "arrogance" and "haughtiness"— and not mere "disbelief."[40] After all, the arch-*kafir* was Satan, who had no shortage of belief in God, but who had an excess of arrogance.[41]

The key question is who exactly are the *kafirs* on earth. The Qur'an used the term for those who rejected the Prophet's message, first in Mecca and then Medina.[42] Later Muslims extended it to all those who reject Islam after hearing "the invitation." Islam is such a universal and obvious truth, they assumed, "the only alternative to having Islamic faith is deliberate and perverse rejection of it."[43]

But there was something missing in this view: the gap between the Qur'an's immediate addressees and all other people. The gap is that, first, the Qur'an's immediate addressees knew the Prophet in person. Meccans used to called him al-Amin, or "The Trustworthy," so they should have known that he was no charlatan. But after his passing, the Prophet became a reported story, not a lived experience.

Similarly, the Qur'an's immediate addressees heard a Qur'an

that spoke in their own language, mindset, and context. Its impact is reflected in the famous conversion story of Umar, who was initially hostile to Islam but then heard a recitation, which blew him away. "My heart was softened and I wept," he later recalled, "and Islam entered into me."[44] Yet people from other languages and cultures don't always have the same connection with the Qur'an in their first encounter. Modern Western readers rather often find it "baffling."[45]

The Qur'an's moral imperative was also unmistakable in its own context. When it condemned female infanticide with powerful words, those who have gone through this horror must have been swept into tears. The same must be true for the Qur'an's compassion for orphans and slaves. Perhaps for this reason, the Qur'an conflated disbelief in God with the oppression of the weak. "Have you seen the person who denies the Judgment?" read one of the early suras. "It is he who pushes aside the orphan and does not urge others to feed the needy."[46]

But today, there are people in the world who "deny the Judgment," who don't believe in any religion, but who still help the orphans or the needy and do many other acts of charity. Also, unlike the Arab pagans who came close to killing all Muslims, these contemporary non-Muslims have nothing against Muslims. So what are we supposed to make of them?

One answer is to take the Qur'an's sharp dichotomy between good Muslims versus bad *kuffar* as a universal blueprint. However, on a careful read, the Qur'an itself mitigates that contrast. After condemning a group of Jews in Medina for their enmity, it adds, "but they are not all alike," that some of them do "good deeds" and "are among the righteous."[47] Similarly, it tells Muslims, "Do not take the Jews and Christians as allies," but then clarifies:

> God forbids you to take as allies those who have fought against you for your faith, driven you out of your homes, and helped others to drive you out. . . . [But] He does not forbid you to deal

kindly and justly with anyone who has not fought you for your faith or driven you out of your homes. God loves the just.[48]

What is even more striking is that the Qur'an does not limit salvation to its own believers. In two almost identical verses, it reads:

The [Muslim] believers, the Jews, the Christians, and the Sabians—all those who believe in God and the Last Day and do good—will have their rewards with their Lord. No fear for them, nor will they grieve.[49]

The exact identity of the "Sabians" mentioned here has been "an unsolved Qur'anic problem."[50] The more important point is that the Qur'an explicitly mentions such non-Muslim communities only to promise them a place in heaven. It is a strikingly universalist view.

However, the post-Qur'anic Muslim tradition got rid of this universalism with its usual method of getting rid of inconvenient verses: abrogation.[51] The verse above was deemed to be canceled out by another one: "If anyone seeks a religion other than Islam, it will not be accepted from him."[52] But the "Islam" here could mean merely "submission" to God, covering all manifestations of monotheism, as some of the earliest exegetes, such as Ibn Abbas (d. 687), thought.[53] Similarly, al-Razi understood this "Islam" as "an active approach on the part of the individual" toward God, and not a "group reference."[54] Only later scholars, beginning with Ibn Kathir (d. 1373), began to define it as "the specific, historical path of Muhammad."[55]

Before the consolidation of this later orthodoxy, there were also Muslims who asked the inescapable question: If Christians, Jews, and others preserved their religion, while learning about Islam but still not being convinced by it, why would God punish them for their sincere beliefs? Mu'tazila scholar al-Jahiz probed this question, and concluded that such non-Muslims must be "excusable." But al-Ghazali, while admitting that this argument rationally makes sense, still rejected it with references to the reported Sunna. Non-Muslims who keep refusing Islam, he concluded, deserve the wrath of God in the afterlife, and the wrath of Muslims in this life.[56]

In the modern era, an array of scholars—such as Musa Jarullah Bigiev, Hasan Askari, Mohammed Arkoun, Mahmoud Ayoub, Farid Esack, Abdulaziz Sachedina, and Seyyed Hossein Nasr—have questioned this "salvific exclusivism" in traditional Islam with arguments based on the Qur'an and also common sense. Others, such as Pakistani scholar Javed Ahmad Ghamidi or the Indonesian organization Nahdlatul Ulama, also called on Muslims to stop using the term *kafir* for all non-Muslims. In return, they are typically blamed by Islamists for groveling to non-Muslims and "selling out" the truth to Islam. What these exclusivists never consider is that their own passion to be the only saved religion—just like the passion to be the only "saved sect"—may reflect a *hawa,* or "whimsical desire," that they typically ascribe to others.

THE RINGS OF NATHAN THE WISE

In all these matters of religious difference and dispute, there is a key passage in the Qur'anic sura "Ma'ida" which may guide us. It begins by presenting a short history of monotheism, telling how God sent other messengers before, such as Moses and Jesus. Then it calls on the Jews to follow the Torah, and the Christians to follow the Gospel—not to convert to Islam. Then it says:

> We have assigned a law and a path to each of you. If God had so willed, He would have made you one community, but He wanted to test you through that which He has given you, so compete in doing good. You will all return to God and He will make clear to you the matters you differed about.[57]

In other words, the religious diversity on earth is not a problem to be solved, but rather an ideal "willed" by God, and what befalls on us is an unmistakably Murji'ite disposition: we should know that God will say the last word on matters on which we differ. Until we hear from Him, in the afterlife, we should compete in "doing good"—which means all people, not just Muslims, can do good.

And this—the Murji'ite disposition—is the Islamic basis for tolerance. It doesn't mean that Muslims should not have religious or moral convictions, by which they may disagree with other people or even disapprove of them. Toleration does not mean evaporation of all difference. But toleration does mean that we should be humble in our judgments, because the ultimate judgment belongs to God. It also means that, beyond our differences, we have a common humanity that connects us.

As we have seen in this chapter, this idea, this Murji'ite disposition, has helped us Muslims, throughout our history, to secure peaceful coexistence. Meanwhile, its absence brought upon us many horrors, from the sword-wielding Kharijites of the first century, to the mosque-bombing jihadists of the more recent past.

Quite remarkably, the same idea also helped the Europeans. Their history of religious conflict was in fact worse than ours, but they found solace in the Enlightenment, thanks to the ideas of thinkers such as Gotthold Ephraim Lessing (d. 1781). The latter's famous play *Nathan the Wise* was a powerful plea for religious tolerance, articulated in the parable of the three rings. Accordingly, the three great Abrahamic religions were like three valuable rings. Only one of them was authentic, but the people who wore them would not be able to tell which one, until God—"the Arbiter"— reveals the truth in the afterlife. "Absolute truth," therefore, was "the prerogative of God alone . . . unattainable by man." Hence man's duty was to "strive towards the truth, in concert with the rest of humanity."[58]

I have not yet seen anyone who noticed the remarkable

resemblance between these themes in Lessing's *Nathan the Wise* and the theology of Murji'ites. Most probably, Lessing himself didn't know anything about his Muslim predecessors. It just seems that good ideas can appear in different traditions, intuitively and independently, as well as the bad ones.

So perhaps, we can add Nathan the Wise, a symbol of tolerance, to our hall of fame, which we opened many chapters ago with Hayy ibn Yaqzan, a symbol of reason. It is a hall that also includes Ibn Rushd, the West's Averroes, as well as many other aforementioned Muslim minds who championed reason, freedom, or tolerance— sometimes at the expense of their lives. They remind us that we Muslims don't have a shortage of good ideas and good values. But, unfortunately, we forgot or ignored some of them, only at our own peril. Long past is the time to wake up, to remember the wisdoms of the past, and to begin to imagine a brighter future.

EPILOGUE

Throughout this book, I have highlighted certain strains from the formative centuries of Islam—such as the Mu'tazila, the *falasifa* (philosophers), and the Murji'a. I argued that they had some significant ideas that the mainstream tradition marginalized or silenced.

This doesn't mean that the opposite should have taken place—that what became the mainstream tradition had to be suppressed. No, not at all. We Muslims should have rather preserved a plurality of ideas, so these different strains could keep debating, to learn from each other and also to refine themselves.

What disallowed this plurality, as I have shown, was political power. It favored what it found helpful and suppressed what it found unhelpful. It was history's curse over our religion that many of us wrongly saw as a blessing.

Therefore, the remedy we need today is not more political intrusion into Islam, but, rather, less. It is not the suppression of the Salafis, Islamists, and rigid conservatives that I have criticized—but the suppression of no one.

The Murji'a vision is important here, for it gives us a basis for that plurality, to coexist with our differences while "postponing" the ultimate verdicts to God.

The Muʿtazila vision is also important, for it reminds us that God blessed us with not just revelation but also reason. The latter can't discover all metaphysical truths, but it can have a sense of earthly ones—such as what is morally "good" and "bad." On that basis, we can reinterpret revelation and reform our tradition.

And the *falasifa* vision is important, for it reminds us that we should be open to all the intellectual achievements of humanity. For Ibn Rushd, that meant studying Aristotle and other "ancients." For us, it would also mean studying all the diverse sciences, philosophies, and disciplines of the moderns.

But why, you may ask, do we need to reopen such long-closed doors, which may only disrupt our peaceful minds?

Because, as a fourteen-century-old *umma,* we have come to a dead end.

Islam is not the powerful, creative, sophisticated, beautiful civilization that it once was. Quite the contrary; today our lands are among the most underdeveloped places in the world. Our wealth is scarce—unless it comes effortlessly from oil—as well as our science, knowledge, justice, and freedom. We are suppressed by authoritarian regimes, whose triumphant rivals often turn out to be new disappointments. We are also torn by hateful divisions and violent conflicts, not to mention the extremists who do unspeakable evils in our name.

Certainly outside powers—colonialists and imperialists—have a share in the making of this modern Muslim crisis. But that is often all we want to hear and see. We don't want to focus on the only thing we can change: our own behavior, our own mindset, our own worldview.

In fact, precisely because of our crisis and the way we interpret it, some of us have become even more resistant to change. The late Fazlur Rahman, who wisely called for "a critical study of our intellectual Islamic past," had spotted the problem well: "Owing to a peculiar psychological complex we have developed vis-à-vis the

West," he wrote back in 1982, "we have come to defend that past as though it were our God."[1]

Today, almost four decades later, it is past time to get over this complex and, frankly, face our challenges.

Here is the core challenge: When Islam appeared in world history, it was a liberating force. We all take pride in that, noting how the Qur'an ended infanticide, uplifted women and slaves, and healed tribal bigotries. It marked a major moral progress in human history, which could be appreciated by all well-meaning human beings.

One of them was Rose Wilder Lane, an American libertarian writer, who saw the birth of Islam as a major step forward in "man's struggle against authority." Islam, she wrote back in 1943, saved Arabs from "pagan gods," only to declare, "men are equal and free." Islam also built a "tolerant" and "humane" civilization, she added, with unmatched "religious freedom."[2]

Yet, today, who would really see Islam as such a liberating force in the contemporary world? Besides its spirituality—which still does inspire and attract souls—to many people in the world, our religion rather connotes violence, oppression, intolerance, or patriarchy. And while the propaganda of ill-meaning people whom we call the Islamophobes have a role in this grim image, it is not totally baseless.

So how are we supposed to address this stark gap between early Islam, in its context, and contemporary Islam, in its own context?

"If they don't like our religion as it is, they can go to hell." That is, in a nutshell, what our fiery Islamists and rigid conservatives are thinking. For them, the gap between our received tradition and the modern human conscience only marks the latter's deviance. And strictly upholding the tradition proves their own righteousness.

Yet, alas, this insularity will only help relegate Islam to a tribal religion—of those who happen to be Muslims—with nothing else to say to humanity. It will also entrap us deeper in our dead end.

As an ordinary Muslim who is concerned with this crisis—and who has been trying to do something about it, rightly or wrongly, for about three decades—I think it is time for us to begin thinking anew. To reopen our minds. To embrace more reason, freedom, and tolerance.

ACKNOWLEDGMENTS

This book was written in a time span of two years, but it was also constructed through an intellectual and spiritual journey of three decades. The number of people whom I must thank for their contributions to this journey is absolutely huge; so, I've had to limit my acknowledgments to only the most recent ones.

First of all, I would like to thank all my colleagues at the Cato Institute, especially Peter Goettler, David Boaz, and Ian Vasquez, who have given me a safe harbor in Washington, D.C., to work on the key issues of Islam and modernity at a time when the world I used to know turned increasingly bleak. That gratitude also goes to the generous donors of the Cato Institute, enabling its principled and unwavering defense of human freedom since 1977.

Then I would like to thank my editor at St. Martin's Essentials, Joel Fotinos, along with Gwen Hawks, and my copy editor, Kate Davis, in addition to my literary agents, Jeff Gerecke and Diana Finch, for making this book possible. I would also like to thank my editors at *The New York Times* over the years—Sasha Polakow-Suranky, Max Strasser, Marc Charney, and Basharat Peer—for giving me the opportunity to share snippets from some of the ideas in this book with a broader audience around the world.

There are many other colleagues and friends to whom I am grateful. They include Thomas Cushman, Caryn Sowa, Simon Grote, and others at Wellesley College, where I spent three semesters in 2017 and early 2018, making a great use of its rich intellectual resources. They include Rev. Robert A. Sirico and Kris A. Mauren of the Acton Institute, which offered me the platform to speak about Islam and liberty on many occasions. Others graciously took the time to read my manuscript and made extremely helpful suggestions. They include Asma Afsaruddin, Yahya Alshamy, Afzal Amin, Mariam Attar, Asma Barlas, Charles Butterworth, Martino Diez, Khaled Abou Fadl, Hillel Fradkin, Usama Hasan, Phillip Holt, David L. Johnston, Enes Karić, Julianne Kelly, Ahmet Kuru, İsmail Kurun, Jack Miles, Ebrahim Moosa, and Gabriel Said Reynolds. Others kindly helped my research by finding and sharing helpful information or insights. They include Nejla Asimovic, Mehmet Evkuran, Nidhal Guessoum, Özgür Koca, Mirnes Kovac, Suleiman A. Mourad, Katherin Rogers, and Noah Feldman.

Then there are people closer to my heart. I am forever indebted to my parents, Taha and Tülin Akyol, who gave me all the love and support a son can dream of, supported all my good endeavors, and also forgave my mistaken ones. The intellectual depth and moral integrity of my father, Taha Akyol, has been my guiding light for decades, as it will remain forever. My young brother Ertugrul has always offered inspiring insights and brought much-needed laughs.

Then there is my own little family. My two beloved little sons, Levent Taha (5) and Efe Rauf (3), can't read this book yet, but I hope they will attentively do so in the future. They are already in it, in Chapter 3, with a theological insight they helped me elucidate, in addition to all the amazing emotions they instilled in my heart. I love them dearly. May God protect them—and, who knows, siblings who may join them in the future.

Finally, the greatest praise should go to my beloved wife, Riada Asimovic Akyol, who is the biggest supporter of my professional work. She has helped me immensely with this book, with her remarkable research skills, her sharp eye for nuances, her incomparably high emotional intelligence. More important, she has also been a wonderful companion and partner in our life together, which has included many joys and blessings, but also unexpected disappointments and extraordinary anxieties. I look forward to continue supporting her own inspiring intellectual journey and her fascinating work on "dignified resilience."

Ultimately, I am thankful to God, to whom we all owe our existence, as I believe. Personally, I held on to His "firmest handhold" decades ago, to falter at times, but never to fall. I hope to keep holding and striving, as long as He keeps granting me this miracle that we call life.

NOTES

Unless stated otherwise, all quotes from the Qur'an in this book are from: M. A. S. Abdel Haleem, *The Qur'an: A New Translation* (Oxford: Oxford World Classics, 2004).

INTRODUCTION

1. Mariam Mokhtar, "Mustafa Akyol Checks Out and Leaves Hotel California," *Malaysiakini,* October 1, 2017.
2. The event titled "Does Freedom of Conscience Open the Floodgate to Apostasy?" was organized by the Islamic Renaissance Front and was hosted by the Royal Selangor Golf Club in Kuala Lumpur on September 24, 2017. I was the main presenter, along with three interveners, most of whom defended the more conservative view on apostasy. All the videos are available at https://www.libertv.net/video/1538/discussion-on-does-freedom-of-conscience-open-the-floodgate-to-apostasy-part-2/1540/.
3. Ramizah Wan Muhammad, "Counseling the Apostates in Selangor: An Overview," *Malaysian Online Journal of Counseling* 3, no. 1 (July 2016): 1, 7.
4. Qur'an, 2:256.
5. In 2013, a Malaysian court gave a bizarre decision: A Catholic newspaper in that country, named the *Herald,* would not be allowed to use the word "Allah" to refer to God. The court's logic was that when Christians pray to "Allah," Muslims get "confused." I had criticized this decision in my column. Mustafa Akyol, "'Allah' Has No Copyright," *Hurriyet Daily News,*

October 19, 2013, http://www.hurriyetdailynews.com/opinion/mustafa -akyol/allah-has-no-copyright-56452.

6. Kamles Kumar, "DPM: Mustafa Akyol's Book Banned for Opposing 'Societal Norms,'" *Malay Mail*, October 6, 2017.

7. The Malay edition of my book is still available for free download at: https://www.cato.org/blog/free-download-banned-malay-edition-islam -without-extremes.

8. Qur'an 2:256.

9. The Saudi-published translation that also "edits" the "no compulsion in religion" clause is what is commonly known as the *Saheeh International*. In the beginning of Baqara 256, it says, "There shall be no compulsion in [acceptance of] the religion." *Translation of the Meaning of the Qur'an*, trans. Saheeh International (Jeddah, Saudi Arabia: Abul-Qasim Publishing House, 1997), 38.

10. This English translation of Qur'an 2:256 is taken from the official website of JAKIM, or the Department of Islamic Advancement of Malaysia, the main official Islamic body of the country. Accessed September 12, 2018 at http://www.islam.gov.my/en/e-jakim/e-quran/al-quran-translation.

11. For more on the interpretations of Qur'an 2:256, see Patricia Crone's "No Pressure, Then: Religious Freedom in Islam," Open Democracy, https://www.opendemocracy.net/en/no-compulsion-in-religion, November 7, 2009. One of the classic sources that declared 2:256 as "abrogated" is al-Wahidi's *Asbab al-Nuzul*. After quoting "no compulsion in religion," he writes, "This was before the Messenger of Allah, Allah bless him and give him peace, was commanded to fight the people of the Book. But then Allah's saying (There is no compulsion in religion . . .) was abrogated and the Prophet was commanded to fight the people of the Book in Surah Repentance." Al-Wahidi, *Asbab al-Nuzul*, (Amman, Jordan: Royal Aal al-Bayt Institute for Islamic Thought, 2008), 25.

12. This view is reportedly from al-Alusi. *Taberi Tefsiri*, trans. and commentary by Kerim Aytekin, Hasan Karakaya, (Istanbul: Hisar Yayınevi, 1996), vol 2, p. 114.

13. This famous hadith exists in the most authoritative hadith collection in Sunni Islam: the 9-volume *Sahih al-Bukhari*, vol. 9, "Book of Dealing with Apostates," hadith 57. (Translation by Muhammad Muhsin Khan, Riyadh: Darussalam, 1994, fully available online at sunnah.com). It also exists in another authoritative hadith collection, *Sunan an-Nasaa'i*, vol. 5, "Book of Fighting" ["The Prohibition of Bloodshed"], hadith 4065 (Translated by Nasiruddin al-Khattab, Riyadh: Darussalam, 2007, fully available at sunnah.com.)

14. The main study one should refer to here is the survey titled *The World's Muslims: Religion, Politics and Society,* published in 2013 by the Pew Research Center in Washington, D.C. The study found that the Muslims who favor making Sharia the law of the land made up 86 percent of the Muslims in Malaysia, 74 percent of those in Egypt, and 84 percent in Pakistan. Among these, those who also favored the execution of apostates made up 62 percent in Malaysia, 86 percent in Egypt, and 76 percent in Pakistan. Muslim societies in South East Europe and Central Asia, who live under secular states, presented lower numbers for both the demand for Sharia as the law of the land and support for its harsh measures, such as the execution of apostates or the stoning of adulterers. See http://www.pewforum.org/2013/04/30/the-worlds-muslims-religion-politics-society-beliefs-about-sharia.

15. Daniel Philpott, a Catholic scholar, offers a good example of that fair-and-balanced approach in his book *Religious Freedom in Islam: The Fate of a Universal Human Right in the Muslim World Today* (New York: Oxford University Press, 1999).

16. Bodin's remarks about Ottoman tolerance are quoted in Daniel Goffman's *The Ottoman Empire and Early Modern Europe* (Cambridge: Cambridge University Press, 2002), 111.

17. See Christopher de Bellaigue, *The Islamic Enlightenment: The Struggle Between Faith and Reason, 1798 to Modern Times* (New York: Liveright Publishing, 2017).

18. Ibid., chap. 6.

CHAPTER 1: A SELF-MADE MAN: HAYY IBN YAQZAN

1. G. A. Russell, ed., *The 'Arabick' Interest of the Natural Philosophers in Seventeenth-Century England*, vol. 47 of *Brill's Studies in Intellectual History* (Leiden: Brill, 1994), 226–27. See also Tom Verde, "Hayy Was Here, Robinson Crusoe," *Aramco World Magazine* 65, no. 3 (May/June 2014).

2. Giovanni Pico della Mirandola had discovered the Hebrew version of *Hayy ibn Yaqzan* two centuries before its publication in Oxford and translated it into Latin for his own use, as Hayy's story was "of great importance" to him. See Francesco Borghesi, Michael Papio, and Massimo Riva, eds., *Pico della Mirandola: Oration on the Dignity of Man: A New Translation and Commentary* (Cambridge: Cambridge University Press, 2012), 207. It is also interesting to note how Mirandola begins the *Oration on the Dignity of Man*: "Most esteemed Fathers, I have read in the ancient

writings of the Arabians that Abdala the Saracen on being asked what, on this stage, so to say, of the world, seemed to him most evocative of wonder, replied that there was nothing to be seen more marvelous than man." The identity of this "Abdala the Saracen," or Abdullah the Muslim, has remained unclear, and various hypotheses have been formulated around the question. See ibid., p. 109.

3. Avner Ben-Zaken, *Reading Hayy Ibn-Yaqzan: A Cross-Cultural History of Autodidacticism* (Baltimore: Johns Hopkins University Press, 2011).

4. Samar Attar, *The Vital Roots of European Enlightenment: Ibn Tufayl's Influence on Modern Western Thought* (Plymouth, UK: Lexington Books, 2007), 19–36.

5. All quotations in this chapter from *Hayy ibn Yaqzan* are from the 1708 translation by Simon Ockley, only with minor editing regarding the capitalization of nouns, which was common in the text. Simon Ockley, *The Improvement of Human Reason: Exhibited in the Life of Hai Ebn Yokdhan* (London: Edm. Powell, 1708).

6. In the Qur'an, "the story of Adam's two sons" are narrated, without mentioning their names (5:27-31). When one of them kills the other out of jealousy, God sends a raven "to show him how to hide his brother's naked corpse" (5:31).

7. The comment is from Baron Carra de Vaux (1867–1953), quoted in A. J. Arberry, *Oriental Essays* (Abingdon, UK: Routledge, 1996), 20.

8. That description of Hayy's epistemological state is from Nadja Germann, "Natural and Revealed Religion," in *The Routledge Companion to Islamic Philosophy*, eds. Richard C. Taylor and Luis Xavier López-Farjeat (Abingdon, UK: Taylor & Francis, 2016), 349.

9. Ockley, trans., *Hayy ibn Yaqzan*, 131.

10. See Ibn Tufayl, *Hayy ibn Yaqzan: A Philosophical Tale,* trans. Lenn Evan Goodman (Chicago: University of Chicago Press, 2009).

11. A. J. Arberry, *Oriental Essays: Portraits of Seven Scholars* (Wiltshire, UK: George Allen & Unwin, 1960), 21.

12. Robert Barclay, *An Apology for the True Christian Divinity: Being an Explanation and Vindication of the Principles and Doctrines of the People Called Quakers* (Birmingham, UK: John Baskerville, 1765), 161.

13. For more on the theological parallels between *Hayy ibn Yaqzan* and Quakerism, see Dan Randazzo and David Russell, "Andalusian Mysticism and Liberal Quakerism?: Bringing *Hayy ibn Yaqzan* and Rufus Jones into Dialogue" (paper presented at the American Academy of Religion 2014 convention, Quaker Studies and Mysticism Group).

14. Conservative Quakers of America, "What Do Friends Mean by the Inward Light?," http://www.quaker.us/inwardlight.html. Accessed June 25, 2020.

15. The quote and the information about the omission of *Hayy ibn Yaqzan* from the later editions of the *Apology* are from: *Quakeriana* (London: Edward Hicks, 1894), 1:108.

CHAPTER 2: WHY THEOLOGY MATTERS

1. Wael B. Hallaq, *A History of Islamic Legal Theories* (Cambridge: Cambridge University Press, 1997), 59.

2. Shaikhul Hadith Mufti Abu Nauman Abdur Raheem, "Ash'ari and Maturidi Aqeeda Explanation," Hanafi Fiqh Channel, January 14, 2012, https://www.youtube.com/watch?v=mexorUrcyc8.

3. Abdullah Saeed, *Islamic Thought: An Introduction* (Abingdon, UK: Routledge, 2006), 71.

4. The term "legal culture" is from Hallaq, *History of Islamic Legal Theories*, 209. The phrase "proper behavior rather than proper belief" is from Suleiman Ali Mourad, "Theology: Freewill and Predestination," in *The Islamic World*, ed. Andrew Rippin (Abingdon, UK: Routledge, 2008), 188.

5. Qur'an, 78:37, 16:43.

6. Montgomery Watt, *The Formative Period of Islamic Thought*, (Chicago: Edinburgh University Press, 1973), 88.

7. Ziauddin Ahmed, "A Survey of the Development of Theology In Islam," *Islamic Studies* 11, no. 2 (June 1972): 97.

8. The term *qadar* comes with certain confusion, as both sides of the controversy used the term, either to defend God's "decree" or the human "power." See Suleiman Ali Mourad, *Early Islam Between Myth and History: Al-Ḥasan Al-Baṣrī (d. 110H/728CE)* (Leiden: Brill, 2006]), 162.

9. The translation of the correspondence between Hasan al-Basri and Caliph Abd al-Malik is from "The Caliph and the Ascetic," *Oasis Magazine* 13, no. 26 (December 2017).

10. Ibid.

11. Michael Schwarz, "The Letter of al-Hasan al-Baṣrī," *Oriens* 20 (1967): 15.

12. The authenticity of the letter is a disputed but unresolved matter. For an evaluation, see Feryal Salem, "Freewill, Qadar, and Kasb in the Epistle of Hasan al-Basri to Abd al-Malik," *Muslim World* 104, no. 1–2 (January/April 2014): 198–219.

13. Steven C. Judd, "Ghaylan al-Dimashqi: The Isolation of a Heretic in Islamic Historiography," *International Journal of Middle East Studies* 31, no. 2 (May 1999): 162.

14. Ibid., 169.

15. From al-Qadi Abd al-Jabbar, *Tabaqat al-Mu'tazilah*, Cairo, date unknown, 334, quoted here from Samuel Hosain, Lamarti, "The Development of Apostasy and Punishment Law In Islam" (PhD thesis, Glasgow University, 2002), 183.

16. Schwarz, "Letter of al-Hasan al-Baṣrī," 29.

17. Mourad, "Theology: Freewill and Predestination," 183.

18. Andrew Rippin, *Muslims: Their Religious Beliefs and Practices* (Abingdon, UK: Routledge, 2012), 77–78.

19. Ibid., 78.

20. This description of Ash'ari "acquisition," or *kasb*, is from David Burell, *Faith and Freedom: An Interfaith Perspective* (Malden, MA: Blackwell Publishing, 2004), 158.

21. For a good critique of the theory of *kasb*, or "acquisition," see Abd al-Jabbar's arguments in his *Mughi*, well summarized in Hazem Y. Salem's "Islamic Political Thought: Reviving a Rationalist Tradition" (PhD diss. University of Denver, 2013), 83–84, https://digitalcommons.du.edu/etd/915.

22. This also includes Saudi rulers referring to "fate" in the wake of deadly accidents in the holy city of Mecca during the Hajj, or "pilgrimage." See Mustafa Akyol, "Islam's Tragic Fatalism," *New York Times*, September 23, 2015. It also includes Islamist Turkish politicians' frequent references to "fate," in the wake of deadly accidents in mines or railroads, which could have been averted by more responsible, and less corrupt, management. See Özgür Korkmaz, "The Unbearable Easiness of Getting Killed in Turkey," *Hurriyet Daily News*, September 4, 2014.

23. As'ad Abu Khalil, "Al-Jabriyyah in the Political Discourse of Jamal 'Abd al-Nasir and Saddam Husayn: The Rationalization of Defeat," *Muslim World* 84, no. 3–4 (July–October 1994): 240.

24. Ibid., p. 247.

25. Ibid.

26. Quoted in Mourad, "Theology: Freewill and Predestination," p. 189.

27. Some have also suggested that the "withdrawal" originally referred to a nonpartisan stance in the face of the bitter political conflicts over the caliphate, similar to that of the Murji'ites. See Mariam al-Attar, "Metaethics: A Quest for an Epistemological Basis of Morality in Classical Islamic Thought," *Journal of Islamic Ethics* 1, (2017): 44–45.

28. Sophia Vasalou, *Moral Agents and Their Deserts: The Character of Mu'tazilite Ethics* (Princeton, NJ: Princeton University Press, 2008), 5.
29. Ibid.
30. Abu'l-Qāsim al-Balkhī *Maqālāt al-Islāmiyyīn*, in *Fadl al-I'tizal watabaqāt al-Mu'tazila*, ed. Ayman Fuad Sayyid (Tunis: Al-Dar al-Tunisiyya lil Nashr, 1974), 63–64, quoted in Vasalou, *Moral Agents,* 2–3.
31. In precise Arabic terms, the Ash'arites held that "the Sharia establishes and indicates" morality (*al-shar' muthabbit wa mubayyin*), whereas the Mu'tazila held that revelation "indicates but does not establish" them (*al-waḥy mubayyin lā muthabbit*). Al-Attar, "Meta-ethics," 39.
32. See Qur'an, 3:7.
33. In fact, there is an argument that the Muslim controversy over the nature of the Qur'an was provoked by the Christian belief in the preexistence of Logos. See Mustafa Akyol, *The Islamic Jesus* (New York: St. Martin's Press, 2017), 159–60.
34. Watt, *Formative Period,* 96. Another definition and an unsurprising critique of *tafwid* is offered by Ayatollah Khomeini in his book *Forty Hadith*: "It means that God, the Exalted, has *na'udhubillah* [God forbid], dissociated Himself in some respect from making any kind of dispositions in the world," resulting in "total human freedom." Ayatollah Kohmeini, *Forty Hadith* (Scotts Valley, CA: CreateSpace Independent Publishing Platform 2014), 448.
35. Lenn Goodman, *Islamic Humanism* (New York: Oxford University Press, 2005), 97.
36. In the words of Walter C. Klein: "It was not among irreverent *zindiqs* (dualists, atheists) or *mulhids* (enemies of religion) that the Mu'tazilite movement began, but among persons of uncommon piety. In Islam the Mu'tazilah were called 'the people of justice and unity,' 'the people of the promise and the threat.' European writers have applied the names 'freethinkers' and 'rationalists' to them. Such designations are hardly admissible without considerable reservation and qualification. At their best they were broad churchmen, who tried to make peace between revelation and reason and maintained the unity of God and His justice in this world and the next against what really seemed to them unworthy beliefs." Walter C. Klein, *Abu'l-Hasan Ali Ibn Ismail al-Ash'ari's Al-Ibanah 'an Usul ad-Diyanah,* [The Elucidation of Islam's Foundation] trans. Walter Conrad Klein, American Oriental Society (New York: Kraus, 1967), 22–23.
37. This definition is from George Hourani, *Reason and Tradition in Islamic Ethics* (Cambridge: Cambridge University Press, 2007), 94.

38. See Violet Moller, *The Map of Knowledge: A Thousand-Year History of How Classical Ideas Were Lost and Found* (New York: Doubleday, 2019), 68–75.

39. For a more detailed discussion of the *mihna*, see my earlier book, *Islam Without Extremes: A Muslim Case for Liberty* (New York: W. W Norton, 2011), 109–10. Recent scholarship has found little indication that the Mu'tazila, as a group, were involved in the *mihna*, which appears to have been an effort at establishing caliphal dominance over all doctrinal schools. See John A. Nawas, "A Reexamination of Three Current Explanations for al-Ma'mun Introduction of the Mihna," *International Journal of Middle East Studies* 26, no. 4 (November 1994); Christopher Melchert, "The Adversaries of Aḥmad Ibn Ḥanbal," *Arabica* 44, no. 2 (April 1997); Muhammad Qasim Zaman, *Religion and Politics Under the Early 'Abbāsids: The Emergence of the Proto-Sunnī Elite*, vol. 16 (Leiden: Brill, 1971); Ulrich Haarmann and Wadad Kadi, *Islamic History and Civilization: Studies and Texts* (Leiden: Brill, 1997).

40. Alfred L. Ivry, *Al-Kindi's Metaphysics: A Translation of Ya'qub ibn Ishaq al-Kindi's Treatise "On First Philosophy"* (Albany, NY: SUNY Press, 1974), 58.

41. Majid Fakhry, *Islamic Occasionalism: And its Critique by Averroës and Aquinas* (New York: Routledge, 1958), 24.

42. Ibn Hanbal, *Musnad*, ed. A. M Shakir, Cairo: Dar al-Ma'arif, 1954, volume 5, page 68, quoted in Mourad, "Theology: Freewill and Predestination," 182. Thanks to Dr. Mourad for confirming the translation of the hadith also in personal correspondence.

43. Klein, *Abu'l-Hasan Ali Ibn Ismail al-Ash'ari's Al-Ibanah* 49.

44. P. M. Holt, Ann K. S. Lambton, and Bernard Lewis, eds., *The Cambridge History of Islam*, vol. 2B, Islamic Society and Civilization (Cambridge: Cambridge University Press, 1970), 594.

45. Imran Aijaz, *Islam: A Contemporary Philosophical Investigation* (Abingdon, UK: Routledge, 2018), 2–10.

46. Shabbir Akhtar, "The Dialogue of Islam and the World Faiths," in *Philosophy Bridging the World Religions*, ed. Peter Koslowski (Dordrecht, Netherlands: Springer Science & Business Media, 2003), 27.

47. Hourani, *Reason and Tradition*, 271–73.

48. Mawdudi, *Tanqihat*, 87, trans. and quoted in Yohanan Friedmann, "Quasi-Rational and Anti-Rational Elements in Radical Muslim Thought: The Case of Abū al-A'lā Mawdūdī," in *Rationalization in Religions: Judaism, Christianity and Islam*, eds. Yohanan Friedmann and Christoph Markschies (Berlin and Boston: Walter de Gruyter GmbH, 2019), 297.

49. Ibid., 297–98.

50. The quote here is from a lecture titled "Understanding The Traditions of The Signs of Judgement Day," by Dr. Yasir Qadhi, a popular Muslim scholar and preacher based in the Al-Maghrib Institute in Texas. (Accessed on June 25, 2020: https://www.youtube.com/watch?v=1W6zHsyoBxc&feature=youtu.be). Granted, the phrase "We hear and we obey" is from the Qur'an (24:51), however early Muslims had the privilege of hearing divine or prophetic commands that came explicitly to guide their lived experience. Any experience after that has to use an interpretative lens, even if it assumes that it is not doing so. See also chapter 10.

CHAPTER 3: ISLAM'S "EUTHYPHRO DILEMMA"

1. Khaled Abou El Fadl, "Islam and the Challenge of Democracy," *Boston Review* 28, no. 2 (April/ May 2003): 21.
2. Research has shown that an "authoritarian" parent "who issues directives, expects children to obey and sometimes hits those who don't," do worse in parenting than "authoritative" ones who "use reasoning to persuade kids to do things that are good for them" and who emphasize "adaptability, problem-solving and independence." See Pamela Druckerman, "The Bad News About Helicopter Parenting: It Works," *New York Times*, February 7, 2019.
3. S. Marc Cohen, "Socrates on the Definition of Piety," *Journal of the History of Philosophy*, vol 9:1, 1971, 2.
4. Quoted in William J. Wainwright, *Religion and Morality* (Abingdon, UK: Routledge, 2005), 74.
5. St. Thomas Aquinas, *On the Truth of the Catholic Faith,* trans. Anton C. Pegis (New York: Image Books, 1955), 1:62.
6. Roger Crisp, *The Oxford Handbook of the History of Ethics* (Oxford: Oxford University Press, 2013), 322–23.
7. John Locke, *An Essay Concerning Human Understanding: And a Treatise on the Conduct of the Understanding* (Philadelphia: Hayes & Zell Publishers, 1856), bk. 2, chap. 21, sec. 49, p. 166. In fact, there has been a scholarly dispute on whether Locke was in favor of voluntarism or intellectualism. I agree with Raghuveer Singh, who thinks that Locke was primarily an intellectualist. See "John Locke and the Theory of Natural Law," *Political Studies* IX, no. 2 (1961): 105–118.
8. Charles de Secondat Baron de Montesquieu, *The Spirit of Laws,* trans. Thomas Nugent (London: F. Wingrave, 1793), 1–2.
9. Quoted in Ayman Shihadeh, *The Teleological Ethics of Fakhr al-Din al-Razi* (Leiden: Brill, 2006), 77.

10. Hourani, *Reason and Tradition in Islamic Ethics* (Cambridge: Cambridge University Press, 2007), 18.

11. Quoted in David J. Theroux, "C. S. Lewis on Mere Liberty and the Evils of Statism," in *Culture and Civilization: Globalism,* ed. Irving Louis Horowitz (New Brunswick, NJ: Transaction Publishers, 2011), 197.

12. Anver M. Emon, "Natural Law and Natural Rights in Islamic Law," *Journal of Law and Religion* 20, no. 2 (2004–2005): 351–95.

13. Mariam al-Attar, "Meta-ethics: A Quest for an Epistemological Basis of Morality in Classical Islamic Thought," *Journal of Islamic Ethics* 1, (2017): 30.

14. Quoted in ibid., p. 111.

15. Quoted in ibid., p. 118.

16. Richard M. Frank, "Moral Obligation in Classical Muslim Theology," *Journal of Religious Ethics* 11, no. 2 (Fall 1983): 208.

17. Ibid., 209.

18. Bāqillānī, *Taqrīb,* 1:253, quoted here from Mairaj Uddin Syed, "Coercion in Classical Islamic Law and Theology" (Phd diss., Princeton University, Department of Religion, 2011), 139.

19. Frank, "Moral Obligation," 210.

20. Mariam al-Attar, *Islamic Ethics: Divine Command Theory in Arabo-Islamic Thought* (Abingdon, UK: Routledge, 2010), 58.

21. In the words of a contemporary Sunni scholar, "Islamic paradigm demonstrates that the problem of evil is not truly a problem," because "God's Wisdom and Knowledge are incomprehensibly beyond our imagination." Sulciman Hani, "The Problem of Evil: A Multifaceted Islamic Solution," yaqeeninstitute.org, April 20, 2020.

22. This view was defended by none other than al-Ghazali. See Hourani, *Reason and Tradition,* 145.

23. Frithjof Schuon, "Dilemmas of Theological Speculation: With Special Reference to Moslem Scholasticism," *Studies in Comparative Religion* 3, no. 2 (Spring 1969): 2.

24. Fazlur Rahman, *Islam* (Chicago: Chicago University Press, 1966), 99.

25. Qur'an, 5:91, Pickthal translation. (Mohammed Marmaduke Pickthall, *The Meaning of the Glorious Koran,* Calcutta, India: Signet Press, 1953.)

26. Qur'an, 6:145, Shakir translation. (Mohammed Habib Shakir, *The Qur'an: Arabic Text and English Translation,* New York: Tahrike Tarsile Qur'an, 1993.)

27. Qur'an, 5:91, Pickthal translation.

28. Khaled Abou El Fadl, *Reasoning with God: Reclaiming Shari'ah in the Modern Age* (Lanham, MD: Rowman and Littlefield), 11–12. Mariam Attar also agrees that the Qur'an gives support of the idea of objective morality known through reason: "The Qur'an used a pre-existing language in

revealing the divine message. It used the particular concepts with their specific meanings and connotations, and addressed many ethical terms to pagans, such as ʿadl (justice), ẓulm (transgression), khayr (goodness), sharr (evil). Therefore, it used ethical terms in a way that people could understand. If good and evil deeds mentioned in verses such as (Q.16:90) 'Surely Allah enjoins the doing of justice and the doing of good (to others) and the giving to the kindred, and He forbids indecency and evil and rebellion; He admonishes you that you may be mindful,' (translation by Shakir 1983) meant only 'obedience to commands,' the whole sentence would be almost tautologous and pointless." Al-Attar, "Meta-ethics," 35.

29. A. Kevin Reinhart, "What We Know about Maʿrūf," *Journal of Islamic Ethics* 1 (2017): 61.
30. Ibid., 68.
31. Ibid., 63.
32. Ahmad Kazemi Moussavi and Karim Douglas, *Facing One Qiblah: Legal and Doctrinal Aspects of Sunni and Shiʾah Muslims,* (Singapore: Pustaka Nasional Pte, 2005), 87–88. The term "Ahl al-Ahwa" is still common in Sunni popular literature. A Turkish Sunni site (http://www.ehlisunnetbuyukleri.com) defines it as those "who follow their inadequate reason."
33. Daniel Brown, "Islamic Ethics in Comparative Perspective," *Muslim World* 89, no. 2 (April 1999): 181–82.
34. Genesis 22:12, New International Version.
35. Ronald M. Green, "Abraham, Isaac, and The Jewish Tradition: An Ethical Reappraisal," *Journal of Religious Ethics* 10, no. 1 (Spring 1982): 1.
36. Robert Bretall, *A Kierkegaard Anthology* (Princeton, NJ: Princeton University Press, 1973), 134.
37. Immanuel Kant, *Religion Within the Boundary of Pure Reason* (Edinburgh: Thomas Clark, 1838), 253.
38. See Esra Yazicioglu, "Engaging with Abraham and His Knife," in *Interpreting Abraham: Journeys to Moriah,* eds. Bradley Beach and Matthew Powell (Minneapolis, MN: Fortress Press, 2014), 70.
39. Ibid.
40. Al-Jabbar's comment is from his *Mutashābih al-Qurān,* which is unfortunately lost. It comes to us thanks to the reporting by one of his immediate pupils, Abū al-Husayn, in his *Kitāb al-Muʿtamad fī Usūl al-Fiqh.* I owe this quote to Mariam al-Attar, who highlighted the importance of the Abraham story for ethical discussions in Islam in *Islamic Ethics: Divine Command Theory in Arabo-Islamic Thought* (Abingdon, UK: Routledge, 2010), 123.
41. See Asma Barlas, "Abraham's Sacrifice in the Qur'an: Beyond the Body," *Religion and the Body* 23 (2011): 59–60.

42. Margaretha T. Heemskerk, *Suffering in the Mu'tazilite Theology: Abd al-Jabbār's Teaching on Pain and Divine Justice* (Leiden: Brill, 2000), 53.

43. Ibn al-Arabi al-Maliki, once a student of al-Ghazali, chided the latter when he said, "Our master Abu Hamid al-Ghazali swallowed philosophy and then tried an emetic but failed to expurgate it." Ebrahim Moosa, *Ghazali and the Poetics of Imagination* (Chapel Hill: University of North Carolina Press, 2005), 171.

44. Ahmad Dallal, "Ghazali and the Perils of Interpretation," review of *Al-Ghazali and the Ash'arite School,* by Richard M. Frank, *Journal of the American Oriental Society* 122, no. 4 (October–December, 2002): 787.

45. For opposite interpretations of al-Ghazali, see Richard Frank, who sees him as departing from orthodox Ash'arism on causality, versus Michael Marmura, who rather sees him as an orthodox Ash'ari. Richard M. Frank, *Al-Ghazālī and the Ash'arite School* (Durham, NC: Duke University Press, 1994); Michael Marmura, "Ghazali and Ash'arism Revisited," *Arabic Sciences and Philosophy* 12 (2002): 91–110.

46. Al-Attar, "Meta-ethics," 30.

47. The term "eclectic" is from Ayman Shihadeh, *The Teleological Ethics of Fakhr al-Din al-Razi* (Leiden: Brill, 2006), 66. For al-Razi's "Universal Principle" on contradictions between reason and revelation, and a critique of it from a more textualist point of view, see Yasir Qadhi, "Reconciling Reason and Revelation in the Writings of Ibn Taymiyya (d. 728/1328)" (PhD diss., Yale University, 2013), 91–99, 197–206.

48. It is really interesting that while Ash'arism was born as a more reasonable version of Hanbalism, some later Hanbalis, such as Ibn Aqil, Ibn Taymiyya, or Ibn Qayyim, rejected the absolute voluntarism of Ash'arism and sought a middle position between that and Mu'tazilism, often thanks to the Qur'anic notion of *fitra,* or "human nature." See Sophia Vasalou, *Ibn Taymiyya's Theological Ethics* (New York: Oxford University Press, 2016), 21–33.

49. The questions on the Ash'ari and Maturidi creeds are paraphrased by Klein, *Abu'l-Hasan Ali Ibn Ismail al-Ash'ari's Al-Ibanah 'an Usul ad-Diyanah* [The Elucidation of Islam's Foundation], *American Oriental Society* (New York: Kraus, 1967), 37.

50. Fazlur Rahman, *Islam and Modernity: Transformation of an Intellectual Tradition* (Chicago: University of Chicago Press, 1984), 27.

51. Despite the fact that Ottoman Turks subscribed to the Hanafi school of jurisprudence, whose theological counterpart is Maturidism, in the initial centuries of the empire, "Ottoman theologians remained largely within the radius of Ash'arism," where a revived interest in Maturidism only emerged toward the end of the sixteenth century. Yahya Raad

Haidar, "The Debates Between Ash'arism and Māturīdism in Ottoman Religious Scholarship: A Historical and Bibliographical Study" (PhD thesis, Australian National University, 2016), iv.

52. Rahman, *Islam and Modernity*, 33.

53. Asim Cuneyd Koksal did not publish the full translation of the treaties, but an evaluation of them in two academic articles: "Osmanlılar'da Mukaddimât-ı Erbaa Literatürü," [The Ottoman Literature on the Four Premises] *Türkiye Araştırmaları Literatür Dergisi* 14, no. 27, (2016): 101–32; "İslâm Hukuk Felsefesinde Fiillerin Ahlâkîliği Meselesi—Mukaddimât-ı Erbaa'ya Giriş " [The moral dimensions of actions according to the philosophy of Islamic law: Introduction to the Four Premises], *İslam Araştırmaları Dergisi* 28 (2012) (İsam, Istanbul): 1–43.

54. The Pew Global Attitudes Project, *47-Nation Pew Global Attitudes Survey*, May 27, 2014, p. 33, https://www.pewresearch.org/wp-content/uploads/sites/2/2007/10/Pew-Global-Attitudes-Report-October-4-2007-REVISED-UPDATED-5-27-14.pdf.

CHAPTER 4: HOW WE LOST MORALITY

1. Amin Maalouf, *Doğu'dan Uzakta* (Turkish translation of the French novel *Les Désorientés*) (Istanbul: Yapı Kredi Yayınları, 2012), 242.

2. Matthew 23–25, New International Version. On how the criticisms Jesus posed to the religious orthodoxy of his time, as we learn from the New Testament gospels, are meaningful to Muslims today, see Mustafa Akyol, *The Islamic Jesus*, chap. 9, "What Jesus Can Teach Muslims Today," (New York: St. Martin's Press, 2017), 196–215.

3. The cultish group in question is the "Gülen Community," named after the US-based cleric it follows, Fethullah Gülen. While the apparent teachings of the group are filled with rosy messages of moderation, ample evidence, including statements by former members, shows that the group has carried out a long and covert operation to infiltrate strategic state institutions with many dirty tactics. For this, including their key role in the failed military coup attempt of June 2016, see Dexter Filkins, "Turkey's Thirty-Year Coup," *New Yorker*, October 17, 2016.

4. Mustafa Öztürk, "Dünyanın Tuzu Olmak" [Being the salt of the earth], *Karar*, January 7, 2017.

5. Mustafa Çağrıcı, "Ahlaksız Dindarlık Olur mu?" [Can there be 'immoral piety'?], *Karar*, January 25, 2017.

6. I have personally heard these hadiths used by various Islamic personalities in Turkey to justify unethical behavior while "at war" with the

forces of evil. In August 2018, a supporter of the ruling party used the purported hadith on social media to justify the self-serving date of the elections announced by the government.

7. A deputy of the ruling AKP made this argument on TV in January 2015. See https://www.demokrathaber.org/siyaset/akpli-vekilden-torpil -savunmasi-ayet-diyor-ki-akrabalarini-koru-kolla-h42846.html.

8. These changes took place under the first sixteen years of the incumbency of the Justice and Development Party (AKP). A critic, Turkish architect Dogan Hasol, jokingly suggested that under the AKP, tenders are not made according to the law, but the law is constantly remade according to tenders. "Kamu İhale Yasası 16 yılda 186 kez değişti, yasaya göre mi ihale, ihaleye göre mi yasa!," T24.com.tr website, May 28, 2018.

9. From Nasr Abu Zayd, "The Crisis of Islamic Discourse" (public lecture in Netherlands, 2009), https://www.youtube.com/watch?v=Dw6mukyd WLg&feature=youtu.be.

10. Ali Allawi, *The Crisis of the Islamic Civilization* (New Haven, CT: Yale University Press, 2009), xii.

11. Omar Edward Moad, "What Is Islamic Analytic Theology?," yaqeeninstitute.org, June 25, 2018, https://yaqeeninstitute.org/omar-edward-moad /what-is-islamic-analytic-theology/#.XegY1JNKgdU.

12. Ali Bardakoglu, "Ahlâkın Fıkıh Kuralları Arasında Buharlaşması" [Vaporization of morals among rules of jurisprudence], *Eskiyeni: A Journal of Social Sciences, 37* (Fall 2017): 90–92.

13. Ibid., 72.

14. Abdullah Saeed, *Islamic Banking and Interest: A Study of the Prohibition of Riba and Its Contemporary Interpretation* (Leiden: Brill, 1996), 38.

15. Saffet Köse, "Hiyel," *İslam Ansiklopedisi* (Istanbul: Türkiye Diyanet Vakfı, 1998), 18: 172.

16. Ali Bardakoglu, *İslam Işığında Müslümanlığımızla Yüzleşme* [Facing our Muslimhood in the light of Islam] (İstanbul: Kuramer Yayınları, 2017), 48. Trans. Mustafa Akyol from the Turkish original text.

17. Sherman A. Jackson, "The Alchemy of Domination? Some Ash'arite Responses to Mu'tazilite Ethics," *International Journal of Middle East Studies* 31, no. 2 (May 1999): 195.

18. Ibid., 195.

19. Ibid. I slightly reworded Sherman's original sentence for simplicity, by changing "one's" into "the."

20. "Is it permissible to shower while standing," Masjid-us-Sunnah, Nov 22, 2018; "Cutting Fingernails," Islamweb, fatwa no: 83722, Feb 6, 2002; "Performing Ghusl while standing," Islamweb, fatwa no: 91182, Feb 20,

2006; "Ruling of being naked before animals," Islamweb, fatwa no: 7605, Dec 24, 2012.

21. Masjid-us-Sunnah, "Is it permissible to urinate while standing? Is there any sunnah which forbids this?," http://www.masjidforyou.com/question-details.aspx?qstID=94.

22. *Sunan Ibn Majah*, "The Book of Purification and its Sunnah," hadith no: 307, narrated on the authority of Aisha. (Translated by Nasiruddin al-Khattab, Riyadh: Darussalam, 2007, fully available online at sunnah.com.)

23. Shabir Akhtar, *Islam as Political Religion: The Future of an Imperial Faith*, (Abingdon, UK: Routledge, 2010), 204.

24. "Confused about suckling wife's breasts," www.islamweb.net, fatwa no: 90612, Oct 6, 2006.

25. Islamweb Fatwas (www.islamweb.net), "Whether bestiality invalidates hajj and fasting," Fatwa No: 325030, Fatwa Date: 17/05/2016.

26. Fadl, *Reasoning with God: Reclaiming Shari'ah in the Modern Age* (Lanham, MD: Rowman and Littlefield), 201.

27. Shireena Al Nowais, "Some Fatwas Are Dangerous . . . and Some Are Ridiculous, Says Renowned Muslim Scholar Hamza Yusuf," *The National* (UAE), June 28, 2018.

28. Romans 2:15, New International Version.

29. Oddbjørn Leirvik, *Human Conscience and Muslim-Christian Relations: Modern Egyptian Thinkers on al-Damir* (Abingdon, UK: Routledge, 2006), 29–30.

30. Patricia S. Churchland, *Conscience: The Origins of Moral Institution* (New York: W. W. Norton, 2019), 152–79.

31. Oddbjørn Leirvik, "Conscience in Arabic and the Semantic History of Damīr," *Journal of Arabic and Islamic Studies* 9 (2009): 19–26. Turkish scholar Osman Demir observes the same fact: the concept of conscience was translated as *vicdan* "during the process of translation of books about Western moral philosophy in the late Ottoman and the Republican period." In "Vicdan," *İslam Ansiklopedisi* (Istanbul: Türkiye Diyanet Vakfı, 2013), 43:100–2.

32. Leirvik, *Human Conscience*, 71.

33. Al-Ghazali, in *Al-Iqtisad fi-l I'tiqad*, eds. İbrahim Ağa Çöpekçi and Hussein Atay (Ankara: Nur Matbaası, 1962), 1, also quoted in Paul L. Heck, "Conscience Across Cultures: The Case of Islam," *Journal of Religion* 94, no. 3 (July 2014): 298.

34. Fazlur Rahman, with whom I respectfully disagree here, defined *taqwa* as an "inner torch" that helps one "discern between right and wrong." *Major Themes of the Qur'an* (Minneapolis, MN: Bibliotheca Islamica, 1980), 6. For Esack's argument, see *Liberation and Pluralism: An Islamic*

Perspective of Interreligious Solidarity Against Oppression (Oxford: Oneworld, 1997), 87. For a more recent and detailed work, see M. Ashraf Adeel, *Epistemology of the Quran: Elements of a Virtue Approach to Knowledge and Understanding* (Cham, Switzerland: Springer, 2019), 43–54.

35. Qur'an, 91:8.

36. "Taqwa," *The Oxford Dictionary of Islam* (Oxford: Oxford University Press, 2019).

37. See Paul L. Heck, "Conscience Across Cultures: The Case of Islam," *Journal of Religion* 94, no. 3 (July 2014): 292–324. Heck, who notes that "there has not been much study of conscience in Islam" (p. 296), compares Christian and Muslim approaches to conscience, trying to bridge them in an ecumenical spirit. Finally, he notes that in Islam, only among the Mu'tazila and the "philosophical circles," one finds the conviction that "the rational workings of the mind can beget moral knowledge," reminiscent of Kantian conscience (p. 321).

38. Abou El Fadl, *Reasoning with God*, 362.

39. Al-Nawawi, *Forty Hadith*, hadith 27, quoted here from Jamaal al-Din M. Zarabozo, *Commentary on the Forty Hadith of al-Nawawi,* vol. 2 (Denver, CO: Al-Basheer Company for Publications & Trans., 1999), 846 Jamal Ahmed Badi, *Commentary of Forty Hadiths of An Nawawi* (Selangor, Malaysia, International Islamic University Malaysia, 2001), 132.

40. The Rumi quote, originally in his *Fihi ma Fih*, is from Jawid Mojaddedi, *Beyond Dogma: Rumi's Teachings on Friendship with God and Early Sufi Theories* (New York: Oxford University Press, 2012), 105.

41. Zarabozo, *Commentary on the Forty Hadith*, 2:848.

42. See al-Nawawi, *Forty Hadith,* hadith 27, quoted from Badi, *Commentary of Forty Hadiths*, 132. The author makes sure to warn that the human soul, which the hadith shows as a guide, "is subject to corruption and can be spoiled due to the influence of bad environment" (p. 133).

43. Zarabozo, *Commentary on the Forty Hadith*, 2:847, 849.

44. Tawfiq Hamid, "The Development of a Jihadist's Mind," *Current Trends in Islamist Ideology*, Hudson Institute, April 6, 2007.

45. The poll was a tweet to which other Twitter users could respond by choosing one of the options: "Question the jurisprudential judgment" or "Question conscience." See https://twitter.com/AkyolMustafa/status /1090655430295146502.

46. Gece Defni, Twitter post, January 30, 2019, 9:11 A.M., https://twitter.com /ivorianze/status/1090658757669998597.

47. Gamal al-Banna was the youngest brother of Hasan al-Banna, the founder of the Muslim Brotherhood, but clearly defended a more liberal and reformist interpretation of Islam. This quote is from David L. Johnston,

Muslims and Christians Debate Justice and Love (Bristol, UK: Equinox Publishing, 2020), 73. I am personally thankful to Dr. Johnston for making the book available to me before its publication.

48. Leirvik, *Human Conscience*, 81–198.

49. For a thoughtful discussion on harmonizing modern sexual ethics with Islamic textual sources, see Kecia Ali, *Sexual Ethics and Islam: Feminist Reflections on Qur'an, Hadith, and Jurisprudence* (Oxford: Oneworld Publications, 2006), especially pp. 151–57. Ali is also right to note the theological reckoning needed for such an effort: "Those Muslims who strive for gender equality . . . must address the central issue: what is justice and on what basis does one know it? Is something good because God says so? Or does God say it is good because it is, inherently, so?" (p. 149).

CHAPTER 5: HOW WE LOST UNIVERSALISM

1. Oddbjørn Leirvik, *Human Conscience and Muslim-Christian Relations:- Modern Egyptian Thinkers on al-Damir* (Abingdon, UK: Routledge, 2006), 39.

2. Necmettin Erbakan, *Davam* (İstanbul: MGV Yayınları, 2013), 18. Original quotes read, "İslamsız akıl, tek başına ilk ve mutlak doğruları bilemez, hayrı ve şerri tayin edemez" and "İslam'ın dışında, hiçbir hak ve hakikat kaynağı yoktur." Svante E. Cornell also offers the translation in *Current Trends in Islamist Ideology, vol. 23*, June 4, 2018.

3. Nicholas Kristof, "Is Islam the Problem?," *New York Times*, March 5, 2011.

4. Toby E. Huff, *The Rise of Early Modern Science* (Cambridge: Cambridge University Press, 2013), 221.

5. Erol Güngör, *İslam'ın Bugünkü Meseleleri* [The Issues of Islam Today] (Istanbul: Ötüken Neşriyat, 1981), 32–33.

6. Quoted in Joel L. Kraemer, *Humanism in the Renaissance of Islam: The Cultural Revival During the Buyid Age* (Leiden: Brill, 1993), xxvii.

7. "Until at least 1000 CE, Christians of various denominations were the majority of population in the Islamic world." (Joseph W. Meri, *Medieval Islamic Civilization: An Encyclopedia*, New York: Taylor & Francis, 2006, vol I, p. 154).

8. Vartan Gregorian, *Islam: A Mosaic Not a Monolith* (Washington, D.C.: Brookings Institution Press, 2003), 28.

9. Ibid., 14.

10. See more at Joel L. Kraemer, "Humanism in the Renaissance of Islam: A Preliminary Study," *Journal of the American Oriental Society* 104, no. 1 (January–March 1984): 135–64.

11. M. S. H. Ma'ṣumi, "Review of the Ethical Philosophy of Miskawayh by M. Abdul Haq Ansari," *Islamic Studies* 4, no. 3 (September 1965): 347.

12. Leirvik, *Al-Damir, Human Conscience and Christian–Muslim Relations*, (New York: Routledge, 2007) 283.

13. Lenn Goodman, *Islamic Humanism* (New York: Oxford University Press, 2005), 119. Goodman also shows how al-Ghazali, who used Miskawayh's work, "systematically expunged" its "courtly humanism." Muhammad Abul Quasem also thinks, "a third of Miskawayh's ethics was unacceptable to al-Ghazali and dropped as quietly as the rest was adopted." Ibid., 112–13.

14. The Qur'anic verse is 17:70.

15. Turkish scholar Recep Şentürk has extensively written on the concept of *adamiyyah*, or "humanity," which he traces in the writings of Abu Hanifa and some other Hanafis, and a few non-Hanafis as well, which he calls the "Universalistic School." The other camp is the "Communalistic School," originating from Malik, Shafi'i, and Ibn Hanbal, who denied that humans have rights by their nature, and set up a more antagonistic view toward non-Muslims. See Recep Şentürk, "'I Am Therefore I Have Rights': Human Rights in Islam Between Universalistic and Communalistic Perspectives," *Muslim World Journal of Human Rights* 2, no. 1 (2005): art. 11 Similarly, while Hanafis argued that a Muslim who murders a non-Muslim should face retaliation, other Sunnis argued to the contrary, on the assumption that Muslim lives are "superior." Al-Mawardi narrates this gap between early Hanafi and Shafi'i jurisprudence in *Al-Ahkam as-Sultaniyyah: The Laws of Islamic Governance*, trans. Asadullah Yate (London: Ta-Ha Publishers, 1996), 326. Also see Yohanan Friedmann, *Tolerance and Coercion in Islam: Interfaith Relations in the Muslim Tradition* (New York: Cambridge University Press, 2003), 197.

16. Qur'an 30:30.

17. The hadith is from *Sahih al-Bukhari*, vol. 2, bk. 23, no. 441.

18. This hadith is from *The Kitab al-Siyar* (298, 549) of Abu Ishaq al-Fazari (d. 802), which was clearly written before *Sahih al-Bukhari* and all other major hadith collections. I am thankful to Asma Afsaruddin for both bringing it to my attention and also publishing it in her important article on the changing views on jihad in early Islam: "Jihad, Gender, and Religious Minorities in the Siyar Literature: The Diachronic View," *Studia Islamica* 114 (2019): 6.

19. Camilla Adang, "Islam as the Inborn Religion of Mankind: The Concept of Fitra in the Works of Ibn Hazm," *Al-Qantara* 21, no. 2 (2000): 408.

20. Gowhar Quadir Wani, "Islamic Perspectives on Human Nature: Ibn Ashur's Fitrah-Based Theory of Maqasid Al-Shari'ah," *Islam and Civilisational Renewal* (IAIS Malaysia) 8, no. 2 (2017): 235–36.

21. Abdulaziz Sachedina, *Islam and the Challenge of Human Rights* (New York: Oxford University Press, 2009), 85.

22. See Bernard Lewis, *The Muslim Discovery of Europe* (New York: W. W. Norton, 2001), 298–307.

23. David Boaz, "Black History Is American History," *Huffington Post*, February 11, 2015.

24. The first comment is from R. Brunschvig, "Abd," *The Encyclopaedia of Islam* (Leiden: Brill, 1:25. The second quote is from Ehud R. Toledano, *The Ottoman Slave Trade and Its Suppression: 1840–1890* (Princeton, NJ: Princeton University Press, 1982), 3.

25. Toledano, *Ottoman Slave Trade*, 67.

26. In his book *Slavery and Islam,* Muslim scholar Jonathan A. C. Brown frankly notes: "Emancipation had certainly always been encouraged in Islam. But this theme, often cited in recent times as evidence for a strong indigenous mandate for abolition in Islam, only rose to such prominence in response to European abolitionist pressure." (See *Slavery and Islam*, Simon and Schuster, 2020, Chapter 5, "Abolishing Slavery in Islam." Apple Books.)

27. BFASS/Mss. Brit. Emp./S20/E2/18/39–40, quoted in Toledano, *Ottoman Slave Trade*, 93.

28. Toledano, *Ottoman Slave Trade*, 95–124.

29. The comparison of *Sergüzeşt* to *Uncle Tom's Cabin* is from Şerif Mardin, "Super Westernization in Urban Life in the Ottoman Empire in the Last Quarter of the Nineteenth Century," in *Turkey, Geographic and Social Perspectives*, eds. Peter Benedict et al. (Leiden: Brill, 1974), 403–46. Also see Toledano, *Ottoman Slave Trade*, 275.

30. Toledano, *Ottoman Slave Trade*, 277.

31. See my book *Islam Without Extremes: A Muslim Case for Liberty* (New York: W. W. Norton, 2011), 140–41.

32. William Gervase Clarence-Smith, *Islam and the Abolition of Slavery,* (New York: Oxford University Press, 2006), 129.

33. The verses in question were 47:4–5. For Sayyid Ahmad Khan's opposition to slavery, see Bernard K. Freamon, *Possessed by the Right Hand: The Problem of Slavery in Islamic Law and Muslim Cultures* (Leiden: Brill, 2019), 181–83.

34. Clarence-Smith, *Islam and the Abolition of Slavery,* 135.

35. Ibid., 146.

36. Ali al-Ahmed, "Author of Saudi Curriculums Advocates Slavery," *Arabia News*, November 7, 2003, available at http:// web.archive.org/web /20120524043027/http://www.arabianews.org/english/article.cfm?qid= 132&sid=2. Khaled Abou El Fadl quotes the scandalous fatwa in his *Reasoning with God: Reclaiming Shari'ah in the Modern Age* (Lanham, MD: Rowman and Littlefield), 118.

37. Clarence-Smith, *Islam and the Abolition of Slavery,* 17.

38. Abou El Fadl, *Reasoning with God,* 185–86.

39. Ibid., 186.

40. On the epistemic basis the drafters of the UDHR assumed in "conscience of mankind," see Johannes Morsink, *The Universal Declaration of Human Rights: Origins, Drafting, and Intent* (Philadelphia: University of Pennsylvania Press, 1999), 281–302.

41. Abul A'la Mawdudi, *Human Rights in Islam* (Lahore, Pakistan: Islamic Publications, Zahid Bashir Printers, 1977), 19–20.

42. See Muhammad Khalid Masud, "Clearing Ground: Commentary to 'Sharia and the Modern State,'" in *Islamic Law and International Human Rights Law,* eds. Anver M. Emon, Mark Ellis, and Benjamin Glahn (Oxford: Oxford University Press, 2012), 113–14.

43. Ebrahim Moosa, "The Debts and Burdens of Critical Islam" in *Progressive Muslims: On Justice, Gender and Pluralism,* ed. Omid Safi (Oxford: Oneworld, 2003), 121.

44. Ibid.

45. Ibid., 122.

46. Muqtedar Khan, "Islam and Four Essential Freedoms," *The Maydan,* August 28, 2019.

47. The term "puritan," that I also referred to in the Introduction, is from Khaled Abou El Fadl.

48. The phrase "no-value-in-the-absence-of-revelation tradition," as a definition of Ash'arism, is from Sherman Jackson, "The Alchemy of Domination? Some Ash'arite Responses to Mutazilite Ethics," *International Journal of Middle East Studies* 31, no. 2 (May 1999): 190.

49. In 2014, the then prime minister of Malaysia said, "Islam is now being tested aggressively by an ideology which can be termed as 'human rights-ism.'" See "Najib: 'Human Rights-ism' Goes Against Muslim Values," *Star Online,* May 13, 2014.

50. Sayyid Qutb, *Milestones,* (Islamic Book Service, 2006), 75.

51. Abou El Fadl, *Reasoning with God,* 213.

52. Ali Bardakoglu, "Ahlâkın Fıkıh Kuralları Arasında Buharlaşması," [Vaporization of morals among rules of jurisprudence], *Eskiyeni: A Journal of Social Sciences,* 37 (Fall 2017): 79.

53. "Islamization of knowledge" was an intellectual project proposed by the late Palestinian American philosopher Ismail al-Faruqi in the 1980s. But more recently, Ziauddin Sardar and Jeremy Henzell-Thomas, in a work supported by the same International Institute of Islamic Thought that had espoused the earlier theory, published *Rethinking Reform in Higher Education: From Islamization to Integration of Knowledge* (London: IIIT,

2017). For a good review of this book, see Charles Butterworth, review essay, *American Journal of Islamic Social Sciences* 36, no. 1 (2019).

CHAPTER 6: HOW THE SHARIA STAGNATED

1. Fazlur Rahman, "Islam and Social Justice," *Pakistan Forum* 1, no. 1 (October–November 1970): 4.
2. For Ramadan's call, see "An International Call for Moratorium on Corporal Punishment, Stoning and the Death Penalty in the Islamic World," April 5, 2005, https://tariqramadan.com/an-international-call-for-moratorium-on-corporal-punishment-stoning-and-the-death-penalty-in-the-islamic-world/. The definition of the reaction is from David L. Johnston, *Muslims and Christians Debate Justice and Love* (Bristol, UK: Equinox Publishing, 2020), 78.
3. Wael Hallaq, *A History of Islamic Legal Theories*, (Cambridge: Cambridge University Press, 1997), 207.
4. Abu l-Qasim Abd al-Karim al-Qushayri, *Lata'if al-Isharat, Subtle Allusions: Great Commentaries of the Qur'an*, trans. Kristin Zahra Sands, Royal Aal al-Bayt Institute for Islamic Thought (Louisville, KY: Fons Vitae, 2017), 90. The quote is slightly modified for a grammatical correction.
5. Qur'an, 4:11. The rest of the verse gives more detail about how the inheritance should be exactly divided.
6. The figures come from a 2017 poll by the International Republican Institute, http://www.iri.org/sites/default/files/2018-01-10_tunisia_poll_presentation.pdf.
7. For a summary of al-Haddad's arguments, see Ziba Mir-Hosseini, "Justice and Equality and Muslim Family Laws: New Ideas, New Prospects," in *Sharia and Justice: An Ethical, Legal, Political, and Cross-cultural Approach*, ed. Abbas Poya (Berlin: Walter de Gruyter GmbH, 2018), 88.
8. Ronak Husni and Daniel L. Newman, eds., *Muslim Women in Law and Society: Annotated Translation of al-Tahir al-Haddad* (New York: Routledge, 2007), 37.
9. Ziba Mir-Hosseini, Kari Vogt, Lena Larsen, and Christian Moe, *Gender and Equality in Muslim Family Law: Justice and Ethics in the Islamic Legal Tradition* (London: I. B. Tauris, 2013), 14.
10. The views of Abd al-Jabbar and Manekdim, expressed in the latter's *Sharh Al-Usul Al-Khamsa*, or the "Explanation of the Five Principles," is paraphrased here by Hazem Y. Salem in "Islamic Political Thought: Reviving a Rationalist Tradition" (PhD diss., University of Denver, 2013), 82, https://digitalcommons.du.edu/etd/915.

11. Yunus Apaydin, "Re'y," *İslam Ansiklopedisi* (Istanbul: Türkiye Diyanet Vakfı, 2008), 35:37–40.
12. Hadith in *Sunan Abu Dawood*, bk. 25, "Kitab al-Aqdiyah," hadith 7:15.
13. See Hallaq, *A History of Islamic Legal Theories*, 19.
14. Ibid.
15. Ibid.
16. Ibid., 32.
17. Ibid., 23.
18. Adis Duderija, *Maqāṣid al-Sharī'a and Contemporary Reformist Muslim Thought: An Examination* (New York: Palgrave Macmillan, 2014), 4.
19. *Maslaha mursala,* or public interest that could discern without any reference to the Qur'an and Sunna, was initially accepted in the Maliki school but was then rejected by latter-day Malikis. See David Johnston, "A Turn in the Epistemology and Hermeneutics of Twentieth Century Usul al-Fiqh," *Islamic Law and Society* 11, no. 2 (June 2004): 248.
20. Hallaq, *A History of Islamic Legal Theories*, 135.
21. In the words of Mamoud Munes Tomeh, "There is significant exegetical support" to think that "what is so wrong with this practice [*riba*] is that the increase in the amount comes *after the maturity date, which tends to put the debtor in* a weaker bargaining position." Tomeh, "Persuasion and Authority in Islamic Law," *Berkeley Journal of Middle Eastern & Islamic Law* 3, no. 1 (2010): 154–55.
22. Rumee Ahmed, "Which Comes First, the Maqāṣid or the Sharī'ah?," in *The Objectives of Islamic Law: The Promises and the Challenges of the Maqasid al-Shariah,* eds. Idris Nassery, Rumee Ahmed, and Muna Tatari (Lanham, Maryland: Lexington Books, 2018), 244.
23. Timur Kuran, *The Long Divergence: How Islamic Law Held Back the Middle East* (Princeton, NJ: Princeton University Press, 2010), x, book jacket.
24. Allison Engel, "Conversation with Timur Kuran," *USC News,* December 18, 2006.
25. See Felicitas Opwis, *Maslaḥa and the Purpose of the Law: Islamic Discourse on Legal Change from the 4th/10th to 8th/14th Century* (Leiden: Brill, 2010), 27–33.
26. Muhammad Khalid Masud, *Islam and Modernity: Key Issues and Debates* (Edinburgh: Edinburgh University Press, 2009), 239.
27. Opwis, *Maslaḥa and the Purpose of the Law,* 116.
28. Ahmed, "Which Comes First?," 243.
29. Ibid., 242.
30. Muhammad Khalid Mas'ud, "Shatibi's Philosophy of Islamic Law" (PhD diss. McGill University, Montreal, 1973).
31. Ibid., 407.

32. Ibid., 413.

33. Hallaq, *A History of Islamic Legal Theories*, 190. David Johnston also notes that Shatibi's work amounted to "classical Ash'ari epistemology being overrun by Mu'tazili rationalism," in "Maqasid al-Shari'a: Epistemology and Hermeneutics of Muslim Theologies of Human Rights," *Die Welt des Islams*, June 2007, 161.

34. Hallaq, *A History of Islamic Legal Theories*, 190.

35. Johnston, "A Turn in the Epistemology and Hermeneutics," 253.

36. Ibid., 254.

37. The analogy to Bentham and Mill is from Felicitas Opwis, "Maslaḥa in Contemporary Islamic Legal Theory," *Islamic Law and Society* (Leiden: Brill) 12, no. 2 (2005) 201.

38. Whether classical Islam did have its own version of natural law has been discussed by Anver Emon. He calls the Mu'tazila "Hard Natural Law theorists," because they gave reason "the ontological authority to analyze and investigate the world around them, and thereby derive new norms." Anver M. Emon, in *Natural Law: A Jewish, Christian, and Islamic Trialogue* (Oxford: Oxford University Press, 2014), 149. In comparison to the Mu'tazila, Emon argues that Ash'arism developed "Soft Naturalism," whose theorists "balanced their theological commitment to God's omnipotence with the need to endow reason with sufficient authority to extend the Sharia." Anver M. Emon, *Islamic Natural Law Theories*, (New York: Oxford University Press, 2010, 32. Yet, in agreement with Mariam al-Attar, I find this "Soft Naturalism" status given to Ash'arism a bit too generous. Emon himself admits that notions of *maqasid al-sharia* and *maslaha* were developed "as a check on the scope of reason." Ibid., 36. For a bold critique of Emon's postulate of "Soft Naturalism" among the Ash'aris see Rami Koujah, "A Critical Review Essay of Anver M. Emon's Islamic Natural Law Theories," *Journal of Islamic and Near Eastern Law*, 14(1), 2015.

39. Hashim Kamali, "Goals and Purposes: Maqasid al-Shari'ah," in *The Objectives of Islamic Law: The Promises and Challenges of the Maqasid al-Shari'a*, eds. Idris Nassery, Rumee Ahmed, and Muna Tatari (Lanham, Maryland: Lexington Books, 2018), 8.

40. "Can Women Travel Without a Mahram?," Fatwa by Mufti Muhammad ibn Adam, http://www.daruliftaa.com/node/4774.

41. See Adis Duderija, *The Imperatives of Progressive Islam*, Taylor & Francis, 2017, p. 144.

42. Ibid.

43. Mariam al-Attar, "Divine Command Ethics in the Islamic Legal Tradition," in *Routledge Handbook of Islamic Law*, eds. Khaled Abou El Fadl, Ahmad Atif Ahmad, and Said Fares Hassan, (New York: Routledge, 2019) 107.

44. Ibid.
45. Ebrahim Moosa, "Recovering the Ethical: Practices, Politics, Tradition," in *The Shari'a: History, Ethics and Law,* ed. Amyn Sajoo (London: Bloomsbury Publishing, 2018), 55.
46. Ibn Ashur quotes this maxim from Shams al-Din al-Shirbini (d. 1570) in his *Treatise on Maqasid al-Shariah*, trans. from Arabic and annotated by Mohamed El-Tahir El-Mesawi, abridged by Alison Lake (Herndon, VA: International Institute of Islamic Thought, 2013), 155. Sixteenth-century Egyptian jurist Shams al-Din Muhammad ibn al-Khatib al-Shirbini had inferred the maxim from "Shari'ah provisions governing marriage between free men and female slaves." Ibid. 399.
47. Ibn Ashur, *Treatise on Maqasid al-Shariah*, 155.
48. For al-Ghazali, for example, punishing an unbeliever "who leads others astray" upholds and protects the value of religion. Al-Ghazali, *Al-Mustasfa*, 1:637, quoted here from Emon, *Islamic Natural Law Theories*, 153.
49. Ibn Ashur, *Treatise on Maqasid al-Shariah*, 160.
50. Ibid., 161.
51. See Hossein Askari, Hossein Mohammadkhan, *Islamicity Indices: The Seed for Change* (New York: Palgrave Macmillan, 2016). Also see http://islamicity-index.org/wp/.
52. Johnston, "A Turn in the Epistemology and Hermeneutics," 252.
53. Shamsuddin Ibn al-Qayyim, *I'lām al-Muwaqi'īn*, annotated by Taha Saad (Beirut: Dar al-jīl, 1973), 1:333, quoted in Jasser Auda, "Realizing Maqāṣid in the Sharī'ah," in *The Objectives of Islamic Law: The Promises and Challenges of the Maqasid al-Shari'a*, eds. Idris Nassery, Rumee Ahmed, and Muna Tatari (Lanham, Maryland: Lexington Books, 2018), 35.

CHAPTER 7: HOW WE LOST THE SCIENCES

1. Said Halim Paşa, *Buhranlarımız* (İstanbul: Tercüman 1001 Temel Eser, 1970), p. 47.
2. *Sahih al-Bukhari*, Book 76, Hadith 43. Translation by Muhammad Muhsin Khan, Riyadh: Darussalam, 1994, fully available online at sunnah.com.
3. One of the fiercest Pakistani opponents of social distancing in mosques, Muhammad Ashraf Asif Jalali, a Barelvi scholar, repeatedly quoted *"la adwa"* in his online sermons available on YouTube, such as in: https://www.youtube.com/watch?v=ab2tbqaQkOs. Pakistani writer Sultan B Mirza also observed that many clerics in his country were "not fully convinced that a disease can be transmitted from one human to another," due to religious texts including the "la adwa" hadith. Sultan B Mirza, "COVID-19

& Religion: Why Are Pakistani Muftis Resisting Closure Of Mosques?," *Naya Daur Media,* April 24, 2020, https://nayadaur.tv/2020/04/covid-19-religion-why-are-pakistani-muftis-resisting-closure-of-mosques/.

4. *Sahih al-Bukhari,* Book 76, Hadith 34. Different definitions are given to *safar* and *hama* in different sources—the ones here are from Lawrence I. Conrad, "Epidemic Disease in Formal and Popular Thought in Early Islamic Society," *Epidemics and Ideas: Essays on the Historical Perception of Pestilence,* eds. Terence Ranger, Paul Slack (Cambridge: Cambridge University Press, 1992) 88.

5. For a discussion of this hadith, also see Ovamir Anjum, "Is Contagion Real? Giving Context to Prophetic Wisdom," yaqeeninstitute.org, April 16, 2020. Anjum concludes, rightly in my view, that "there is no indication that the Final Apostle of God was sent to instruct humanity in germ theory."

6. For the most comprehensive study of this matter, which I have relied on here, see Justin Stearns, *Infectious Ideas: Contagion in Premodern Islamic and Christian Thought in the Western Mediterranean,* Johns Hopkins University Press, 2011, especially chapters I and V. Also see Adel Allouche, "Epidemics," in *Medieval Islamic Civilization: An Encyclopedia,* vol I, pp. 235–236.

7. Lawrence I. Conrad, "A Ninth-Century Muslim Scholar's Discussion of Contagion," in *Contagion: Perspectives from Pre-Modern Societies* (London: Routledge, 2017) 170–71.

8. This was the position of Ibn Rushd al-Jadd (d. 1126), the grandfather of the more famous Ibn Rushd we address in the next chapter. See Russell Hopley, "Contagion In Islamic Lands: Responses from Medieval Andalusia and North Africa," *Journal for Early Modern Cultural Studies,* vol. 10, no. 2, Fall/Winter 2010, p. 50.

9. Justin Stearns, *Infectious Ideas,* p. 34.

10. Ibid.

11. Justin Stearns, *Infectious Ideas,* see chapter V, especially 116, 118.

12. *Sahih Muslim,* Book 39, Hadith 143. Translated by Abdul Hamid Siddiqui, New Delhi: India, Kitab Bhavan, 2000, fully available online at sunnah.com.

13. Justin Stearns, "Contagion in Theology and Law: Ethical Considerations in the Writings of Two 14th Century Scholars of Nasrid Granada," *Islamic Law and Society,* vol 14:1, 2007, 117.

14. Ibid.

15. On how Ibn al-Khatib "echoed" Ibn Tufayl, see Ali Humayun Akhtar, "The Political Controversy Over Graeco-Arabic Philosophy and Sufism in Nasrid Government: The Case of Ibn Al-Khatib in Al-Andalus," *International Journal Middle East Studies,* vol 47:2, May 2015, 328.

16. Thomas Arnold, Alfred Guillaume, *The Legacy of Islam* (London: Oxford University Press, 1931), 340.
17. Justin Stearns, "Contagion In Theology and Law," 112–113.
18. Ibid.
19. Joseph Patrick Byrne, *Encyclopedia of the Black Death* (Santa Barbara, CA: ABC-CLIO, 2012), 182.
20. The persecution and execution of Ibn al-Khatib may also have political reasons, but his "heresy" certainly played "a clear role . . . in escalating the rivalry between him and the chief qadi." (Ali Humayun Akhtar, "The Political Controversy Over Graeco-Arabic Philosophy and Sufism in Nasrid Government," p. 324).
21. Robert Irwin, *The Alhambra* (Cambridge, MA: Harvard University Press, 2012), 86.
22. These reasonable voices included Ottoman top cleric Ebusuud Efendi and Kurdish scholar Idris-i Bitlisi, both of whom referred to Ibn al-Khatib in their writings. For their views, and the Ottoman Quarantine Reform, including the quote "turning point," see Birsen Bulmuş, *Plague, Quarantines and Geopolitics in the Ottoman Empire* (Edinburgh: Edinburgh University Press, 2012) 15–29, 97. Bulmuş also shows how the "no contagion" view was championed by Ottoman officials such as Osman bin Süleyman Penah (d. 1817), and how others challenged his "fatalist" views. It is also worth noting the 1838 reform was justified by a fatwa from the Shaikh-ul Islam, but it faced popular resistance, sometimes violently, as it was seen as an intrusive invention of "the Franks," or Europeans. See Nuran Yildirim, "Karantina İstemezük!," [We don't want quarantine], *Toplumsal Tarih*, vol 150, 2006, 18–27.
23. Al-Ghazali, *The Incoherence of the Philosophers / Tahâfut al-falâsifa: A Parallel English-Arabic Text*, ed. and trans. M. E. Marmura, 2nd. ed. (Provo, UT: Brigham Young University Press, 2002), 167.
24. Ibn Ḥazm, *al-Faṣl fī al-Milal wa-l-Ahwā' wa-n-Nihal* trans. into Turkish by Halil İbrahim Bulut, (Istanbul: Türkiye Yazma Eserler Kurumu Başkanlığı, 2017), vol 3, 638. I am thankful to Özgür Koca, author of *Islam, Causality, and Freedom,* for helping access this quote.
25. Al-Kiyâ' al-Harrâsi, *Usul ad-dîn* (Cairo: MS Dar al-Kutub al-Misriyya) 295, quoted in Richard M. Frank, "Moral Obligation in Classical Muslim Theology," *Journal of Religious Ethics* 11, no. 2 (1983): 209.
26. Majid Fakhry, *Islamic Occasionalism and Its Critique by Averroes and Aquinas* (New York: Routledge, 2013; originally published in 1953), 9.
27. Koca, *Islam, Causality, and Freedom,* 26.

28. Mehmet Bayrakdar, "Al-Jahiz and the Rise of Biological Evolutionism," *Islamic Quarterly,* vol 27, (1983), 149–155. Also see Aamina H. Malik, Janine M. Ziermann, and Rui Diogo, "An Untold Story in Biology: The Historical Continuity of Evolutionary Ideas of Muslim Scholars from the Eighth Century to Darwin's Time," *Journal of Biological Education,* Jan 2017, 4–6.

29. Uthman Sayyid Ahmad Ismail al-Bili, *Some Aspects of Islam in Africa* (Reading, UK: Ithaca Press, 2008), 14.

30. The comment on occasionalism being first developed by Muslim theologians is from Koca, *Islam, Causality, and Freedom,* 10. For Maimonides being an intermediary, see Majid Fakhry, *Islamic Occasionalism: And Its Critique by Averroes and Aquinas* (New York, Taylor & Francis, 2008) 14.

31. Nicolas Malebranche, *The Search After Truth: With Elucidations of The Search After Truth,* trans. and eds. Thomas M. Lennon and Paul J. Olscamp (Cambridge: Cambridge University Press, 1997), 448.

32. "Gottfried Leibniz: Causation," *Internet Encyclopedia of Philosophy,* https://www.iep.utm.edu/leib-cau/.

33. Charlotte Johnston, "Locke's Examination of Malebranche and John Norris," *Journal of the History of Ideas* (University of Pennsylvania Press) 19, no. 4 (October 1958): 558.

34. Ibid.

35. The essay was later published in *Posthumous Works of Mr. John Locke* (London: A. and J. Churchill, 1706). The quote is from the preface of the book.

36. Saint Thomas Aquinas, *Summa Theologica* (New York: Cosimo Classics, 2007), vol I, part I, 124.

37. "Occasionalism," *Stanford Encyclopedia of Philosophy,* first published Monday, October 20, 2008, https://plato.stanford.edu/entries/occasionalism. For contemporary Christian critiques of occasionalism, see Katherine A. Rogers, "What Is Wrong with Occasionalism?," *American Catholic Philosophical Quarterly* 75, no. 3 (2001); Stephen Meredith, "Looking for God in All the Wrong Places," *First Things,* February 2014.

38. The description is from by Stephen H. Webb, "Intelligent Design Might Be Wrong, but Not The Way You Think," *First Things,* February 20, 2014.

39. Rogers, "What's Wrong with Occasionalism?," 352.

40. Toby Huff, *The Rise of Early Modern Science: Islam, China, and the West* (New York: Cambridge University Press, 2003), 89.

41. "Muslim theological tradition remains occasionalist for the most part." Koca, *Islam, Causality, and Freedom,* 11–12.

42. *The Essays of Adam Smith* (London: Alex Murray, 1872), 353.

43. A. I. Sabra, "The Astronomical Origins of Ibn al-Haytham's Concept of Experiment," in *Actes du XIIe. International d'Historie des Sciences,* Tome IIIa (1971), 133–36, quoted in Huff, *Rise of Early Modern Science,* 91.

44. Whether al-Ghazali's occasionalism was a "modified" one, which denied not causation but only *necessary* causation, has been a matter of debate. See Jon McGinnis, "Occasionalism, Natural Causation and Science in al-Ghazali," in *Arabic Theology, Arabic Philosophy, from Many to the One: Essays in Celebration of Richard M. Frank,* ed. James E. Montgomery (Leuven, Belgium: Peeters Publishers, 2006), 441–63. There may also be a gap between what al-Ghazali wrote and what others understood. Lenn Goodman finds it "regrettable" that "what stuck in the minds of Ghazali's readers through the centuries . . . was not the potential he left behind for the opening of the universe but the rhetorical emphasis on God's ultimate causality, at the expense of proximate causes." (Lenn Goodman, *Islamic Humanism* [New York: Oxford University Press, 2005], 97.)

45. This third view, referred and quoted in this paragraph, is offered, most forcefully, by Dimitri Gutas, the eminent Arabist at Yale University whose earlier views were in the opposite direction. See "Avicenna and After: The Development of Paraphilosophy: A History of Science Approach," in *Islamic Philosophy from the 12th to the 14th Century,* ed. Abdelkader Al Ghouz (Göttingen, Germany: V&R Unipress, 2018), 19–66. Quotes are from pp. 37, 43, 59.

46. Ahmad Dallal, *Islam, Science, and the Challenge of History* (New Haven, CT: Yale University Press, 2012), 120.

47. Ibid., 122.

48. Ibid.

49. A. I. Sabra, "Science and Philosophy in Medieval Islamic Theology: The Evidence of the Fourteenth Century," *Zeitschrift für Geschichte der Arabisch-Islamischen Wissenschaften,* vol 9, 1994, 36.

50. Y. Tzvi Langermann, "Arabic Cosmology," *Early Science and Medicine* 2, no. 2, Medieval Cosmologies (1997): 209.

51. Robert G. Morrison, "Natural Theology and the Qur'an," *Journal of Qur'anic Studies* (Edinburgh University Press) 15, no. 1 (2013): 2.

52. Langermann, "Arabic Cosmology," 209.

53. Abdelhamid I. Sabra, "The Appropriation and Subsequent Naturalization of Greek Science in Medieval Islam: A Preliminary Statement," *History of Science* 25, no. 3 (September 1987): 240. (Emphasis added.)

54. Quoted in John J. Esposito, *Islam: The Straight Path* (New York: Oxford University Press, 1991), 57.

55. Sabra, "Appropriation and Subsequent Naturalization," 239.

56. Ibid., 241.

57. *Sahih Muslim,* no. 2722, bk. 48, hadith 99. (Translated by Abdul Hamid Siddiqui, New Delhi: India, Kitab Bhavan, 2000, fully available online at sunnah.com.)

58. Enmity against all secular knowledge, which has been wrongly attributed to al-Ghazali by some early Orientalists, was in fact not a feature of him but others, such as Imam Rabbani: "Unlike al-Ghazali, Sirhindi does not discuss separately the merits or otherwise of each science; he lumps together all the philosophers and all their sciences and rejects them in toto. While al-Ghazali approaches the question with a well-balanced argument and uses relatively moderate language, Sirhindi's approach is emotionally charged and his language largely vituperative." Yohanan Friedmann, "Shaykh Ahmad Sirhindi: An Outline of His Thought and a Study of His Image in the Eyes of Posterity" (PhD diss., McGill University, Montreal, June 1966), 79.

59. Mufti Ali, "A Statistical Portrait of the Resistance to Logic by Sunni Muslim Scholars Based on the Works of Jalal al-Din al-Suyuti (849–909/1448–1505)," *Islamic Law and Society* 15, no. 2 (2008): 253.

60. See Joel L. Kraemer, "Humanism in the Renaissance of Islam: A Preliminary Study," *Journal of the American Oriental Society* 104 (1984): 150. Also see D. S. Margoliouth, "The Discussion Between Abu Bishr Matta and Abu Sa'id al-Sirafi on the Merits of Logic and Grammar, *The Journal of the Royal Asiatic Society of Great Britain and Ireland* 1 (January 1905): 79–129.

61. Rabbani quote is from Sufi Irshad Alam, *Faith Practice Piety: The Great Mujaddid Ahmad Sirhindi* (Dhaka, Bangladesh: Aklima Akter, 2010), 114. The book is a partial translation of Rabbabi's *Maktubat* with the author's commentary. The author defends Rabbani's condemnation of geometry with the following explanation: "It must be understood from the context that the Mujaddid vilified geometry as 'useless' only because he could not find any practical use for it; and so he rejected the study of geometry as an end in itself or as a means of God-realization. . . . So the Mujaddidi view is that no science is worth studying as an end in itself; instead they should help one either in one's path towards God-realization or in the practical world." Ibid., 115.

62. As Ottoman reformist Katip Çelebi had pointed out, the "elimination from the madrasa curriculum of the rational and mathematical sciences" was one of the very causes of the decline of the Ottoman Empire. See Ekmeleddin Ihsanoglu, *The Madrasas of the Ottoman Empire* (Manchester: UK, Foundation for Science, Technology and Civilization, April 2004), 15.

63. See Hasan Yıldız, "An Evaluation on Reform Attempts in Ottoman Madrasahs," *International Journal of Historical Researches* 4, no. 1 (Spring 2019): 433–35.

64. Ethan L. Menchinger, "Free Will, Predestination, and the Fate of the Ottoman Empire," *Journal of the History of Ideas* 77, no. 3 (July 2016): 445–66.

65. There is one thesis that Muteferrika "was enslaved and forced to convert to Islam," but it seems more probable that "he took refuge in the Ottoman Empire and converted voluntarily," as some other Unitarians did at

that time. See Vefa Erginbaş, "Enlightenment in the Ottoman Context: İbrahim Müteferrika and His Intellectual Landscape," in *Historical Aspects of Printing and Publishing in Languages of the Middle East: Papers from the Third Symposium on the History of Printing and Publishing in the Languages and Countries of the Middle East*, ed. Geoffrey Roper (Leiden: Brill, 2014) 64. For the broader connection between early Unitarians and the Ottoman Empire, see my book *The Islamic Jesus* (New York: St. Martin's Press, 2017), 176–80.

66. The terms "one of the founding fathers" and "Ottoman Enlightenment" are from Erginbaş, "Enlightenment in the Ottoman Context."

67. Menchinger, "Free Will, Predestination, and the Fate of the Ottoman Empire," 455.

68. Ibid., 457.

69. The original quote, which Menchinger presents in his article but I preferred to translate myself, reads: "Tedbirde noksan oldı, takdire buhtan etdiler." Ibid.

70. See Ethan L. Menchinger, *The First of the Modern Ottomans: The Intellectual History of Ahmed Vasif* (Cambridge: Cambridge University Press, 2017).

71. Menchinger, "Free Will, Predestination, and the Fate of the Ottoman Empire," 459.

72. Ibid., 462.

73. Ibid., 461.

74. Ibid. Also see Marlene Kurz, *Ways to Heaven, Gates to Hell: Fazlızade Ali's Struggle with the Diversity of Ottoman Islam* (Berlin: EB Verlag, 2011).

75. Menchinger, "Free Will, Predestination, and the Fate of the Ottoman Empire," 461. For more on Fazlızade Ali, see Marlene Kurz, *Ways to Heaven, Gates to Hell.*

76. Ibid., 464.

77. See Christopher de Bellaigue, *The Islamic Enlightenment: The Struggle Between Faith and Reason, 1798 to Modern Times* (New York: Liveright Publishing, 2017) 53–106.

78. H. R. Dalafi and M. H. A. Hassan, eds., *Renaissance of Sciences in Islamic Countries: Muhammad Abdus Salam* (London: World Scientific Publishing, 1994), 59–60.

79. Mehmet Evkuran, "İslam Düşüncesinde Nedensellik Problem" [The problem of causality in Islamic thought]," *Eskiyeni* 21 (Spring 2011): 22.

80. Nasr Hamid Abu Zayd, *Critique of Religious Discourse,* trans. Jonathan Wright (New Haven, CT: Yale University Press, 2018), 53–54.

81. This was a comment by the Islamist Zaynab al-Ghazali on the Arab defeat at the Six-Day War. John Calvert, *Sayyid Qutb and the Origins of Radical Islamism* (New York: Columbia University Press, 2010), 268.

82. Thomas R. Paradise, "Islam and Earthquakes: Seismic Risk Perception in a Muslim City," *Journal of Islamic Law and Culture* 10, no. 2 (2008): 213.

83. Ahmad Dallal, *Islam, Science, and the Challenge of History,* 162.

84. For a brief and succinct critique of "Islamic science," and how it goes against Islam's own historical experience, see S. Irfan Habib, "Viability of Islamic Science: Some Insights from 19th Century India," *Economic and Political Weekly,* vol. 39, no. 23, June 2004, 2351–5.

85. Edward Said quote is from *Arab Human Development Report 2003,* (Amman, Jordan: United Nations Publications, 2003), 2003, 35.

CHAPTER 8: THE LAST MAN STANDING: IBN RUSHD

1. Charles Butterworth, "Averroës, Precursor of the Enlightenment?," *Alif: Journal of Comparative Poetics* 16 (1996): 6.

2. *Al-Ghazali's Tahafut al-Falasifah* [Incoherence of the philosophers], trans. Sabih Ahmad Kamali (Lahore, Pakistan: Pakistan Philosophical Congress, 1963), 249. Here al-Ghazali also rebukes the Mu'tazila, whose parallels to the philosophers he points out, as "innovators," or the proponents of *bid'a.* But he doesn't go as far as condemning the "innovators" for "infidelity," while reminding that some Muslims do that as well.

3. Abū-Ḥāmid Muḥammad Ibn-Muḥammad al-Ġazzālī, *Imām al-Ghazālī's Deliverance from Error and the Beginning of Guidance,* trans. W. Montgomery Watt (Kuala Lumpur, Malaysia: Islamic Book Trust, 2005), 30.

4. The first quote is from İhsan Süreyya Sırma, *Müslümanların Tarihi* [History of Muslims] (İstanbul: Beyan Yayınları, 2016), 4:49; the second quote is from a 2017 textbook used in Morocco, taken from Souleymane Bachir Diagne, *Open to Reason: Muslim Philosophers in Conversation with the Western Tradition,* trans. Jonathan Adjemian (New York: Columbia University Press, 2018), 102.

5. Yohanan Friedmann and Christoph Markschies, eds., *Rationalization in Religions: Judaism, Christianity and Islam* (Berlin: Walter de Gruyter GmbH, December 17, 2018), 217.

6. George N. Atiyeh, "Ibn Masarra, Muhammad ibn 'Abd Allah," *Routledge Encyclopedia of Philosophy,* 1998, https://www.rep.routledge.com/articles/biographical/ibn-masarra-muhammad-ibn-abd-allah-883-931/v-1.

7. Friedmann and Markschies, *Rationalization in Religions,* 217.

8. The argument that decentralization in Muslim Spain helped the philosophers is from Amira K. Bennison, a historian of the Middle East at the University of Cambridge. See BBC, In Our Time, "Averroes," https://www.bbc.co.uk/programmes/p0038x79.

9. The quote from Alain de Libera is taken from Nidhal Guessoum, *Islam's Quantum Question: Reconciling Muslim Tradition and Modern Science* (London: I. B.Tauris, 2010), xiii.

10. Both the definition of Ibn Tufayl's role in the court of Caliph Abu Yusuf Ya'qub al-Mansur and the quote from Ibn Rushd are from Seyyed Hossein Nasr and Oliver Leaman, *History of Islamic Philosophy* (New York: Routledge, 1996), 313–14.

11. Qur'an, 88:17–18.

12. The quotes are from George Hourani, trans., *Decisive Treatise Determining the Nature of the Connection Between Religion and Philosophy* (London: Luzac and Co., 1961), 1, 2.

13. Ibid., 4.

14. Qur'an, 3:7.

15. *The Philosophy and Theology of Averroes*, trans., from Arabic, Mohammad Jamil-Ub-Behman Barod (Baroda: Manibhai Mathurbhal Gupta, 1921), 119.

16. Hourani, *Decisive Treatise*, 12.

17. Ovamir Anjum, *Politics, Law, and Community in Islamic Thought* (Cambridge: Cambridge University Press, 2012), 163.

18. Ibn Rushd pointed to verses such as 11:7, 41:11, and 65:48, which imply that objects such as a "throne," "water," and "smoke" existed before the formation of the world.

19. Ibn Rushd quote is from: Matteo Di Giovanni, "Averroes, Philosopher of Islam," *Interpreting Averroes: Critical Essays*, eds. Peter Adamson, Matteo Di Giovanni (Cambridge: Cambridge University Press, 2018), 25.

20. Simon Van Den Bergh, trans., *Averroes' Tahafut al-Tahafut, The Incoherence of the Incoherence* (Oxford: Ejw Gibb Memorial Trust, 2008), 416.

21. Ibid, 423.

22. Matteo Di Giovanni, "Averroes: Philosopher of Islam," in *Interpreting Averroes: Critical Essays* (Cambridge: Cambridge University Press, 2018), 16.

23. Ibid.

24. Özgür Koca, *Islam, Causality, and Freedom,* (Cambridge: Cambridge University Press, 2020), 87.

25. Ibrahim Kalın, "Will, Necessity and Creation as Monistic Theophany in the Islamic Philosophical Tradition," in *Creation and the God of Abraham*, eds. David B. Burrell, Carlo Cogliati, Janet M. Soskice, and William R. Stoeger (New York: Cambridge University Press, 2010), 116.

26. Ibid.

27. See Ibn Rushd, *The Distinguished Jurist's Primer* trans. Imran Ahsan Khan Nyazee (Reading, UK: Garnet Publishing, 2000.) 1:465.

28. One example is R. Brunschvig, "Averroes juriste," in *Etudes d 'orientalisme dediees a la memoire de Levi-Proverycal* (Paris: G. P. Maisonneuve & Larose,

1962), 1:35–68. See more on this in George Hourani, *Reason and Tradition in Islamic Ethics* (New York: Cambridge University Press, 1985.), 268–69.

29. Hourani, *Reason and Tradition,* 268.

30. Averroes in *Paraph. Rhetoric* II. 84–5 (§§I.10.5–6); Feriel Bouhafa, "Averroes' Corrective Philosophy of Law," in *Interpreting Averroes: Critical Essays,* eds. Peter Adamson and Matteo Di Giovanni (Cambridge: Cambridge University Press, 2019), 72–73.

31. This is a paraphrase of Ibn Rushd's views by George Hourani, *Reason and Tradition,* 264.

32. Averroes, *Paraph. Rhetoric* II.113 (§I1.13.2), in Bouhafa, "Averroes' Corrective Philosophy of Law," 73.

33. Averroes, *Paraph. Rhetoric* II.117 (§1.13.10), in ibid., 75.

34. Also see Karen Taliaferro, "Ibn Rushd and Natural Law: Mediating Human and Divine Law," *Journal of Islamic Studies* (Oxford University Press), September 22, 2016, 11–24. Taliaferro here also shows the parallelism between the Mu'tazila and Ibn Rushd in their common belief in "unwritten law."

35. The quotes are from Rushd, *The Distinguished Jurist's Primer,* 464, 458, 460, 457.

36. See chapter 10. Also see Asma Afsaruddin, *Striving in the Path of God: Jihad and Martyrdom in Islamic Thought* (New York: Oxford University Press, 2013.)

37. This quote from Ibn Rushd survived only in Hebrew, whose translation was offered by Noah Feldman in his PhD thesis: "Reading the Nicomachean Ethics with Ibn Rushd," Faculty of Oriental Studies, Oxford University, 1994, 238. With special thanks to Dr. Feldman and his assistant Shannon Whalen-Lipko for access to this text. The quote is also in Bouhafa, "Averroes' Corrective Philosophy of Law," 76.

38. In this passage, to whom Ibn Rushd refers by the term "the legislator" has been a matter of discussion. The full phrase reads, "this is ignorance on their part of the intention of the legislator, may God watch over him." This seems to suggest that the legislator isn't God himself, as a Muslim would typically assume when talking about the Sharia. But Ibn Rushd might have Prophet Muhammad in mind, whose hadiths make up an important source of the jihad doctrine, as well as the Muslim jurists who interpret Sharia to develop *fiqh,* or jurisprudence.

39. Anver M. Emon, "Natural Law and Natural Rights in Islamic Law," *Journal of Law and Religion* (Cambridge: Cambridge University Press) 20, no. 2 (2004–2005): 361.

40. See Bouhafa, "Averroes' Corrective Philosophy of Law," 78.

41. See Alan Verskin, *Islamic Law and the Crisis of the Reconquista: The Debate on the Status of Muslim Communities in Christendom* (Leiden: Brill,

2015), 97–98. Verskin notes that while many Malikis believed "the property, children, and wives of Muslims living in the abode of war may all be taken as booty," Ibn Rushd, along with Ibn al-Arabi, opposed this view, which sanctioned "the actions of the powerful . . . without regard to the demands of justice" (p. 97).

42. Hourani, *Reason and Tradition*, 264.

43. Noah Feldman, "Reading the Nicomachean Ethics with Ibn Rushd," 257. Feldman suggests that Hourani read too much pacifism and rational departure from the Sharia into Ibn Rushd's remarks on the matter (pp. 255–56). According to Feldman, Ibn Rushd did not "overturn positive law," i.e., the Sharia, but argued that "positive law provides space for authorized rectification." (ibid., 256).

44. Al-Ghazali, *Revival of the Religious Sciences* [*Ihya Ulum ad-Din*], trans. Mohammad Mahdi al-Sharif, (Beirut: Dar al-Kotob al-Ilmiyah, 2011), 2:94.

45. *The Stanford Encyclopedia of Philosophy,* "Feminist History of Philosophy," substantive revision, Monday, March 9, 2015, https://plato.stanford .edu/entries/feminism-femhist/.

46. See Nicholas D. Smith. "Plato and Aristotle on the Nature of Women," *Journal of the History of Philosophy* 21, no. 4 (1983), 467–78.

47. Erwin I. J. Rosenthal, *Political Thought in Mediaeval Islam: An Introductory Outline* (Cambridge: Cambridge University Press, 1962), 191.

48. Ibid.

49. For a commentary on Ibn Rushd's views on these themes in his *Bidayat*, see Catarina Belo, "Some Considerations on Averroes' Views Regarding Women and Their Role in Society," *Journal of Islamic Studies* 20, no. 1 (January 2009): 13–17.

50. Ibid., 20.

51. The notion that women are "deficient in intelligence and religion" comes from a hadith: *Sahih al-Bukhari*, vol.2, bk. 24, hadith 541.

52. Rabbi Sacks gives this quote from Loewe's book: Maharal, *Be'er haGolah* (Jerusalem: 1972), 150–51. I have not been able to trace the same quote in the known works of Ibn Rushd; but it is quite possible that it is a saying of his that has survived in the Hebrew tradition. See Jonathan Sacks, *Not in God's Name: Confronting Religious Violence* (New York: Schocken Books, 2015), 234–35.

53. Jonathan Sacks, *Not in God's Name*, 235.

54. Ibid., 236.

55. Paul Kurtz, "Intellectual Freedom, Rationality, and Enlightenment: The Contributions of Averroes," in M. Wahbah and M. Abousenna (eds.), *Averroes and the Enlightenment* (Amherst, NY: Promethius Books, 1996), 32.

56. See David Sorkin, *The Religious Enlightenment: Protestants, Jews, and Catholics from London to Vienna* (Princeton, NJ: Princeton University Press, 2011).

57. Charles Butterworth, "Averroës and the Rational Legacy in the East and the West," *Alif: Journal of Comparative Poetics* 16 (1996): 15.

58. Erwin I. J. Rosenthal, "The Place of Politics in the Philosophy of Ibn Rushd," *Bulletin of the School of Oriental and African Studies* (University of London) 15, no. 2 (1953): 254.

59. On the Ashʿari beliefs of Ibn Rushd's opponents in Al-Andalus, see Delfina Serrano Ruano, "Explicit Cruelty, Implicit Compassion: Judaism, Forced Conversions and the Genealogy of the Banū Rushd," *Journal of Medieval Iberian Studies* 2, no. 2 (2010): 223.

60. Ibid., 222, 224.

61. See Maribel Fierro, "Ibn Rushd's (Averroes) 'Disgrace' and His Relation with the Almohads," in *Islamic Philosophy from the 12th to the 14th Century*, ed. Abdelkader Al Ghouz (Göttingen, Germany: V&R Unipress, 2018), 84–85.

62. The original quote is from a book from the early fourteenth century, Imam al-Dhahabi, *Siyar Aʿlaam an-Nubala* [The lives of noble figures] (Lebanon: Muʾassassat al-Risalah, 2014 repr.) 21:307. The English-language quote is from https://islamqa.info/en/answers/130484/some-criticisms-of-the-belief-of-ibn-rushd-averroes.

63. One key misunderstanding of the Christian Averroists was their notion of "double truth," that there are two kinds of truth—religious and philosophical. What Ibn Rushd argued, however, was a vision of single truth, which can be accessed both by religion and philosophy in their own ways.

64. Arthur Herman, *The Cave and the Light: Plato Versus Aristotle, and the Struggle for the Soul of Western Civilization* (New York: Random House, 2013), 252–53.

65. Peter Leuprecht, *Reason, Justice and Dignity: A Journey to Some Unexplored Sources of Human Rights* (Leiden: Martinus Nijhoff Publishers, 2012), 50.

66. Oliver Leaman, *An Introduction to Classical Islamic Philosophy* (Cambridge: Cambridge University Press, 2004) 30.

67. H. Chad Hillier, "Ibn Rushd (Averroes) (1126–1198)," *The Internet Encyclopedia of Philosophy*, https://www.iep.utm.edu/ibnrushd/.

68. Oliver Leaman, *Averroes and His Philosophy* (Richmond, UK: Curzon Press, 1988), xv.

69. See Mourad Laabdi, "The Other Averroes: Revealed Law and the Craft of Juristic Disagreement" (PhD thesis, Department for the Study of Religion, University of Toronto, 2017), 179–83.

70. The term is used by Fazlur Rahman in his *Islam and Modernity: The Transformation of an Intellectual Tradition* (Chicago: University of Chicago Press, 1982), 158.
71. According to Rosenthal, Ibn Rushd "resembles Maimonides among the Jews." Erwin I. J. Rosenthal, "The Place of Politics in the Philosophy of Ibn Rushd," *Bulletin of the School of Oriental and African Studies* (University of London) 15, no. 2 (1953): 262.
72. Moses Maimonides, *The Guide for the Perplexed*, trans. M. Friedlander (New York: E. P. Dutton, 1904), 108.
73. Ibid.
74. See Sabine Schmidtke, "Mu'tazilism in Islam and Judaism: Why Did Jewish Thinkers in the Tenth Century Start to Adopt Rationalist Doctrines?" *IAS The Institute Letter*, Fall 2017, 8–9.
75. See Jonathan Jacobson, *Law, Reason, and Morality, in Medieval Jewish Philosophy: Sadia Gaon, Bahya ibn Pakuda, and Moses Maimonides* (NewYork: Oxford University Press, 2010), 111, 152.
76. Heinrich Graetz, *History of the Jews* (Philadelphia Jewish Publication Society of America, 1894), 3:542.
77. See Adrian Sackson, "From Moses to Moses: Anthropomorphism and Divine Incorporeality in Maimonides's *Guide* and Mendelssohn's *Bi'ur*," *Harvard Theological Review* 112, no. 2 (April 2019): 209–34.
78. Raphael Patai, *The Jewish Mind* (Detroit: Wayne State University Press, 1996) 272.
79. For a discussion on how being a minority gave Jews the predisposition to think unconventionally, thus creatively, see Norman Lebrecht, *Genius & Anxiety: How Jews Changed the World, 1847–1947* (New York: Scribner Books, 2019).
80. Among them was the Egyptian Islamist thinker al-Jundi, who depicted modernity and Enlightenment as a "Jewish idea," and their impact on the Muslim world a "Jewish conspiracy." Quoted in Bassam Tibi, *Islam's Predicament with Modernity* (New York: Routledge, 2009), 237.

CHAPTER 9: WHY WE LOST REASON, REALLY

1. Al-Kawakibi, *The Character of Despotism*, 50–51, quoted in *Arab Human Development Report 2003*, (Amman, Jordan: United Nations Publications, 2003), 120.
2. "The Islamist Spring and the West's Decline: An Interview with Robert R. Reilly," *European Conservative*, Winter 2013. Also published in *Catholic World Report*, September 4, 2013, https://www.catholicworldreport.com/2013/09/04/the-islamist-spring-and-the-wests-decline/.

3. Qur'an, 2:30, 35:39, 38:26.
4. Qur'an, 2:34, 7:11, 15:29, 17:61, 18:50, 20:116, and 33:72.
5. For more on the *mihna*, see Mustafa Akyol, *Islam Without Extremes* (New York: W. W. Norton, 2011), 107–10.
6. "Createdness of the Qur'an," *Encyclopedia of the Qur'an* (Leiden: Brill, 2001), 1:469.
7. Bahjat Kamil al-Tikriti, "The Religious Policy of al-Mutawakkil" (master's thesis, McGill University, 1969), 50–51.
8. Ibid., 51.
9. George Makdisi, *Ibn 'Aqil: Religion and Culture in Classical Islam*, (Edinburgh: Edinburgh University Press, 1997), 8.
10. Ibid.
11. Ibid., 9.
12. Ibn al-Jawzi, *Al-Muntazam fi ta'rikh al-muluk wa al-umam* (Beirut: Dar al-kutub al-ilmiyya, 1992), 15:125–26, quoted in Eric J. Hanne, *Putting the Caliph in His Place: Power, Authority, and the Late Abbasid Caliphate* (Madison, NJ: Fairleigh Dickinson University Press, 2007), 70.
13. Ziauddin Sardar, *Islam Beyond the Violent Jihadis: An Optimistic Muslim Speaks* (London: Biteback Publishing), 2016.
14. Makdisi, *Ibn 'Aqil*, 15.
15. Omid Safi, *Politics and Knowledge in Premodern Islam: Negotiating Ideology and Religious Inquiry* (Chapel Hill, NC: University of North Carolina Press, 2006), xxv.
16. For the collapse of "theology" into "creed" under the "Sunni unity" of Mamluks, see J. Halverson, *Theology and Creed in Sunni Islam* (New York: Palgrave Macmillan; 2010), 53–54.
17. Ibid., 53.
18. Al-Maqrīzī, *Al-Khiṭaṭ*, 2:343, quoted here from Yasir Qadhi, "Reconciling Reason and Revelation in the Writings of Ibn Taymiyya (d. 728/1328)" (PhD diss., Yale University, 2013), 75.
19. Margaretha T. Heemskerk, *Suffering in the Mu'tazilite Theology: 'Abd al-Jabbār's Teaching on Pain and Divine Justice* (Leiden: Brill, 2000), 69.
20. *The Fatwas of Ibn al-Salāh*, 34–35, cited in Mustafa Abd al-Rāziq, *Tamhīd li-Tārīkh al-Falsafa al-Islāmiyya*, 3rd ed. (Cairo: Maktabat al-Nahdha al-Misriyya, 1966), 85–86. Quoted here from: Nasr Hamid Abu Zayd, *Critique of Religious Discourse*, trans. Jonathan Wright (New Haven: Yale University Press, 2018], 83–84.
21. On this topographic factor, see my book *Islam without Extremes* (New York: W. W. Norton, 2011) pp. 133–134.
22. Patricia Crone, "Ninth-Century Muslim Anarchists," *Past and Present* (Oxford University Press) 167 (May 2000), 1.

23. Ibid.
24. Ibid., 5.
25. Ibid., 13.
26. Ibid., 22.
27. Ibid., 18.
28. Ibid., 17.
29. Ibid., 15. For an Islamic view on Mu'tazila "anarchists," also see Yahya Alshamy, "Islam and State-Skepticism," Libertarianism.org, Sep 21, 2020, https://www.libertarianism.org/articles/islam-and-state-skepticism.
30. Averroes on Plato's *Republic*, trans., with intro. and notes, Ralph Lerner (Ithaca and London: Cornell University Press, 1974), 4.
31. See Muhammad Ali Khalidi, "Al-Farabi on the Democratic City," *British Journal for the History of Philosophy* 11, no. 3 (2003): 379–94. Khalidi carefully shows that "Farabi departs significantly from Plato, according the democratic city a superior standing and casting it in a more positive light" (p. 379). For a summary of Farabi's argument on the democratic city, also see Franz Rosenthal, *Man Versus Society in Medieval Islam*, ed. Dimitri Gutas (Leiden: Brill, 2015), 112.
32. Anthony Robert Booth, *Islamic Philosophy and the Ethics of Belief* (London: Palgrave Macmillan, 2016), 81. Booth only adds that Farabi's political theory is "a kind of liberalism that resembles something more like anarchism." "Libertarianism" may be the right word.
33. Anthony Black, *The History of Islamic Political Thought* (Edinburgh: Edingurgh University Press, 2011), 75.
34. Ibid.
35. Maribel Fierro, "Ibn Rushd's (Averroes) 'Disgrace' and his Relation with the Almohads," in *Islamic Philosophy from the 12th to the 14th Century*, ed. Abdelkader Al Ghouz Göttingen, Germany: V&R Unipress, 2018), 87.
36. Charles Butterworth, "Political Teachings of Averroes," *Arabic Sciences and Philosophy*, Volume 2 Issue 2, 1992],192, 198.
37. Al-Jabiri makes that argument. See Fierro, "Ibn Rushd's (Averroes) 'Disgrace,'" 87.
38. Ibn Rushd's commentary on Plato's *Republic*, 133–34:97, in Hazem Y. Salem, "Islamic Political Thought: Reviving a Rationalist Tradition" (PhD diss., University of Denver, 2013), 160.
39. Hazem Y. Salem, "Islamic Political Thought: Reviving a Rationalist Tradition", 162.
40. It was none other than Abd al-Raziq who had this observation: "It is quite noticeable in the history of scientific movement of Muslims that the chance of political science among them was the worst compared to

other sciences." Souad T. Ali, *A Religion, Not a State* (Salt Lake City: University of Utah Press, 2009), 75.

41. Rosenthal, *Man Versus Society in Medieval Islam,* 112.
42. Robert Irwin, *Ibn Khaldun: An Intellectual Biography* (Princeton, NJ: Princeton University Press, 2018), xi.
43. Ibn Khaldun, *The Muqaddimah: An Introduction to History*, trans. Franz Rosenthal, (Princeton, NJ: Princeton University Press, 1958) 2:92. For "forced labor" and "forced sales and purchases," see 2: 108–109.
44. Ibid., 89.
45. Irwin, *Ibn Khaldun,* 151.
46. Abdul Azim Islahi, "Al-Asadi and His Work al-Taysir: A Study of His Socio-economic Ideas" (Jeddah, Saudi Arabia: Islamic Economics Institute, King Abdulaziz University, April, 14, 2016).
47. Trans. and quoted in Fatih Ermiş, *A History of Ottoman Economic Thought: Developments Before the Nineteenth Century* (New York: Routledge, 2014), 57.
48. Ibid., 59.
49. The term "proto-quasi-socialist Ottoman system" has been coined by Turkish historian Murat Çızakça, an expert on Islam's economic heritage, who thinks that the Ottomans abandoned the more market-oriented traditions of that heritage only to their detriment. See Murat Çızakça, "Long Term Causes of Decline of the Ottoman/Islamic Economies" (paper submitted at the *Settimana di Studi*, "Religion and Religious Institutions in European Economy, 1000–1800," 2011), 20. Also see Murat Çızakça, *Islamic Capitalism and Finance: Origins, Evolution and the Future* (Cheltenham, UK: Edward Elgar, 2011). Another Turkish scholar, Ahmed Güner Sayar, adds that until the nineteenth century, Ottoman economic thought "limited the economic activity of the individual," to whom it rather advised *zühd*, or ascetism. *Osmanlı İktisat Düşüncesinin Çağdaşlaşması* [The Modernization of Ottoman Economic Thought] (Istanbul: Otuken, 2009), 11.
50. Irwin, *Ibn Khaldun,* 162.
51. Ibid., 106.
52. Fazlur Rahman quotes this incident, from Abduh's al-A'mal al Kâmila (3:117) in his *Islam and Modernity: Transformation of an Intellectual Tradition,* 64.
53. Arthur Laffer himself notes his debt to Ibn Khaldun in "The Laffer Curve: Past, Present, and Future," June 1, 2004, https://www.heritage.org/taxes /report/the-laffer-curve-past-present-and-future.
54. Robert D. McFadden, "Reagan Cites Islamic Scholar," *New York Times,* October 2, 1981; Ronald Reagan, "There They Go Again," *New York Times,* February 18, 1993. The quote here is from the latter article.

55. Ibn Hajar, *Fath al-bari* (Dar al-Ma'rifa, 1379), 13: 208; quoted here from Ovamir Anjum, *Politics, Law, and Community in Islamic Thought: The Taymiyyan Moment* (New York: Cambridge University Press, 2012), pp. 138–139.

56. Qur'an 4:59.

57. See Asma Afsaruddin, *Contemporary Issues in Islam* (Edinburgh: Edinburgh University Press, 2015), 29–38.

58. The hadith is quoted by al-Mawardi: Al-Mawardi, *The Ordinances of Government*, trans. Wafaa H. Wahba (Reading, UK: Garnet Publishing, 1996), 3.

59. Montgomery Watt, *The Formative Period of Islamic Thought* (Edinburgh: Edinburgh University Press, 1973), 292. For another, similar, translation, see Imaam Ahmed ibn Hanbal, *Foundation of the Sunnah: By the Revered Imaam, the Scholar, the Teacher, the Reviver of the Sunnah, the Subduer of Innovations*, (Al-maktabah As-Salafiyyah Publications, 1997) Here, on p. 45, the statement reads: "We do not set out [in revolt] against the Rulers with the sword, even if they are unjust and oppressive."

60. This is a Mu'tazila text from the ninth century and it refers to *ashab al-hadith*, or the hadith followers, which was a reference to Hanbalites and also Ash'arites. Patricia Crone, *God's Rule: Government and Islam: Six Centuries of Medieval Islamic Political Thought* (New York: Columbia University Press, 2005), 137.

61. al-Hakim al-Jishumi, *Sharh: Uyun al-Masail*, ms. Leiden, Or. 2,584–B, quoted in Michael Cook, *Commanding Right and Forbidding Wrong in Islamic Thought* Cambridge: (Cambridge University Press, 2004), 224.

62. Antony Black, *The History of Islamic Political Thought: From the Prophet to the Present* (Edinburgh: Edinburgh University Press, 2011), 29.

63. Antony Black, *The History of Islamic Political Thought*, 89.

64. Ovamir Anjum, *Politics, Law, and Community in Islamic Thought: The Taymiyyan Moment* (New York: Cambridge University Press, 2012), 132.

65. Ibid., 168.

66. Ibid., 131. It is worth noting that Anjum himself is a modern-day student of Ibn Taymiyya, who, in Anjum's words, took a "middle position" between Mu'tazila intellectualism and Ash'arite voluntarism (p. 207).

67. Ali Mabrook, "The Ash'arite Dogma: the Root of the Arab/Muslim Absolutism," *Al-Jami'ah* 46, no. 1 (2008): 16.

68. Soud T. Ali, *A Religion, Not a State: Ali Abd al-Raziq's Islamic Justification of Political Secularism* (Salt Lake City: Utah University Press, 2009), 74.

69. See more on this in Akyol, *Islam Without Extremes*, 67–70.

70. See Gerhard Bowering, *Islamic Political Thought: An Introduction* (Princeton, NJ: Princeton University Press, 2015), 81.

71. Al-Ghazali quotes the hadith, from *Al-Hakim* and *At-Tirmidhi*, his *Revival of the Religious Sciences* [*Ihya Ulum Ad-Din*], trans. Mohammad Mahdi al-Sharif, (Beirut: Dar al-Kotob al-Ilmiyah, 2011), 2:545.

72. Ibid.

73. Ahmet Kuru, *Islam, Authoritarianism, and Underdevelopment: A Global and Historical Comparison* (Cambridge: Cambridge University Press, 2019).

74. Malcolm H. Kerr, *Islamic Reform: The Political Theories of Muhammad Abduh and Rashid Rida* (Los Angeles: Universtity of California Press, 1966), 108.

75. *Saudi Government & People: What Others Do Not Know* (Riyadh: Center for Global Thought on Saudi Arabia, 2013), 124–25. Emphasis added.

76. Ibid., 128.

77. This was an observation by Richard Burton, who was the British consul in Aleppo from 1869 to 1871. Quoted in Robert Carver, "The Great Divide," *History Today* 69, no. 8 (August 2019).

78. Turkish theologian İlhami Güler makes this argument in *Allah'ın Ahlakiliği Sorunu* [*The problem of God's moralness*] (Ankara: Ankara Okulu Yayınları, 2017), 77–79.

79. Al-Ash'arī, *al-Luma'*, 73, quoted in Mona Siddiqui, *The Good Muslim: Reflections on Classical Islamic Law and Theology* (Cambridge: Cambridge University Press, 2012), p. 131. Emphasis added.

80. Habib Ahmad Mashhur al-Haddad, *Key to the Garden*, trans. Mostafa al-Badawi (Beirut: Starlatch Press, 1997), 43. Emphasis added. It is worth noting that al-Haddad immediately added the verse "Your Lord is never unjust to His servants." But from this he understood that whatever God does is just; not that He does whatever is just.

81. Moses Maimonides, *The Guide for the Perplexed*, trans. M. Friedlander (New York: Dover Publications, 1956), 128.

82. Ibid.

83. Derk Pereboom, "Theological Determinism and the Relationship with God," in *Free Will and Classical Theism*, ed. Hugh J. McCann (New York: Oxford University Press, 2017), 201–2.

CHAPTER 10: BACK TO MECCA

1. Fazlur Rahman, *Islam and Modernity: Transformation of an Intellectual Tradition* (Chicago: University of Chicago Press, 1982), 141.

2. Qur'an, 111:1–5. It should be noted that "Abu Lahab," which means "Father of Fire," is not a proper name but a nickname for Abd al-'Uzzā ibn Abd al-Muttalib. One narration is that the man was called "Father of Fire" by his own father, because of his beauty and charm due to his

red ("inflamed") cheeks. Another theory is that he was called "Father of Fire," by the Qur'an itself, for he was condemned to hell fire.

3. See Fahruddin er-Razi, *Tefsir-i Kebir* (Ankara: Huzur Yayınevi, 2002), 23:538–39.

4. Osman Aydınlı, "İlk Mu'tezile'nin Özgür İrade Söylemi: Amr B. Ubeyd ve Kader Anlayışı" [The narrative of freewill in early Mu'tazila: Amr b. Ubayd and his notion of fate], *Çorum İlahiyat Fakültesi Dergisi*, 2002, 136–38. Montgomery Watt also mentions Ibn Ubayd's argument in *The Formative Period of Islamic Thought* (Edinburgh: Edinburgh University Press, 1973), 108.

5. Qur'an, 85:22.

6. Qur'an, 43:4. The same term is also used in 13:39.

7. It is notable that the Qur'an says it was revealed "of the book." (35:31). For a detailed study of this issue, see Daniel A. Madigan, *The Qur'an's Self-Image: Writing and Authority in Islam's Scripture* (Princeton, NJ: Princeton University Press, 2001). Madigan shows that by the term *kitab,* or "book," the Qur'an actually refers not to the *mushaf* (the Qur'an between the covers), but the divine wisdom and will, which is the source of both the Qur'an as well as former revelations. The distinction between the Qur'an and "the Book" was also highlighted by Muhammad Shahrur. See his *The Essential Muhammad Shahrur: The Qur'an, Morality and Critical Reason*, trans., ed., and intro. Andreas Christmann (Leiden: Brill, 2009), 120–50. Shahrur argued that while parts of the Qur'an are "not subject to occasions of revelation," other parts "[respond] to change and alterations in nature and [record] human history reflecting its peculiar fluctuations and unpredictable movements" (p. 142).

8. Qur'an, 9:1.

9. "Esbab," *İslam Ansiklopedisi* (Istanbul: Türkiye Diyanet Vakfı, 1995), 11:360.

10. See Barbara Stowasser, "The Qur'an and Its Meaning," *Arab Studies Journal* 3, no. 1 (Spring 1995): 5. It is also quite interesting that the word *sabab*, plural *asbab*, can mean both "occasion" or "cause," which point to two different ways of understanding both the nature of Qur'an and that of the universe.

11. See Mohammad Fadel, "Is Historicism a Viable Strategy for Islamic Law Reform?," *Islamic Law and Society* (Leiden: Brill) 18 (2011): 147. Fadels add that "a minority of scholars" disputed this generalization of words, whereas the majority upheld it.

12. This is a definition by Egyptian jurist Muhammad Said Ashmawi, professor of Islamic and comparative law at the University of Cairo. Wael Hallaq, *A History of Islamic Legal Theories*, (Cambridge: Cambridge University Press, 1997) 230.

13. See Watt, *Formative Period,* 179.

14. Qur'an, 5:97, 9:5, 9:36–37.

15. Qur'an, 2:194.

16. Qur'an, 24:58.

17. Qur'an, 4:3, 4:24, 4:36, 24:33, 24:58, 30:28.

18. Qur'an, 4:36, 24:33.

19. Qur'an, 24:33, 90:13. For a more detailed explanation of the major improvement Islam brought to the reality of seventh-century slavery, see Ibn Ashur, *Treatise on Maqasid al-Shariah*, trans. Mohamed El-Tahir El-Mesawi (King's Lynn, UK: International Institute of Islamic Thought, 2006), 156–60.

20. Asma Barlas and David Raeburn Finn, *Believing Women in Islam: A Brief Introduction* (Austin: University of Texas Press, 2019), 12.

21. Qur'an, 2:231–32, 65:1, 6.

22. See Adis Duderija, "A Case Study of Patriarchy and Slavery: The Hermeneutical Importance of Qur'ānic Assumptions in the Development of a Values-Based and Purposive Oriented Qur'ān-sunna Hermeneutic," *Journal of Women of the Middle East and the Islamic World* 11 (2013): 58–87. Also see Asma Lamrabet, *Women and Men in the Qur'an* trans. Muneera Salem-Murdock, (Cham, Switzerland: Palgrave Macmillan, 2018), 90–91, 96.

23. Lamrabet, *Women and Men in the Qur'an*, 102.

24. The verse is 4:34. For the discussions on whether it is descriptive or prescriptive, see Aysha A. Hidayatullah, *Feminist Edges of the Qur'an* (New York: Oxford University Press, 2014), 70–74.

25. Qur'an, 2:229, 230.

26. Qur'an, 2:228–35, 65:1–7.

27. *Jami at Tirmidhi*, book on divorce and Li'an, chap. 16, here taken from the English edition trans. Abu Khaliyl and ed. Hafiz Abu Tahir Zubair Ali Zai (Riyadh: Darussalam, 2007), 2:561.

28. Qur'an, 2:229.

29. The description, "keep [a woman] hanging," is from Khaled Abou El Fadl, *Reasoning with God: Reclaiming Shari'ah in the Modern Age* (Lanham, MD: Rowman and Littlefield), 385.

30. Yvonne Yazbeck Haddad and Barbara Freyer Stowasser, *Islamic Law and the Challenges of Modernity* (Walnut Creek, CA: Altamira Press, 2004), 163–64. To their credit, Hanbalis have been the only Sunni school that has categorically disallowed *tahlil* marriages.

31. For an example, see the Turkish novel *Hülle ve Töre* by İsmail Polat (İstanbul: Kora Yayın, 2012). *Hülle* is the Turkish word for "tahlil marriage."

32. Athar Ahmad, "The Women Who Sleep with a Stranger to Save Their Marriage," BBC Asian Network, April 5, 2017. https://www.bbc.com/news/uk-39480846.

33. "What Is 'Triple Talaq' or Instant Divorce?," AlJazeera.com, August 22, 2017. https://www.aljazeera.com/indepth/features/2017/05/tripple-talaq -triple-divorce-170511160557346.html.

34. See Fazlur Rahman, *Islam and Modernity*, 5–7.

35. Qur'an, 58:1.

36. Qur'an, 58:2–4.

37. Nasr Abû Zayd, *Rethinking the Qur'ân: Towards a Humanistic Hermeneu-tics*, Kindle ed. (Utrecht: Humanistics University Press, 2004).

38. Qur'an, 5:101.

39. Qur'an, 16:103.

40. Qur'an, 109:1–6. Emphasis added.

41. Qur'an, 18:29. Emphasis added.

42. See Qur'an, 2:119, 7:188, 11:12, 13:17, 15:89, 22:49, 26:115, 27:92, 28:46, 29:50, 33:45, 34:28, 35:23, 35:24, 38:65, 37:80, 41:4, 46:9, 48:8, 50:2, 53:56, 67:26, 79:85.

43. Qur'an, 6:104. Emphasis added.

44. Qur'an, 10:99.

45. Quran, 6:35.

46. Qur'an, 6:107.

47. For an example, see Hayrettin Karaman, "Sol Yanağını mı Çevireceksin?" [Will you turn the left cheek?], *Yeni Şafak*, October 12, 2012.

48. Qur'an, 41:34.

49. See Gabriel Said Reynolds, *The Emergence of Islam: Classical Traditions in Contemporary Perspective* (Minneapolis: Fortress Press, 2012), 22–23. "The issue," Reynolds says, based on Quraysh's accounts, "was not Meccan trade but Meccan pride."

50. Qur'an, 53:19–23.

51. Ibn Kathir, *Stories of the Prophets: From Adam to Muhammad*, trans. Sayed Gad, Tamir Abu As-Su'ood, and Muhammad A. M. Abu Sheishaa (Cairo, Egypt: Dar Al-Manarah, 2001), 373.

52. Al-Ghazali, too, makes the same point when he says pagans of Mecca were enraged against the Prophet for "disgracing their gods and abusing their religion." *Revival of the Religious Sciences*, 2:585.

53. Narrated by al-Ghazali in ibid.

54. Qur'an, 22:39–40.

55. "Ghazw," *The Encyclopedia of Islam* (Leiden: Brill, 1991), 2:1055.

56. Fred Donner argues that from all the battles of Prophet Muhammad, one cannot infer an intention of conquest beyond Arabia, but one can certainly map out a strategy for survival. Donner, *The Early Islamic Conquests* (Princeton, NJ: Princeton University Press, 2014), 102.

57. Qur'an, 9:5, 8:12.

58. Montgomery Watt, *Muhammad in Medina* (Oxford: Oxford University Press, 1956), 223. The clause also includes the sentence, "The Jews of Banu Awf are a community (*ummah*) along with the believers," where the term *ummah* signifies a multireligious political community, not just the Muslim community.

59. The historical accuracy of the reports about the massacre of the men of Banu Qurayza has been disputed by some modern Muslim authors. See my *Islam Without Extremes* (New York: W. W. Norton, 2011), 57–58.

60. Qur'an, 5:64.

61. That prominent member was Ka'b ibn al-Ashraf, who is also addressed in chapter 11. For his connection with Mecca, see Uri Rubin, "The Assassination of Ka'b b. al-Ashraf," *Oriens*, no. 32, 1990.

62. "Hamas Covenant 1988," https://avalon.law.yale.edu/20th_century/hamas .asp.

63. Qur'an, 5:45.

64. Ibid.

65. Qur'an, 5:38, 5:33.

66. Ibn Qutayba, a Muslim historian who died in 889, wrote that it was the Meccan polytheist leader Walid ibn al-Mughira who established the rule of amputation of hands for theft. See Michael Cook, *Islam and Its Past: Jahiliyya, Late Antiquity, and the Qur'an*, eds. Carol Bakhos and Michael Cook (New York: Oxford University Press, 2017) 235.

67. Qur'an, 7:124, 20:71, 26:49.

68. Muhammad Abid al-Jabiri, *Democracy, Human Rights and Law in Islamic Thought* (London, UK: I. B. Tauris, 2008), 85.

69. There are reports of short-term captivity in Medina under the Prophet, but only in private houses or the mosque, none of which were formal prisons. See Sean Anthony, "The Domestic Origins of Imprisonment: An Inquiry into an Early Islamic Institution," *Journal of the American Oriental Society*, October–December 2009, vol. 129, no. 4, 575–580.

70. Franz Rosenthal, *Man versus Society in Medieval Islam*, ed. Dimitri Gutas (Leiden: Brill, 2015), 57.

71. Qur'an, 8:60.

72. Qur'an, 9:60.

73. Timur Kuran, "Zakat: Islam's Missed Opportunity to Limit Predatory Taxation" (Working Paper No. 284, Economic Research Initiatives at Duke [ERID], Duke University, Durham, NC, April 2019) 11.

74. Suliman Bashear, "On the Origins and Development of the Meaning of Zakāt in Early Islam," *Arabica* 40, no. 1 (January 1993): 103, 107.

75. Quoted by al-Ghazali in *Revival of the Religious Sciences*, 2:587.

76. Bashear, "On the Origins and Development of the Meaning of Zakāt," 107.

77. Ibid., 101.
78. Quoted by al-Ghazali in *Revival of the Religious Sciences*, 2:587.
79. See Taha Jabir Alalwani, *Apostasy in Islam: A Historical and Scriptural Analysis*, trans. Nancy Roberts (London: International Institute of Islamic Thought, 2011), 99.
80. Even ISIS magazine *Dabiq* happily quotes some Salafi references to Abu Bakr's campaign as an argument against those who opposed the punishment of sins. "Irja: The Most Dangerous Bidah," *Dabiq* 8 (March 2015): 45.
81. The description of the "Constantinian revolution" is from Christian C. Sahner, *Christian Martyrs Under Islam: Religious Violence and the Making of the Muslim World* (Princeton, NJ: Princeton University Press, 2018), 23.
82. Sherko Kirmanj, "Challenging the Islamist Politicization of Islam: The Non-Islamic Origins of Muslim Political Concepts," in *Political Islam from Muhammad to Ahmadinejad: Defenders, Defractors, and Definitions*, ed. Joseph Morrison Skelly (Santa Barbara, CA: Praeger Security International, 2009), 42.
83. The name of al-Raziq's book was *Al-Islam wa 'Usul al-Hukm [Islam and the principles of governance]*, and its main thesis was that the caliphate is a historical institution, not a requirement of Islam. The phrase "a religion, not a state" is repeatedly used in the book and has become the title of a book about al-Raziq: Souad Tagelsir Ali, *A Religion, Not a State: Ali 'Abd al-Raziq's Islamic Justification of Political Secularism* (Salt Lake City: University of Utah Press, 2009).
84. Sayyid Abul A'la Mawdudi, *Let Us Be Muslims* (London: The Islamic Foundation, 1985), 288.
85. Rasim Özdenören, "İslam Kıskançtır" [Islam is jealous], *İzlenim* vol 28, Dec 1995, 26–28.
86. See Al-Sayyid Abū al-Qāsim al-Mūsawī al-Khūī, *The Prolegomena to the Qur'an*, trans. with intro. A. Sachedina (New York: Oxford University Press, 1998), 186.
87. Asma Afsaruddin, *Contemporary Issues in Islam* (Edinburgh: Edinburgh University Press, 2015), 191.
88. Which verses are exactly the "verses of the sword" are disputed, but a commonly acceptable list would include 2:191, 193; 4:89, 91; 8:39; 9:29, 36, 73, 123; and 66:9. Meanwhile, 9:5 has been often seen as the "sword verse" par excellence.
89. Khalid Yahya Blankinship, "Sword Verses," *The Oxford Encyclopedia of the Islamic World*, ed. John Esposito (New York: Oxford University Press, 2009), Oxford Islamic Studies Online.
90. Afsaruddin, *Contemporary Issues in Islam*, 118; Asma Afsaruddin,

"Jihād, Gender, and Religious Minorities in the Siyar Literature: the Diachronic View," *Studia Islamica* 114 (2019): 11.

91. Afsaruddin, *Contemporary Issues in Islam*, 118–21.
92. Qur'an, 2:106, Sahih international translation. (The Quran: Arabic Text With Corresponding English Meaning, [Jeddah: Saheeh International, 1997]) A parallel verse is 16:101. An alternative explanation to these verses is that the Qur'an itself was "abrogating" earlier scriptures, not that Qur'anic verses were abrogating each other.
93. Afsaruddin, *Contemporary Issues in Islam*, 191.
94. Thameem Ushama, "The Phenomenon of Al-Naskh: A Brief Overview of the Key Issues," *Jurnal Fiqh* 3 (2006): 123–24.
95. Roslan Abdul-Rahim, "Demythologizing the Qur'an Rethinking Revelation Through Naskh al-Qur'an," *Global Journal Al-Thaqafah* 7, no. 2 (December 2017): 60.
96. For the execution of Taha, and the key role played in it by Sudan's Islamist ideologue Hasan al-Turabi, see George Packer, "The Moderate Martyr," *New Yorker,* September 3, 2006. Also see the article by Abdullahi Ahmed An-Na'im, a student of Taha and an important reformist scholar himself: Na'im, "The Islamic Law of Apostasy and Its Modern Applicability," *Religion* 16, no. 3 (1986): 197–224.
97. "Fitna," *Encyclopedia of Islam*, 2:930–31.
98. The term *fitna* is translated as "persecution" or "oppression" by Muhammad Marmaduke Pickthall, Abdullah Yusuf Ali, Shakir, Arthur John Arberry, and M. A. S. Abdel Haleem in their well-respected Qur'an translations. Arguably this translation is closer to the meaning of *fitna*, which comes from the process of exposing metals to fire to shape them, as in "trial by fire." It has several other uses in the Qur'an as "temptation or trial of faith." Cleary, persecution can be a trial, but "disbelief" not. See "Fitna," *Encyclopedia of Islam*, 2:930.
99. See Asma Afsaruddin, *Striving in the Path of God: Jihad and Martyrdom in Islamic Thought* (New York: Oxford University Press, 2013), 45–52. Also see Mustafa Öztürk, "Cihad Ayetleri: Tefsir Birikimine, İslam Geleneğine ve Günümüze Yansımaları, [Jihad Verses: Their Reflections on Exegesis, Islamic Tradition and Today]" in *İslam Kaynaklarında, Geleneğinde ve Günümüzde Cihad [Jihad in Islamic Sources, Tradition and Today]* (İstanbul: Kuramer Yayınları, 2016), 145–46.
100. Qur'an, Yusuf Ali translation, 9:33, 48:28, and 61:9. (The Holy Qur'an, Hertfordshire, UK: Wordsworth Editions Ltd, 2001).
101. See Pickthall, Shakir, Muhammad Sarwar, and Mohsin Khan translations. (All fully available at http://corpus.quran.com) Similarly, most Turkish translations use the term *üstün kılmak*, which is "to make superior." The

problem was noted by Jamal Badawi, the Egyptian-born Canadian Muslim scholar, who wrote, "a better translation of the original Qur'anic Arabic term *li-yuzhirahu* is 'to proclaim it,' rather than 'to make it prevail.'" (Jamal Badawi, "Muslim/Non-Muslim Relations," December 3, 2012, The Fiqh Council of North America, http://fiqhcouncil.org/muslim-non-muslim-relations.

102. Mawdudi, *Tafhim al-Qur'an*, commentary on 9:33. (Leicestershire, UK: Islamic Foundation, 2007) Available online at https://quranx.com/tafsirs/9.33.

CHAPTER 11: FREEDOM MATTERS I: *HISBAH*

1. Alija Izetbegović, *Izetbegović of Bosnia and Herzegovina: Notes from Prison, 1983–1988,* (Westport, CT: Praeger, 2002), 50.

2. This a paraphrase of a common narrative. For its examples in Iran, see Reza Afshari, *Human Rights in Iran: The Abuse of Cultural Relativism* (Philadelphia: University of Pennsylvania Press, 2011), 5–6.

3. "'Gerçek özgürlük: Allah'a kulluk,' [True freedom: Slavery to Allah]" *Yeni Şafak,* May 19, 2017.

4. Iain Taylor, *Pannenberg on the Triune God* (London: T&T Clark, 2007), 151.

5. Roger Olson, "The Bonds of Freedom," *Christianity Today,* October 5, 2012.

6. "What Is Freedom?—Answered by a Zen Master," https://medium.com/@Jos91/what-is-freedom-answered-by-a-zen-master-e82d3a63d24d.

7. See "Inner and Outer Freedom," *Cato Unbound: A Journal of Debate,* October 2018, https://www.cato-unbound.org/print-issue/2410.

8. F. A. Hayek, *The Constitution of Liberty* (Chicago: The University of Chicago Press, 1978), 12.

9. Bernard Lewis, *What Went Wrong?: Western Impact and Middle Eastern Response* (New York: Oxford University Press, 2002), 156.

10. Noah Feldman, "Does Shariah Mean the Rule of Law?," *New York Times,* March 16, 2008.

11. For the function of Sharia in classical Islam as "rule of law," see my book *Islam Without Extreme,* (New York: W. W. Norton, 2011), 67–70.

12. Michael Weiss, "Inside ISIS's Torture Brigades," *The Daily Beast,* November 17, 2015, https://www.thedailybeast.com/inside-isiss-torture-brigades.

13. Ramizah wan Muhammad, "Hisbah in Malaysia: Preventing Vices and Immoralities," *International Journal of Islamic Thoughts* 5, no. 2, 62.

14. Al-Mawardi, *Al-Ahkam as-Sultaniyyah: The Laws of Islamic Governance* (London: Taha Publishers, 1996), 313.

15. Al-Ghazali, *Revival of the Religious Sciences (Ihya Ulum Ad-Din])*, trans. Mohammad Mahdi al-Sharif, (Beirut: Dar al-Kotob al-Ilmiyah, 2011), 2:539.

16. Ibid., 465–66.

17. The verse is 24:27, which reads, "O you who believe! Do not enter houses other than your own, until you have asked permission." Another verse that limited the zeal for *hisbah* is 49:12, which reads, "Do not spy on each other." Al-Ghazali quotes both verses in his discussion of *hisbah* to establish the principle of the privacy of homes. *Revival of the Religious Sciences*, 2:555–56.

18. Ibid., 2:556. Slightly reworded for a grammatical correction.

19. For an extensive and meticulous study of the classical heritage on *hisbah*, see Michael Cook, *Commanding Right and Forbidding Wrong in Islamic Thought* (Cambridge: Cambridge University Press, 2011).

20. M. J. Kister, "The Market of the Prophet," *The Journal of the Economic and Social History of the Orient* 8 (1965): 274.

21. Al-Tabari argues that the first verses of the sura "Mutaffifin" were revealed in the face of such frauding in Medina, which existed in the city before the Prophet came. Ebu Cafer Muhammed ibn Cerir et-Taberi, *Taberi Tefsiri*, trans. Kerim Aytekin and Hasan Karakaya (Istanbul: Hisar Yayınevi, 1996), 9:33. But other sources think that "Mutaffifin" is a Meccan sura dealing with frauds in Mecca. Both seem possible.

22. R. P. Buckley, "The Muḥtasib," *Arabica* (Leiden: Brill) 39 (1992): 60.

23. Ibid., 4:183, where Buckley refers to ibn Abd al-Barr.

24. Ibid., 39 (1992): 60.

25. Ibid., 62

26. Ibid., 63.

27. "Hisba," *Encyclopedia of Islam* (Leiden: Brill, 1986), 3:487–88.

28. B. R. Foster, "Agoranomos and Muhtasib," *Journal of the Economic and Social History of the Orient* 13 (1970): 128–44.

29. "Hisba," *Encyclopedia of Islam*, 3:487.

30. Yassine Essid, *Critique of the Origins of Islamic Economic Thought* (Leiden: Brill, 1995), 115.

31. Ahmad bin Che Yaacob, "The Development of the Theory of the Institution of Hisbah in Medieval Islam" (Phd thesis, University Of Edinburgh, 1996), 29.

32. The incident is narrated in *Sahih Muslim*, bk. 17, hadith 4226; *Sunan Abu Dawud*, bk. 38, hadith 4474; *Sunan Ibn Majah*, bk. 20, hadith 2571. Yet still, even classical commentators couldn't agree on whether the Prophet instituted this punishment as a *hadd*. Ibn Abbas is on the record for saying, "the Prophet did not fix any punishment for wine drinking," which,

according to Hashim Kamali, means that "it is a flexible *ta'zir* punishment," rather than a more strict *hadd*. Mohammad Hashim Kamali, *Crime and Punishment in Islamic Law: A Fresh Interpretation* (New York: Oxford University Press, 2019), 162. The number of lashes was later fixed as eighty under Caliph Umar. *Sahih Muslim*, bk. 17, hadith 4231.

33. *Asbab al-Nuzul by Ali ibn Ahmad al-Wahidi* (Amman, Jordan: Royal Aal al-Bayt Institute for Islamic Thought, 2008), 72.
34. Ibid., 72–73. The incident about Hamza is narrated also in *Sahih al-Bukhari*, vol. 3, bk. 40, no. 563.
35. Qur'an, 5:91.
36. Qur'an, 3:104, Abdullah Yusuf Ali translation. (*The Holy Qur'an*, Hertfordshire, UK: Wordsworth Editions Ltd, 2001).
37. Cook, *Commanding Right*, 22–23.
38. Ibid., 22.
39. Ibid., 39.
40. W. Madelung, "Amr be Ma'ruf," *Encyclopædia Iranica*, ed. Ehsan Yarshater, (London, etc.: Routledge & Kegan Paul, 1985), I/9, 992–95.
41. Al-Tabari makes this point in his exegesis of Qur'an, 9: 112. The quote here is from Cook, *Commanding Right*, 24. Emphasis in the original.
42. Al-Ghazali, *Revival of the Religious Sciences* 2:556.
43. Abu Hanifa reasoned that alcoholic beverages other than *khamr*, or "wine," are forbidden only when they are taken in an intoxicating amount. He described intoxication as the state when "the person loses his rational capacity (*aql*) altogether; he cannot tell the difference between a small and a large amount, cannot distinguish the earth from the sky, nor a man from a woman." See Hashim Kamali, "Issues over Drinking Wine, in *Crime and Punishment in Islamic Law: A Fresh Interpretation* (New York: Oxford University Press, 2019).
44. Al-Ghazali, *Revival of the Religious Sciences* 2:559.
45. Ibid., 4:556–57.
46. Ibid., 4:558.
47. Mairaj Uddin Syed, "Coercion in Classical Islamic Law and Theology" (PhD diss., Princeton University, 2011), 17–18.
48. 'Abd al-Jabbār, *Mughnī*, 11:393. Quoted here from Mairaj Uddin Syed, "Coercion in Classical Islamic Law and Theology," 78, 95.
49. Syed, "Coercion in Classical Islamic Law," 17–18.
50. Patricia Crone notes how "the Mu'tazila argument" for metaphysical freedom has been updated by Islamic modernists such as Ibn Ashur to argue against social coercion in religion. "No Compulsion in Religion: Q. 2:256 in Mediaeval and Modern Interpretation," in *The Qur'ānic Pagans and Related Matters* (Leiden: Brill, 2016), 374–75.

51. "8 Shiites Say Saudi Religious Police Beat Them," *New York Times*, August 11, 2007.
52. "Sunni Muslims Banned from Holding Own Eid Prayers in Tehran," *The Guardian*, August 31, 2011.
53. Naser Ghobadzadeh, *Religious Secularity, A Theological Challenge to the Islamic State* (New York: Oxford University Press, 2015), 91–92.
54. "Politician in Iran Says Banning Alcohol Is a 'Failed Policy,'" *Radio Farda*, Radio Free Europe/Radio Liberty, April 1, 2019.
55. See Mustafa Akyol, "How Islamism Drives Muslims to Convert," *New York Times*, March 25, 2018.
56. H. Montazeri, *Hokumat-e Dini va Hughogh-e Ensanha* [*Religious state and human rights*] (Tehran: Saraei, 2008), 142–43, quoted here from Ghobadzadeh, *Religious Secularity*, 94.
57. Al-Ghazali, *Revival of the Religious Sciences*, 2:556.
58. Cook, *Commanding Right*, 214; W. Madelung "Amr be Ma'ruf," 992–95.
59. Kevin Reinhart, "What We Know About Ma'rūf," *Journal of Islamic Ethics* 1 (2017): 60.
60. Ibid., 63.

CHAPTER 12: FREEDOM MATTERS II: APOSTASY

1. Chandran Kukathas, *The Liberal Archipelago: A Theory of Diversity and Freedom* (Oxford: Oxford University Press, 2003), 96.
2. The al-Qaradawi interview is available on YouTube with English subtitles: https://www.youtube.com/watch?feature=player_detailpage&v=tB9UdXAP82o.
3. Rudolph Peters and Gert J. J. De Vries, "Apostasy in Islam," *Die Welt des Islams* (Leiden: Brill), n.s., 17, no. 1–4 (1976–1977): 5.
4. See Qur'an, 2:217, 3:86–87, 90; 4:137; 16:106; 47:25–28.
5. Qur'an, 2:256.
6. This English translation of Qur'an 2:256 is taken from the official website of JAKIM, or the Department of Islamic Advancement of Malaysia, the main official Islamic body of the country. Accessed September 12, 2018, http://www.islam.gov.my/en/e-jakim/e-quran/al-quran-translation.
7. See Jonathan A. C. Brown, "Even If It's Not True It's True: Using Unreliable Ḥadiths in Sunni Islam," *Islamic Law and Society* 18 (2011): 1–52. For a brief evaluation of classical hadith collections, also see my book, *Islam without Extremes* (New York, W. W. Norton, 2011), 98–107.
8. *Sahih al-Bukhari*, vol. 4, bk. 52, no. 260.
9. Ibid., vol. 9, bk. 83, no. 17.

10. Samuel Hosain Lamarti, "The Development of Apostasy and Punishment Law in Islam, 11 AH/632AD–157AH/774AD" (PhD thesis, Glasgow University, 2002),188–89.

11. *Sahih al-Bukhari*, vol. 9, bk. 89, no. 316. Exegetes differed on what the man exactly meant by saying, "Cancel my pledge." While some argued that it meant canceling the pledge of staying in Medina, others said it meant canceling the pledge to Islam, i.e., apostasy. Nihat Dalgın, "İrtidat ve Cezası," *Kur'an Mesajı İlmi Araştırmalar Dergisi* 10 (Summer 1998): 183–84. There are a few other individuals who also apostatized from Islam during the time of the Prophet, but received no punishment. For a short discussion, see Abdullah Bin Hamid Ali, "Preserving the Freedom for Faith: Reevaluating the Politics of Compulsion," *The Review of Faith & International Affairs*, vol. 9:2 (2011): 6.

12. Qur'an, 3:72.

13. Qur'an, 3:73. For the use of this verse by Muslim scholars against the ban on apostasy, see Declan O'Sullivan, "The Interpretation of Qur'anic Text to Promote or Negate the Death Penalty for Apostates and Blasphemers," *Journal of Qur'anic Studies*, Vol. 3, No. 2 (2001), 69–70.

14. Muhammad Shahrur makes this much-overlooked point. See *The Essential Muhammad Shahrur: The Qur'an, Morality and Critical Reason*, trans., ed., with intro. Andreas Christmann, (Leiden: Brill, 2009), 346–47.

15. Samuel Hosain Lamarti, "The Development of Apostasy and Punishment Law in Islam, 11 AH/632AD—157AH/774AD," PhD Thesis, Glasgow University, 2002, p. 184. For al-Awzai's political views on "obedience to the state" and his anti-Qadari stance, see Abdulhadi Alajmi, "Transcending Legitimacy: Al-Awza'i and His Interaction with the 'Abbasid State" (PhD thesis, Durham University, 2004), 58–62, 195–206, available at Durham E-Theses online, http://etheses.dur.ac.uk/1736/.

16. Mohammad Hashim Kamali, *Crime and Punishment in Islamic Law: A Fresh Interpretation* (New York: Oxford University Press, 2019), 148–49.

17. Demetrios J. Constantelos, "Paganism and the State in the Age of Justinian," *Catholic Historical Review*, 50, no. 3 (October 1964), 372–80.

18. Procopius, *Anecdota*, XI. 26, quoted in ibid., 377.

19. Rudolph Peters and Gert J. J. De Vries, "Apostasy in Islam," *Die Welt des Islams* (Leiden: Brill), n.s., 17, no. ¼ (1976–1977): 4.

20. Ibid.

21. See *No Place to Call Home: Experiences of Apostates from Islam, Failures of the International Community* (New Malden, UK: Christian Solidarity Worldwide, 2008).

22. Yusuf al-Qaradawi, "Apostasy: Major and Minor," Islamonline.net, April 13, 2006 [Last access June 2019.]

23. Ibid.

24. Ironically, the author defends this view as part of the "true freedom" that Islam offers: Spahic Omer, "All Islam Ever Wanted Was Freedom," Islamicity.org, April 30, 2019. https://www.islamicity.org/19496/all-islam-ever-wanted-was-freedom/.

25. Rached Ghannochi, *Al-Hurriyat al-Ammah fi al-Dawlah al-Islamiyya* (Beirut: Markaz Dirasat al-Wihdah al-Arabiyyah, 1993), 48–51; the English translation here is quoted from David Johnston, "Maqasid al-Shari'a: Epistemology and Hermeneutics of Muslim Theologies of Human Rights," *Die Welt des Islams* 47, no. 2 (June 2007): 175.

CHAPTER 13: FREEDOM MATTERS III: BLASPHEMY

1. The line by K. H. Mustofa Bisri is quoted from: Abdurrahman Wahid, "God Needs no Defense," in Kelly James Clark (ed.), *Abraham's Children: Liberty and Tolerance in an Age of Religious Conflict* (New Haven: Yale University Press, 2012), 211.

2. The Supreme Court Pakistan's Judgment on Criminal Appeal No. 39-L of 2015, published on the court's website, http://pid.gov.pk/site/news_detail/333

3. Mohammed Hanif, "Blasphemy, Pakistan's New Religion," *New York Times*, November 2, 2018.

4. Qur'an, 15:6. Emphasis added.

5. Qur'an, 46:7. Emphasis added.

6. Qur'an, 74:2. Emphasis added.

7. Qur'an, 8:31. Emphasis added.

8. Qur'an, 5:64, 2:116, and 37:152. I must add that the word for "child" in both verses is *walad,* which denotes a biological son, different from the honorary term "son" used in the Bible for certain persons, including King David or Jesus of Nazareth. For more, see my book *The Islamic Jesus* (New York: St. Martin's Press, 2017), 167–68.

9. Qur'an, 5:64.

10. Qur'an, 21:22.

11. Qur'an, 10:38.

12. Qur'an, 6: 68.

13. Qur'an, 4:140.

14. Qur'an, 3:186.

15. Fahruddin er-Razi, *Tefsir-i Kebir* (Ankara: Huzur Yayınevi, 1991), 7:257.

16. Qur'an, 45:14.

17. Qur'an, 25:63.
18. Mark S. Wagner, "The Problem of Non-Muslims Who Insult the Prophet Muhammad," *Journal of the American Oriental Society* 135, no. 3 (July–September 2015): 538–39.
19. Krithika Varagur, "The Islamic World Has a Blasphemy Problem," *Foreign Policy*, May 25, 2017.
20. James Arlandson, "Muhammad's Dead Poets Society," *American Thinker*, March 8, 2006.
21. Rizwi Faizer, *The Life of Muhammad: Al-Waqidi's Kitab al-Maghazi* (New York: Routledge, 2011), 91.
22. Ibid., 92.
23. Montgomery Watt, *Muhammad in Medina* (Oxford: Oxford University Press, 1956), 18.
24. Uri Rubin, "The Assassination of Ka'b b. al-Ashraf," *Oriens*, no. 32, 1990, 65.
25. Faizer, *The Life of Muhammad*, 53.
26. *Sahih al-Bukhari*, bk. 64, hadith 86.
27. Maulana Wahiduddin Khan, *Muhammad: A Prophet for All Humanity* (New Delhi: Goodword Books, 2001), 327–28.
28. A. Guillaume, *The Life of Muhammad: A Translation of Ibn Ishaq's Sirat Rasul Allah*, (Oxford: Oxford University Press, 2002), 773.
29. "Hija': Poetic Genre," Britannica.com, https://www.britannica.com/art/Arabic-literature/Genres-and-themes#ref945071.
30. *Sahih al-Bukhari*, vol. 9, bk. 84, no. 60.
31. Ibid., vol. 8, bk. 75, no. 404.
32. The incident is narrated in al-Wahidi's *Asbab al-Nuzul*, 137. The Qur'anic verse is 45:14.
33. The incident is narrated in *Sahih al-Bukhari*, Book 61, Hadith 117. The Salafi website in question is Islamqa.info, where the quoted comment is at: https://islamqa.info/en/answers/197919/dhul-khuwaysirah-at-tameemi-was-a-hypocrite.
34. Al-Ayni [855] 2001, 24:121, quoted here from Ismail Royer, *Pakistan's Blasphemy Law and Non-Muslims* (Lamppost Education Initiative, 2018), 17.
35. Abu Hanifa as quoted in ibn Taymiyya, *al-Ṣārim al-maslūl*, 3, quoted here from Wagner, "The Problem of Non-Muslims," 530.
36. Christian C. Sahner, *Christian Martyrs Under Islam: Religious Violence and the Making of the Muslim World* (Princeton, NJ: Princeton University Press, 2018), 3–4, 118–19, 140–54.
37. Janina M. Safran, "Identity and Differentiation in Ninth-Century al-Andalus," *Speculum* 76, no. 3 (July 2001): 590. Also see Wagner, "The Problem of Non-Muslims," 531.

38. Mustafa Akyol, "How Islamists are Ruining Islam," *Current Trends in Islamist Ideology,* vol. 26, June 12, 2020

39. *Sahih al-Bukhari,* "Believing," 42. The term here is *nasihah,* which can be translated as "sincerity" or "advice." I preferred the latter and more common one.

40. For Bosnia's experiment of civil Islam, see Riada Asimovic Akyol, "Want to Cultivate a Liberal European Islam? Look to Bosnia," *The Atlantic,* January 13, 2019.

41. According to al-Tirmidhi and al-Tabari, this was said by Caliph Umar ibn al-Khattab at a sermon. Umayyads are known to have used it widely. See Abbas Barzegar, "Adhering to the Community" [Luzūm al-Jamāʿa]: Continuities Between Late Umayyad Political Discourse and 'Proto-Sunni' Identity," *Review of Middle East Studies* 49, no. 2 (2015): 144.

42. Omar Saif Ghobash, *Letters to a Young Muslim* (New York: Picador Books, 2016), 238.

43. Ghobash makes this comment based on his personal experience in the West in ibid., 156.

CHAPTER 14: THE THEOLOGY OF TOLERANCE

1. Peter Berger and Anton Zijderveld, *In Praise of Doubt: How to Have Convictions Without Becoming a Fanatic* (New York: HarperOne, 2010), 113.

2. Khaled Abou El Fadl, *Speaking in God's Name* (London: Oneworld Publications, 2014), 10.

3. "Irja: The Most Dangerous Bid'ah," *Dabiq* 8 (March 2015): 39.

4. A derivative of the term *irja, mur'jawna,* is used in Qur'an 9:106: "And [there are] others *deferred* until the command of Allah; whether He will punish them or whether He will forgive them." For its use for the explanation of the theological term "Irja," see Joseph Givony, "The Murji'a and the Theological School of Abu Hanifa: A Historical and Ideological Study" (PhD thesis, University of Edinburgh, 1977), 6. Givony himself, though, doubts the terms are related.

5. Sönmez Kutlu, "Mürcie," *İslam Ansiklopedisi* (Istanbul Türkiye Diyanet Vakfı,) 32 (2006): 41–42.

6. This is although the Muʿtazilities, in practice, came close to many Murji'ite positions. Montgomery Watt, *The Formative Period of Islamic Thought* (Edinburgh: Edinburg University Press, 1973), 140.

7. W. Madelung, "Murdji'a," *Encyclopedia of Islam* (Leiden: Brill, 1993), 7:605.

8. Ibid., 606.

9. See Watt, *Formative Period,* 125.

10. *Aqidat us-Salaf wa Ashabul-Hadith*, 109, quoted in "Observations Against the Book Supporting the Madhhab of the Khawaarij," 6, http://www.sahihmuslim.com/sps/sp.cfm?subsecID=GSC02&articleID=GSC020001&articlePages=1.

11. Toshihiko Izutsu, *The Concept of Belief in Islamic Theology* (Kuala Lumpur: Islamic Book Trust, 2006), 130.

12. Daniel Law, *Radical Islam and the Revival of Medieval Theology*, Cambridge: Cambridge University Press, 2012), 26.

13. Ibid., 25.

14. According to Daniel Law, there is "a certain ambivalence in classical Sunnism with regard to the Murji'a. On the one hand, they were classified as a heretical school; on the other hand, the signature Murji'ite doctrine that acts are not a condition for faith was assimilated into the dominant Ash'ari and Ma'turidi schools." Law, *Radical Islam*, 29) According to Watt, while al-Ash'ari himself added "acts" to belief, his followers toned down this doctrine. Watt, *Formative Period*, 135–36.

15. Law, *Radical Islam*, 18.

16. Ibid., 30–41.

17. This summary of al-Hudaybi's argument is from ibid., 62.

18. See ibid., the chap. "The 'Murji'ite' Muslim Brotherhood," 41–85.

19. Law, *Radical Islam*, 80–82.

20. Ibid., 75.

21. The original title is *Imta' al-Nazar fī kashf Shubuhat Murji'at al-'Asr.* Ibid., 135.

22. "The Devil's Deception of the Murjia," by Shaikh Abdullah Faisal, July 14, 2012, https://archive.org/details/TheDevilsDeceptionOfTheMurjia.

23. Joe Carter, "Being on God's Side," *First Things*, December 22, 2010.

24. *Jami at-Tirmidhi*, vol. 5, bk. 38, "The Book on Faith," hadith 2640. Here taken from the English edition trans. Abu Khaliyl and ed. Hafiz Abu Tahir Zubair Ali Zai (Riyadh: Darussalam, 2007).

25. Josef Van Ess's 1500-page work *Der Eine und Das Andere* is summarized by Christian Lange, from which these quotes are taken. Lange, "Power, Orthodoxy, and Salvation in Classical Islamic Theology," in *Islamic Studies in the Twenty-First Century: Transformations and Continuities*, eds. Léon Buskens and Annemarie van Sandwijk (Amsterdam: Amsterdam University Press, 2016), 150.

26. Ibid.

27. Ibid.

28. Al-Ḥasan ibn Mūsá Nawbakhtī, *Shi'a Sects: Kitab Firaq al-Shi'a* (London: ICAS Press, 2007), 43. Also see Toshihiko Izutsu, *The Concept of Belief in Islamic Theology* (Kuala Lumpur: Other Press, 2006), 55.

29. Christian Lange, "Power, Orthodoxy, and Salvation in Classical Islamic Theology," in *Islamic Studies in the Twenty-First Century: Transformations and Continuities*, eds. Léon Buskens and Annemarie van Sandwijk (Amsterdam: Amsterdam University Press, 2016), 150.

30. Qur'an, 30:31–32. Emphasis added.

31. Geneive Abdo, *The New Sectarianism: The Arab Uprisings and the Rebirth of the Shi'a-Sunni Divide*, (New York: Oxford University Press, 2017), 1.

32. Yohanan Friedmann, *Tolerance and Coercion in Islam: Interfaith Relations in the Muslim Tradition* (Cambridge: Cambridge University Press, 2003), 93.

33. See Benny Morris and Dror Ze'evi, *The Thirty-Year Genocide: Turkey's Destruction of Its Christian Minorities, 1894–1924* (Cambridge, MA: Harvard University Press, 2019), 494–95.

34. The text of the Marrakesh Declaration is online at: http://www.marrakesh declaration.org/files/Bismilah-2-ENG.pdf. For a discussion on it, see Vebjørn L Horsfjord, "The Marrakesh Declaration on Rights of Religious Minorities: Opportunity or Dead End?," *Nordic Journal of Human Rights*, 36:2, 2018, 151–166. Horsfjord argues: "Although the declaration falls short of the ideals of the international liberal human rights discourse, it may move Islamic theological discourse towards greater recognition of equal rights for all through the promotion of the concept of citizenship."

35. Qur'an, 59:20, Yusuf Ali translation. *The Holy Qur'an*, (Hertfordshire, UK: Wordsworth Editions Ltd, 2001) Only "garden" is reworded here as "heaven."

36. Anver M. Emon, "The Limits of Constitutionalism in the Muslim World: History and Identity in Islamic Law," Research Paper Series, New York Law School, 2008, 24.

37. Ibid.

38. Aan Anshori, "Reviewing 'Kafir' to End Intolerance, Inequality," *Jakarta Post*, April 26 2019.

39. Islamweb Fatwas, "Appropriate Way to Address non-Muslims," Fatwa no.: 86974, Fatwa date: 12/02/2004, https://www.islamweb.net/emainpage /PrintFatwa.php?lang=E&Id=86974&lang=E&Id=86974.

40. Toshihiko Izutsu, *Ethico-Religious Concepts in the Qur'an* (Montreal: McGill-Queen's University Press, 2002), 120, 121, 142.

41. The Qur'an calls Satan, namely Iblis, "*kafir*" twice, at 2:34 and 38:74. The latter verse also notes that Iblis revolted against God's commandment to bow down to Adam out of *istikbar*, which is arrogance.

42. According to Qur'anic exegete Muhammad Husayn Tabatabai, "the words *kuffār* (infidels) or *alladhīna kafarū'* (those who disbelieve) in the

Koran, without exception refer to the Meccan Arabs at the beginning of the Prophet's mission, unless there are contextual aspects to suggest otherwise." Abdulaziz Sachedina, *The Islamic Roots of Democratic Pluralism* (New York: Oxford University Press, 2001), 150.

43. Imran Aijaz, "Traditional Islamic Exclusivism: A Critique," *European Journal for Philosophy of Religion* 6, no. 2 (Summer 2014), 193.

44. A. Guillaume, *The Life of Muhammad: A Translation of Ibn Ishaq's Sirat Rasul Allah*, (Oxford: Oxford University Press, 2002), 158.

45. Karen Armstrong gives a good description of that Western bafflement with the Qur'an in *The Lost Art of Scripture* (New York: Alfred A. Knopf, 2019), 266.

46. Qur'an, 107:1–3.

47. Qur'an, 3:113–14.

48. Qur'an, 60:9, 8. The verse about not taking Jews and Christians as "allies," or *awliya*, is 5:51.

49. Qur'an 2:62. The same verse is repeated, almost verbatim, in 5:69.

50. The most likely candidate for the "Sabians" are the Mandeans, a gnostic tradition also dubbed as "Christians of St. John." See Christopher Buck, "The Identity of the Ṣābi'ūn: An Historical Quest," *The Muslim World* 74, no. 3–4, (July/October 1984), 172, 174–75.

51. See, for instance, al-Tabari's *The Commentary on The Qur'an*, ed. J. Cooper (Oxford: Oxford University Press, 1989), 1:364.

52. Qur'an, 3:85.

53. Jane Smith, *A Historical and Semantic Study of the Term 'Islam' as Seen in a Sequence of Qur'an Commentaries* (Missoula, Montana: Scholars Press for Harvard Theological Review, 1975), 43–44, quoted here from Jerusha Tanner Lamptey, "Toward a Muslima Theology of Religious Pluralism" (PhD diss., Georgetown University, 2011), 33–34.

54. Smith, *A Historical and Semantic Study*, 117.

55. Lamptey, "Toward a Muslima Theology," 34.

56. Both the argument by al-Jahiz and the response by al-Ghazali is from the latter's final work: Imam Gazali, *El-Mustasfa* (Turkish translation by Yusuf Apaydin) (Kayseri: Rey Yayıncılık, 1994), Vol II, pp. 329–330. Ghazali, in a chilling line in the same discussion, also shares a report: "the Prophet launched war on Jews and Christians . . . who insisted on their own beliefs. He raised the skirts of those men who reached puberty, to check if they reached puberty, and killed them if they did."

57. Qur'an, 5:48.

58. This paraphrasing of the lesson of Nathan the Wise is from Noel Clark, *Two Jewish Plays: The Jews, Nathan the Wise* (London: Oberon Books,

2002), "Introduction." The term "the Arbiter" is from George Alexander Kohut, *Nathan the Wise: A Dramatic Poem* (New York: Bloch Publishing, 1917), 117.

EPILOGUE

1. Fazlur Rahman, *Islam and Modernity: The Transformation of an Intellectual Tradition* (Chicago: University of Chicago Press, 1982), 147.
2. Rose Wilder Lane, *The Discovery of Freedom: Man's Struggle Against Authority* (New York: John Day, 1943), 83, 86, 108, 106. For an annotated version of the book's chapter on Islam, see Imad ad-Dean Ahmad, *Islam and the Discovery of Freedom* (Beltsville, MD: Amana Publications, 1997).

INDEX